# The Complete Book of Entertaining

## from The Emily Post Institute

# The Complete Book of Entertaining

### from The Emily Post Institute

## by Elizabeth Post
## and Anthony Staffieri

*illustrations by Lori L. Lambert*

HARPER & ROW, PUBLISHERS

NEW YORK

Cambridge · London
Hagerstown · Mexico City
Philadelphia · São Paulo
San Francisco · *1817* · Sydney

# Contents

# Acknowledgments

For slightly more than five years a host of individuals have assisted us in the conception and writing of this reference book. We extend our thanks to the following:

The team at Abbey Rents, past and present, including Herman Stein, Karl Levin, Darwin Wilson, Ray Cusato, Bob Walter, Jim Hall, Jim Gottheardt and Nancy Lightman.

John Woytowicz at Vera Linen, The Belgian Linen Association, Roy Kilgillan at The Candle Shop, Ms. Nesta DiSisa at The Candle Galleria, Don Schriber of Atlas Pool Scaffolding Company, Arnold Mendick of Baskin & Robbins (Boston), Diane Delmonte of Diane at the Parker House (Invitations), Walter Kelly at County-Wide Beverage, Jessie Willis of Jessie Willis Tents, Donn Roy and Joe Omaggio of S. S. Pennock Flowers (New York City), Dr. Edwin Dombrowski for his assistance with allergy information, Ms. Smoki Bacon of Bacon/Concannon Associates (Boston), Joe Miller for his guidance, Sally Malobabie of The Whirlpool Corporation, Linda Green of Brooke Bond Foods, Inc., Ms. Susan J. Wanbaugh of The State of Maine Publicity Bureau, the ever-helpful staff at the reference desk of the New York Public Library. We would like to extend a special thank-you to Burton J. Braff of New York City for his expert assistance in conceiving and researching the floral chapter of this book. Quinion Books in New York City, and Barbara Weinstein for reproducing and collating thousands of pages, Mrs. Frances Staffieri and Mrs. Ethel R. Hurley for a number of useful pointers, and Janet Langhart and Betty Levin formerly of WCVB–TV, Boston.

The bibliography was the product of many hours of dedicated research and we extend our thanks to Mary Peacock, Joe Slakas and Tony Maglione. Our research team was unceasing in its efforts to obtain important and often hard to locate information—hats off to Beth Weinstein and Richard Protovin and a very special thanks to Carol Binen, who single-handedly located all of the entries in the Source Manual and whose support kept the momentum of the research progressing.

We also wish to thank all of the companies listed in the Source Manual for their gracious assistance and cooperation.

We would also like to acknowledge those professionals in the publishing business who encouraged and supported us: Robert Donald, Cynthia Vartan, Arnold Dolin and Carol Cohen. We particularly acknowledge Ms. Cohen for tying together the enormous quantity of information contained in this work. Her efforts were unceasing.

Finally, and certainly not the least of those we thank, are the team of women who typed draft after draft of manuscript throughout the sixty plus months of this undertaking: Stella Brandt, Linda Adams, Marla Gerstein, Phyllis Denigris, Mary Crampsey, Carol Binen, Isabel Paul and Patti Robb. Special thanks to Joan Whitman, copyeditor, and to Kathleen Hyde of Harper & Row, who supervised the copyediting and oversaw the many details of putting this text in order.

Elizabeth Post and Tony Staffieri

*New York City*

*March, 1981*

# Introduction

Several years ago I was a guest on a television program in Boston. The producers had arranged for a beautifully set dinner table and I discussed the placement of the silver, china, and crystal, and the correct use of various utensils. On the same program, a young man named Tony Staffieri had been invited to demonstrate methods of folding napkins. He was, at the time, a party planner and coordinator for one of the nation's largest catering and party equipment rental agencies. Our program was a great success and the station was deluged with requests for more information on table settings, napkin folds, decorations, and the like. Tony and I had so much fun doing the show that the idea sprang up immediately: with my knowledge of proper procedure and the hostess's role in party giving, and his experience with equipment and decorating, a book by the two of us could tell people just about everything there is to know about entertaining. (In using "I" throughout the book I am speaking for the Emily Post Institute and Tony Staffieri as well as myself.) There is only one thing we can't do, and this, of course, is what differentiates a superb hostess from a merely good one: we cannot inject your personality, your inventiveness, your taste into each party. That you must do yourself.

This is basically a book about entertaining at home. Business entertaining, and entertaining in places like clubs, hotels, and halls, is another subject. There are usually professionals handling those events who are available to guide and to help the party giver, so the host or hostess needs to know very little about the technical aspects. Their responsibility is related only to the choices that must be made—the guest list, the hours, the menu, and so forth. Once these decisions are made, the implementation is taken out of their hands and they may devote themselves to being gracious hosts—and paying the bills!

A great deal of business entertaining *is* done at home, of course. Entertaining an out-of-town client, introducing a new executive to his staff and their families, a party to celebrate a co-worker's birthday or retirement—any of these may be held at home. They are very much like purely social parties and the information in this book applies to them, too. The same problems confront the host and hostess, and the same solutions can be found in these pages.

Whenever I am asked (and I often am) "What is the secret to giving a superb party?" my answer is always the same: *"Advance preparation."* I truly believe that the idea of a party is to give everyone, *including the hostess,* a good time. And that is possible only if she can devote most of her time and her energy to her guests. The hostess who spends most of her time in the kitchen, or running in and out of it, who is harried and nervous, cannot help but make her friends nervous, too. But the hostess whose meal is essentially ready ahead of time, whose help (if she has any) operates smoothly, and who is relaxed and having a good time, spreads that atmosphere quickly, and hers are the invitations that are sought after.

That is why we have chosen a step-by-step format for the parties described in this book. Whether you plan to give a cocktail party or a luau, a BYOB party or a Chinese dinner, you will find a model to follow. If you choose to use our menu, the timetable is all worked out for you, and you will have very little to do the night of the party. If you wish to substitute your own favorite dishes, try to select ones that can be prepared in the same general way. I have tried and tested all recipes and almost all have been served to my own guests with great success.

Because we all tend to have our favorite dishes and ones that we know we do well, I would like to make a suggestion here that does not appear later in the text. If you entertain often, or even three or four times a year, keep a party file. List the date of your party, the guests, the menu, and any further information you think might be useful. I find this an invaluable aid in not inadvertently asking the same couples together time and again, or serving the same dish to the same people two or three times in a row.

For those of you who are familiar with *The New Emily Post's Etiquette,* you will find certain sections here that duplicate some of the information found in that original work. This was inevitable because there are simply no better ways to describe such things as a table setting or making good tea. This book, however, contains a wealth of information that can be found in no other, and we hope that it will be a useful addition to the reference shelf of all aspiring hosts and hostesses.

*Elizabeth L. Post*

# part one

# Party Preparations

# *1*

# *Food and Drink*

## Planning the Menu

**Basic rules for food and its service**   Beneath the enviable coolness of a superb hostess is someone who is well organized and methodical, who knows the rules and how to follow them. Her table setting, whether simple or elegant, is perfectly balanced and coordinated. Her food, whether for a one-dish buffet or a five-course seated dinner, is exquisite, and she is relaxed, gracious, and obviously having a good time. Putting together an outstanding menu requires careful planning, imagination, and a knowledge of certain general rules. For example, the experienced hostess knows that:

Food that must be cut (usually meat) requires that guests be seated. Finger foods and casserole dishes may be eaten standing at a buffet, but almost everyone prefers to sit down, and, if possible, to have table space on which to rest a plate.

Foods with sauces and gravies should be served only on hard (china, pottery, etc.) surfaces. Paper plates absorb liquids, and the coatings of some plasticized paper plates dissolve in hot gravy.

Food with bases of butter and mayonnaise cannot be left unrefrigerated for very long.

The addition of nuts or shellfish to party dishes should never be disguised. Many people are allergic to these ingredients and must avoid them. The danger arises when the shrimp is puréed or the nuts ground up, so that they are unrecognizable.

When space is limited, food service should be decentralized by arranging two service areas, or some of the food may be passed on trays.

Each course requires its own silver and china, whether for a seated dinner or a buffet. The hostess must be sure in advance that her supply is adequate for the number of courses and the number of guests.

There must be enough electrical outlets for heating or cooling foods. For example, a buffet table should be near an outlet so that an electric hot tray can be used. The hot tray is an invaluable aid in keeping serving dishes warm.

A buffet table near an open window or a drafty location is unsuitable for chafing dishes or fondue pots heated by an open flame.

Ventilation is important, especially in the area where food is prepared. Even in cold weather, a window or two opened slightly at the top makes guests more comfortable.

Each course served makes more debris. If you have no help, courses should be limited to what you can comfortably clear away and clean up yourself.

**Menu notes**  Although in the 1880s, gourmands like Diamond Jim Brady may have eaten their way through eight or ten courses and still lived to a ripe old age, our menus today are limited by our knowledge of what is good for us, our pocketbooks and our life style. Five courses are *maximum,* and that number would be served only at the most elaborate official dinner. They are:

1. Soup *or* fruit *or* shellfish
2. Fish course (never served if shellfish is the first course or fish is the entrée)
3. The entrée, or main course
4. Salad
5. Dessert

Coffee (regular and/or decaffeinated) should be served after every dinner party, but it is not considered a course.

Note that salad is course number 4. This is correct, even though restaurants have tried to turn it into a first course. At a dinner party, salad may be served with the entrée on a separate salad plate or as a separate course between the main course and dessert. It may also be served instead of dessert, usually accompanied by fruit and cheese.

The menu should be well balanced. A rich dish should be accompanied or followed by simple dishes. For example, a creamy coquilles St. Jacques as a first course might be followed by roast lamb or chicken, or filet mignon; a consommé or madrilène could be followed by boeuf bourguignonne or beef stroganoff.

The appearance of the food is most important. Avoid a dinner that is "white" from beginning to end—creamed soup, breast of chicken, white rice and cauliflower, for example. Put color into salads by mixing dark spinach leaves with light Boston lettuce, or by adding white mushrooms, red tomatoes, radishes, a few slivers of red cabbage, etc. Sprinkle paprika lightly on creamed dishes, and add a parsley sprig or a sprinkling of chopped parsley to any white or yellow dish to brighten it up. Lay chops in a neat pattern rather than a heap, arrange asparagus or string beans in the same direction, and surround roast meat or poultry with alternating rings of carrots or beets or a green vegetable.

Combine flavors carefully. Never serve all sweet dishes, such as a pumpkin soup, duck à l'orange, fruit salad, and chocolate mousse.

If you are serving a buffet, or if you have no help, try to avoid dishes that require a number of condiments or sauces. Restrict your courses to two or three to eliminate extra plates and silverware. A main course of a hearty stew and a fresh vegetable followed by ice cream or fruit compote can be a satisfying meal and a simple one to serve. You might add a salad, or start out with soup if you can cope with a third course.

To simplify serving in the dining room, some hostesses bring individual servings of soup, fruit cup or appetizer to the living room, and guests enjoy a first course there as they finish their cocktails. In this case, the host should remove the plates while the hostess seats her guests in the dining room; otherwise she must excuse herself during dessert to clean up the living room before the guests return.

Let your imagination be your only limitation in planning an interesting, innovative menu. But don't experiment with a new dish at a party! No matter how good or how easy the recipe sounds, try it on your family first.

**Special notes for summer entertaining** We are all aware that summertime and outdoor entertaining go hand in hand. However, there are certain considerations unique to summertime that we point out, not only as a warning, but as a reminder.

Warm weather promotes food spoilage. Too often we read of cookouts and other events ruined by cases of food poisoning. To prevent a tragedy of that sort, be absolutely certain that foods such as fish, raw meats, mayonnaise, and egg or cream sauces are refrigerated or chilled until just before cooking or serving. Any dishes made with mayonnaise or eggs—and these include potato and macaroni salads—should be kept on ice or in a well-insulated ice chest. The only safe rule to follow is:

When in doubt, throw it out. Otherwise, the risks of food spoilage are too high and too disastrous.

To insure that your ice chest stays cool, fill a plastic container or a used milk carton with water and freeze it. Place that, or a plastic bag filled with ice cubes, in the cooler and keep the lid tightly closed.

Place cold cuts, hot dogs, beef patties, and the like in airtight containers close to the ice in the cooler.

## The Bar and the Liquor

**Setting up the bar**   Most hosts and hostesses at informal parties know the liquor preferences of their friends, provide an ample supply of those choices, and, after serving the first drink themselves, tell their guests to help themselves to refills. If, however, you are planning a larger or more formal party you will want to have a bar supplied for a wide variety of drinks. Here is a list that will take care of all but the most exotic requests.

*Liquors*

Blended whiskey (*domestic or Canadian*)
Bourbon
Scotch
Vodka
Gin
Rum (*light and dark*)
Vermouth (*dry and sweet*)
Brandy
Drambuie
Crème de menthe
Triple sec
Curaçao
Tequila
Kahlua or Tia Maria
Sherry (*dry and sweet*)
Wine (*red, white and rosé*)
Champagne
Beer

*Garnishes and Mixes*

Pitted green cocktail olives
Maraschino cherries
Pearl onions
Orange and lemon slices
Lemon peel
Worcestershire sauce
Tabasco
Sugar
Pepper and salt
Coarse salt for dipping rims of glasses
Ginger ale
Club soda
Cola and diet sodas
Tonic water and/or bitter lemon
Tomato juice
Bottled lemon juice
Canned, bottled, or packaged cocktail mixes may be included if you wish.

## Bar Tools

| | |
|---|---|
| Cocktail shaker | Toothpicks |
| Muddler | Knife |
| Strainer | Cutting board |
| Martini pitcher and stir rod | Ice pick |
| Juice squeezer | Shot glass |
| Spoons | Measuring cup |
| Bar cloth and sponge | Corkscrew |
| Ice crusher | Bottle cap and beer can opener |
| Coasters and napkins | Blender |
| Swizzle sticks | Water pitcher |

## Glasses

Pilsener.    Beer stein.

All-purpose.    On-the-rocks.    Highball.    Shot glass.

Sherry.  All-purpose wine.  Standard champagne.  Tulip champagne.  Brandy.  Liqueur.  Stemmed martini.

Plenty of coasters and cocktail napkins should be available on or near the bar. Allow at least three napkins per person as the guests will often take a fresh one with each new drink.

To hold all of these ingredients and materials without crowding, the surface of the bar must be at least five feet long and three feet wide. A wider bar is inconvenient for the bartender, who must pass the drinks across it.

One bar, tended by a competent professional, can serve between forty and fifty guests comfortably. You would need at least two self-service bars to accommodate the same number. At a party of a hundred or more, self-service bars will suffice only if there are a number of them, and the use of professional bartenders is recommended.

If the bar must be located in a small area, again you will need a bartender to keep the crowd moving rapidly. More space makes it easier to provide a number of self-service bars.

**Purchasing liquor** Purchasing the liquor can be a frustrating experience. "How much liquor do I need?" is always the question. The following formulas should help you arrive at the answer:

One quart of liquor will make twenty-one one-and-a-half-ounce drinks or sixteen two-ounce drinks. You should allow three to five drinks per person, depending on the duration of the party, your friends' drinking habits, and whether it is a cocktail party or a dinner party. For example, if you have two friends in for an evening of cocktails, dinner and bridge, and you all drink bourbon throughout the evening, you should be prepared to use a full quart, or five drinks apiece. You should also be prepared for some outrageous bidding!

There are two kinds of liquor labels—house brands and name brands. Some well-known name brands are more expensive simply because of their advertising and packaging costs. However, others are truly superior to the less expensive house brands. If you are unaccustomed to buying liquor, you would be wise to ask a more experienced friend to suggest the best choices in the price range you can afford.

There are three ways to purchase liquor—from local liquor (package) stores, from chain stores, or direct from a wholesaler.

The local package store is often in competition with the big chain stores. While chain stores provide diversity, immediate supply and some savings, the package store survives because it offers delivery, convenience, and a personal touch. If it is legal in your state, package stores may also give regular customers a discount on large orders by the case. Chain stores and discount stores are best for the purchase of mixes, beer, and some wines.

Buying from a wholesaler is out of the question for a hostess giving a small party. But in some cities there are semi-wholesale operations to which the public has access, and this type of purchase would be well worth your while if you are expecting one hundred or more guests. The prices would be cheaper than either the package or chain store, and only slightly higher than a general wholesaler. In areas where the sale of liquor is not controlled by the state, these outlets are listed in the yellow pages.

If it is legal in your state, buying liquor on consignment is very convenient. Buying on consignment simply means that the seller will refund the purchase price and tax (if any) of any unopened bottles returned to his store within a specified time after the party. Consignment purchases are made by prearrangement only. Without this agreement, you must not assume that you can return unused liquor or expect a refund. Consignment purchases, like all liquor purchases, are paid for in full on or before delivery.

This type of purchase is recommended for the hostess who is unsure of the drinking habits of her guests, or how many guests will be present. On the other hand, liquor is one item that never spoils, so the leftovers can be used for your next party. The liquor will keep indefinitely if you put the tops on tightly and seal the open edges with masking tape.

**Cocktails and before-meal drinks**  The drinks that are served at cocktail parties or preceding dinner parties vary greatly according to the season, the climate, and the ethnic background of the drinkers. Russians, for example, are apt to prefer vodka, while most English people enjoy Scotch without ice. There are, however, many other guidelines that can help you select the liquor that your friends will enjoy most. If you do not know your guests well, you may occasionally be surprised by someone who always drinks gin and tonic—summer or winter—or never touches anything but white wine. But, in general, if you have two or three choices in the summer and winter categories you will be able to please everyone.

In summer, and in hot climates at all times, tall, cold drinks are naturally first choices. Gin or vodka with tonic water or bitter lemon, served with a slice of lemon or lime, is probably the most popular hot weather tall drink. However, a collins—whiskey, rum, gin, or vodka mixed with lemon juice, sugar and soda water—is delicious, and the mix can be purchased so that you need add only the liquor. White wine and soda, known as a spritzer, has become very popular with wine drinkers. Daiquiris and sours are also good summer cocktails.

In cold winter months, martinis, manhattans, and whiskey-on-the-rocks take precedence over the summer drinks. Highballs made of Scotch, bourbon, or a blended whiskey mixed with water or soda and served in a tall glass are offered at all seasons and are equally good for sipping after dinner.

Martinis and manhattans may be served "straight up"—in a stemmed glass with no ice—or "on the rocks"—in an Old Fashioned glass filled with ice cubes. Martinis are garnished with a cocktail onion or olive, or a twist of lemon peel, and manhattans with a slice of orange and a maraschino cherry.

There are, of course, innumerable more exotic drinks. Piña coladas, mai tais, margaritas, and mint juleps, for example, have become popular all over the country although they originated in definite locales—Hawaii, Mexico, and the South. The mint julep is described in detail in the chapter on seasonal parties under "Kentucky Derby Cocktail Party," as it is the traditional drink for that day. Mai tais and piña coladas would be served before a luau (see Labor Day Luau). So you need not stick to the ubiquitous martini, vodka and tonic, and whiskey-on-the-rocks, but you will be safe if you do and your friends will be content. If you are inexperienced at making drinks but would like to try some new ones, get a good drink recipe book. (See bibliography.)

Bloody Marys are undoubtedly the most popular preluncheon drink. There are excellent mixes available necessitating only the addition of vodka, but you may also vary the recipe by mixing bouillon or clam juice with the tomato juice. Chilled white wine, either plain or with ice, is also popular at this hour because it is light and not too intoxicating.

**Wines** As you undoubtedly know, red wine is traditionally served with "red" meat and white wine with fish and chicken. For many, many years it was unthinkable to break that rule. Today, however, almost everyone drinks wine, and almost everyone has a definite preference as to white or red. If that is so in your case, it is not incorrect to serve either red or white with any food. However, that tradition was established because most people felt that red wine really tasted better with red meat, and white with fish or chicken, and the majority of your guests will probably still agree. Therefore, when you give a party with a number of people of different tastes, it is safer to stick to the old rule.

Vin rosé or pink wine is not generally considered as good as a fine red or white wine, but there are many who enjoy it thoroughly and it is a good compromise for "in between" meats such as pork or veal, which are not truly either red or white meat.

In purchasing your wine, you may certainly choose an expensive imported wine if you wish. It is not, however, necessary. There are excellent domestic wines at a somewhat lower cost, and there are also many moderately priced imported wines that are superb. If you do not recognize the names on the labels or know what you are looking for, ask the advice of a knowledgeable friend or a dealer whose judgment you trust. A bad choice of wine can ruin an otherwise superb meal.

Since wine is such an important adjunct to your dinner party, here are some brief descriptions of and recommendations for the use of dinner wines.

*Sherry* is offered when a clear soup or a soup prepared with sherry in it is the first course. This might be a clear consommé, black bean, or turtle soup, but it is not served with a cream soup such as vichyssoise. Sherry is often served before luncheon, and is offered as an alternative to a cocktail before dinner. It is served at room temperature in a small, stemmed v-shaped glass. At a formal dinner, sherry should be served from a decanter.

*Dry white wine* is served with the fish course, and/or when fish or chicken is the main course. It is also served almost exclusively at luncheons. Sweet white wines should be served only with desserts.

White wine should always be served well chilled. The quickest way to chill it if you have forgotten to refrigerate it for several hours is to place it in a bucket of water filled with a mixture of ice cubes and cold water. The melting of the ice in the water actually cools the wine faster than surrounding it with ice only.

White wine does not produce sediment and the bottle or decanter may be emptied to the last drop. Wine bottles may be wrapped in a white napkin when served at a formal dinner although many hosts prefer to let their guests see the label on the bottle.

*Red wine* is traditionally served with red meats such as beef, lamb or venison, and with duck and game birds. It is also the preferred wine with Italian pastas. Claret, a light red wine, is preferred if only one wine is served throughout the meal; burgundy, a heavier wine, is usually the choice with the red meat course.

Red wine is served at room temperature (although some people like it slightly chilled) and it should be opened an hour or two before serving to allow it to "breathe." Aged red wine produces considerable sediment, so it should be laid in a tilted wine holder some time before serving to allow the sediment to settle. The mouth of a bottle of aged red wine must be carefully wiped to remove dirt and grime. The cork, after being pulled, may be laid beside the bottle in the basket to show that it is undamaged. Because of the sediment, the bottle is never emptied. For the same reason, red wine is often served from a decanter, and even then, the decanter should be filled a day ahead of the party, so that any sediment inadvertently poured into it will settle.

When you have no help, opened bottles of wine may be placed at either end of a large table on a coaster or wine holder. The host and someone at the other end pour the wine for the people at their own end, starting with the person on their right. Or, if you prefer, the host or hostess may serve the wine as soon as the guests are seated, starting with the guest of honor and going around the table counterclockwise.

*Champagne* is the most elegant of all the wines, and is generally served only on very special occasions. There are several excellent domestic brands on the market today, making it possible for everyone to enjoy what used to be the privilege of only the very wealthy.

Champagne is served chilled, in either wide-brimmed, stemmed glasses or tulip-shaped glasses. The former are traditional, but the latter are now considered preferable by many connoisseurs as the life of the bubbles is better preserved in the elongated shape. The glasses should be as thin as soap bubbles; if you do not have such fine glasses, chill the thicker ones you are using to keep the chill of the champagne from dissipating.

Champagne is always kept on ice until it is served. To open the bottle, carefully unwind and remove the wire holding the cork and the foil covering the cork. Then grasp the cork firmly with one hand and turn the bottle—not the cork—with your other hand. When the cork begins to loosen, let the gas hiss out slowly until there is no more pressure. Then it is easy to remove the cork.

**Beer**  Whether you choose to serve beer or ale, imported or domestic, regular or light, the most important thing is that it be icy cold. Cans or bottles of beer should *never* be put on the bar but should be kept in the refrigerator or buried in ice cubes until the moment they are opened.

Purchasing beer by the keg can be a great money saver if you need a large quantity. But if ordering the keg, consider how it will be cooled, whether you can order it already chilled, and how you will maintain its chill throughout the party.

This is best done by surrounding the keg with crushed ice. A tub large enough to hold the keg and the ice is usually provided by the distributor. If kegs of beer are to be used over a long period of time, one should be chilling while another is being used. If that is impossible and the keg must be chilled while it is in use, keep in mind the weight of the keg and the fact that it will move around as the ice melts.

If you have never tapped a keg of beer, be sure to get directions from the supplier.

**Ice and refrigeration** The items that need to be kept chilled on or near the bar are soft drinks, soda and other mixers, as well as wines (white and rosé), and beer. Mixers and soft drinks may be kept in the refrigerator, but when you run out of space there, they can easily be chilled in large clean buckets or trash cans lined with plastic and partly filled with ice cubes. Be sure to arrange beer and soda in equal amounts per layer. If you put all the soda on the bottom layer and cover it with a layer of beer (or vice versa), you'll be in real trouble!

Bottles of wine may be chilled and then put out on the bar; they need not be kept on ice the entire time. Nor is it necessary for all the wine to be displayed at once. You can replenish the bar with chilled wine from the refrigerator or ice chest as needed.

You will need ice cubes for mixed drinks and these should be kept separate from the ice being used to cool the beer and soft drinks. Figure on two-thirds of a pound of ice per guest for the average cocktail party; one pound per guest for a dinner party, because the dinner party lasts longer. This allows for consumption and some loss by melting, but not for the cooling of mixers and soft drinks. Remember, ice cubes melt faster than block ice and for cooling anything in large quantities, a combination of the two is ideal.

**Soft drinks** Up to now we have been discussing alcoholic beverages, but it is essential that soft drinks be available. A six-pack of ginger ale and a six-pack of cola will suffice at the average cocktail or dinner party of ten to twenty guests, but if you know that there are a number of nondrinkers in the crowd, count on two or three soft drinks apiece, just as you would if they were cocktails.

For larger numbers of nondrinkers, a bowl of nonalcoholic punch is both welcome and economical. A personal favorite of mine is made of equal parts of grape juice and ginger ale poured over ice, but there are many other excellent punches to be found in collections of drink recipes.

**Some final bar guidelines** Although every type of wine technically has its own glass, with the current move toward informality, many hostesses are managing very nicely with one basic wine glass.

If you use plastic glasses, you'll need many more than if you use real glasses. People tend to bring real glasses back to the bar for a refill, but leave plastic glasses where they empty them. Real glasses are preferable to plastic glasses, but the latter are acceptable for large parties when a caterer is not providing the equipment.

Don't stint on ice. Go out and buy as much as you need, or make it in your ice trays ahead of time and store it in tightly sealed plastic bags in the freezer.

Provide ice tongs and/or a scoop so that guests do not need to use their fingers to pick up the ice cubes.

If you are making clear drinks like martinis, stir gently, don't shake. Stir highballs made with soda only once or twice or all carbonation will be dispersed.

Arrangement of a self-service bar: Stand behind the bar, as if you were the bartender. Leave a working space of approximately two feet square in the middle. Set up glasses on one side, liquor and mixers on the other—most popular brands in front. Utensils are arranged in the rear center. Place garnishes at the front of the bar to lend a touch of color. It's a good idea to have a drink recipe book at hand. Put paper clips on pages describing the most popular drinks for quick and easy reference. Put ice containers on the floor, or on the bar on the same side as the glasses.

## Food and Drink Professionals

Fortunately for the inexperienced hostess, there are a number of people who make their living by supplying and coordinating food and drink for party givers. They are caterers, banquet managers, and consultants. In order to help you choose which of these professionals might best fit your needs, we have prepared a description of the work each does and a list of the details that should be discussed with them.

**Caterers**   Caterers will provide you with a list of menus that they are prepared to serve, from which you can make your selection. They supply all the food for a party, and they may also supply the liquor and other beverages. Some caterers prepare the food in their kitchens and bring it to your home, others prepare it "on site," or they may combine "on site" preparation with prepared foods.

Most caterers also supply help, dishes, silverware, tables, chairs, and even the location. Some smaller organizations simply plan the menu, cook the food, and ready it for serving.

Most caterers are self-employed. They may have agents and assistants, but for the most part caterers are their own bosses. They will bill you directly based on the number of guests actually served or guaranteed in advance. The bill will cover food, preparation, service, equipment, and wages. A fixed amount (generally 15 percent) is usually added for gratuities, but most hostesses give an additional tip to those who actually work at the party. A deposit will be required.

*When do you need a caterer?*

• When you expect twenty-five or more guests, especially if you plan an intricate menu. (Dinners for as few as six or eight may be catered, but it is a very expensive way to entertain.)

• When you have limited cooking facilities and a large number of expected guests.

• When a large function is held at a public hall. If the hall in question is part of a hotel, you would use the hotel's banquet manager, but halls are often rented just for the space and the food is served by outside caterers hired by the hostess.

• When the hostess is physically incapacitated.

• When the hostess is arriving in the area shortly before the party is to take place; for example, rehearsal dinners given by the parents of the groom.

• When a party is impromptu—if you can find a caterer who is available.

• When the host or hostess does not cook.

• When the occasion dictates a menu consisting of specially prepared foods, such as official receptions for visiting foreigners.

**Banquet managers**   Banquet managers usually work for someone else—hotels, restaurants, function halls, clubs, and large companies, where they are sometimes called dining room directors.

A banquet manager's fee is included as part of the bill that comes from the organization that employs him. Special services may also be billable and should be agreed upon in advance. A generous tip for him will be expected, as well as an additional 15 percent of the total bill to be divided among the other help, unless it is already included in the bill.

You should never ask a banquet manager to supply the hall and services while you bring your own caterer. An exception to this rule might be when the menu demands certain exotic dishes.

*When do you need a banquet manager?*

• When the hostess prefers to hold the function in a hotel or club.

• When neither the selected caterer nor the hostess can adequately handle the basic requirements, namely room, tables and chairs, linen, place settings, and help.

• When the guest list is very large (although banquet managers are quite effective at supervising more intimate parties, too). Most big catering firms are equipped to handle at least 300 guests, but their capabilities are strained as the number grows beyond this point.

• When a hostess is planning to have a party in a city other than her own. She may find that planning it is easier through a banquet manager, since the hotel, club, or function hall he services will provide all the facilities, rather than having to go to a number of individual sources.

• When the meal is part of a larger function such as a conference, show, or exposition. Coordinating the meals around these events is a complicated matter, and it is made considerably easier by dealing with an experienced banquet manager of the host hotel.

**Party consultants** Some parties are so elaborate that only a party consultant is capable of handling all the details involved.

Party consultants are like theatrical directors. They combine the talents of individual professionals, producing the desired effect for the hostess. Some of the better known party consultants are capable of orchestrating functions for thousands of guests, but many party consultants specialize in less massive events. They plan the party from a design and/or a food concept.

You may retain a party consultant with the understanding that specific suppliers be used, such as your favorite florist, caterer, or dance band. However, some party consultants insist on working only with their own suppliers. This practice is more common for the higher priced consultants.

Finally, party consultants may simply do just that—consult. In that case their fee is in addition to the other services you engage.

*When do you need a party consultant?*

• When the hostess is unavailable to coordinate all the details of large-scale entertaining.

• When the hostess is unfamiliar with the intricacies of large-scale entertaining.

• When the hostess wishes some part of the duties to be assumed by one coordinator. A skilled hostess might, for example, want to supervise and/or prepare the food for fifty or sixty guests, but would need help with all the other details.

• When the hostess wishes an elaborate design and theme for her party. In this case, the consultant would probably come from a design (often floral design) background. The party concept would begin with the theme, and menu selections would follow accordingly.

• When the function's purpose is a promotional one. Major retailers and large corporations often entertain to create publicity. Newspapers are filled with gossip-column bits from opening night parties, embassy parties, testimonial dinners, and so on. In these instances, the party consultant might be hired not only to create the party, but also to generate some of the coverage.

• When the budget allows for elaborate entertaining.

• When the affair is very formal, perhaps a charity-sponsored debut, or a reception for a visiting dignitary. In this capacity, the party consultant functions much like a master of ceremonies in that he designs the party to accommodate the formal requirements, such as receiving lines, toasts, religious rites, etc.

**How to find the party professionals** No amount of advertising will prove how good a caterer, florist, banquet manager or any other party professional is. Their careers are built on word of mouth. Since they all deal in service, their business is to please and the best party businessmen are obviously those who please the most.

The very best source for finding the right professional is those friends of yours who have used these services and whose parties you have attended and enjoyed, or even just heard about.

The finer caterers usually have a staff of regular workers. It's these regulars whose experience may save you many hours and dollars. It pays to shop around.

When you are considering hiring caterers, party consultants, and the like, don't hesitate to ask for references from previous clients.

Good hostesses know that when all is said and done, it's the thanks that count. A party professional who truly produces will most certainly appreciate a thank-you note and some small token. Cash tips are appropriate as well as items of clothing such as ties and scarves, fine cologne, desk fixtures, and such. A thoughtful gift will certainly show your appreciation.

**Paying the bill**   You *must* get a written quote from the caterer, banquet manager, or party consultant that itemizes all of the points negotiated. In listing the services, the party professional will arrive at a cost per head, including negotiated extras.

Extras may turn out to be hidden costs, and there are some you should be aware of in advance:

Gratuities                          Coat check
Valet parking                       Damage liability deposits
Overtime service charges            Ordinances requiring firemen
Local taxes                            or policemen at certain func-
Delivery charges                       tions

The budget for a party of any magnitude must be discussed and agreed upon *in advance*. It's essential that you and your food and drink professional work within defined financial perimeters.

Some large catering organizations have their own standard contracts, but if not, the written estimate need not read like a formal legal document. It may simply include the date, time, and location of the party, the listing of duties and responsibilities, cost per head, and the professional's signature and date of signing.

You may also wish to have in writing a liability clause in case of injury to guests or members of the catering team.

Be certain to discuss the terms of payment. You may be required to place a small down payment, followed by as much as one-half in advance and the remainder on the completion of the event. Or, you may arrange to be billed for everything. However, only the very best regular clients are extended the courtesies of credit. Never assume that you will be extended credit by a party professional.

**What to ask the party professionals**   (These questions apply to all professionals unless otherwise noted.)

Where will food be prepared?

Can the caterer service hot *and* cold dishes?

What equipment is supplied as part of the cost per guest—tables, chairs, linen, silver, china, crystal, buffet tables, serving pieces (chafing dishes, serving spoons, platters, trays, etc.)? If the caterer does not supply the equipment, ask him to prepare a list of all the equipment that will be needed, including possible sources and estimated cost per person.

What package plans are available—that is, plans that include photographers, dance bands, dance floors, florists, etc.?

Is the help included as part of the cost per person and does this price include waiters and bartenders? When dealing with caterers who do not provide the help, ask them for recommendations.

When is the deadline for the head count?

How many extra guests are figured in?

Can the liquor be bought on consignment?

If either the caterer's or banquet manager's existing equipment is unacceptable, and the host makes a substitution with rented equipment, will the caterer's bill be adjusted since his equipment is not being used?

What is their time schedule? For example, a caterer may not need to be in your home until three or four hours before the event, but a party consultant and her decorator may need to have access several days beforehand.

How much will the tax and gratuity come to?

Is the gratuity included in the bill?

## Religious Dietary Restrictions

There are very strict rules concerning dietary restrictions of certain religious groups. You should know them if you plan to entertain persons of those faiths. It is important, however, to inquire as to the preferences of your guests as there are many who make exceptions to the rules. Please refer to the chart opposite.

## Walking Through the Party

One of the best ways to anticipate your needs is to create the event, step by step, in your imagination and to simulate, insofar as possible, the experience. In other words, actually walk through each stage: preparation, serving, and clearing away. Make notes, and where potential trouble points arise go back at the end and solve the problems. Walk through one more time, eliminating any remaining obstacles and watching for areas that can be improved.

This system may sound foolish, but it does help to spark the memory for little things you may have forgotten, and to suggest others that you might not have thought of at all.

### RELIGIOUS DIETARY RESTRICTIONS*

| | Meat | Fish | Alcohol | Cigarettes | **Tableware** |
|---|---|---|---|---|---|
| *Catholic* | No meat during Lent on Wed. & Fri., and on special holidays such as Holy Saturday. | | | | |
| *Jewish* | No pork or pork products. No meat or poultry unless prepared by a Kosher butcher. | No shellfish. | | | Two sets—one for dairy and one for meat. |
| *Hindu* | No beef. Strictly observant do not eat fish or fowl, some refrain from eggs. | | No. | | |
| *Buddhist* | No dietary restrictions. | | | | |
| *Muslim* | No pork or pork products. No flesh of scavenger animals. | No shellfish. | No. | No. | |
| *Christian Scientist* | | | No. | No. | |

*\* Since not all members of a religion are strictly observant, it is wise to ask your guests beforehand which dietary restrictions they follow.*

# 2

# *Space and Equipment*

It is very easy for an inexperienced hostess to over- or underestimate the number of guests she can entertain in her available space. A room that is too crowded—or, conversely, a large room with too few people "rattling around" in it—can be disastrous. And pity the poor hostess who discovers as she sets her table at 4 o'clock that her supply of wine glasses falls short of the number of guests. To help you avoid these crises, here are some guides to planning your space and equipment needs.

## Your Space Requirements

**For seated guests** To calculate the number of square feet available, multiply the length by the width of the cleared area in which the tables will be set up. Divide this total by 10 to arrive at the number of guests who can be seated in the space. If the room or area is irregular, you will find it easier to divide it into rectangular forms, calculate the number of square feet in each rectangle, then add the results together to determine the area of the entire space, and again divide by 10.

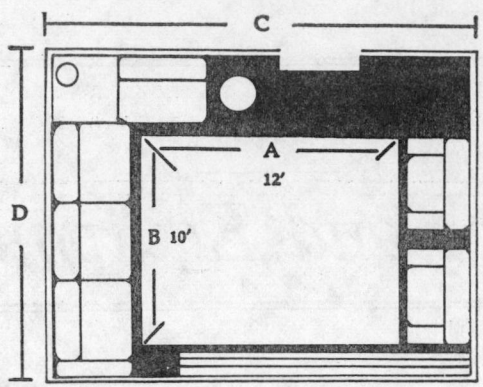

**Sample Room Layout.** *To determine the available number of square feet, and subsequently the number of seated guests a particular area can accommodate, measure the net length and width of the area. That is the area free of furniture, built-in fixtures and architectural features. The A and B figures in the illustration are the net length and width, while the C and D figures are the gross length and width. Multiply A by B. The resulting number is the net total of usable square feet. Since guests seated at tables require 10 square feet per person, divide the total usable square feet by 10.*

$$\frac{12' \text{ (net length)} \times 10' \text{ (net width)}}{10} = 12$$

*Thus, no more than 12 guests could be accommodated at tables in this room.*

**The buffet table**   A single access buffet table is one that is placed against the wall, or that for some other reason the diners will file past on only one side. There should be at least five feet of space in addition to the width of the table available.

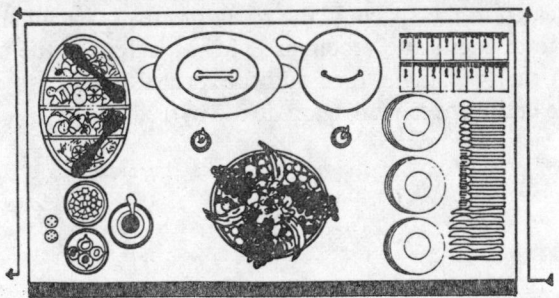

A double access buffet table stands in the middle of the room and the lines file by on both sides, or a server stands on one side and hands the plates to two lines of guests on the other. The table width plus ten feet are necessary, or five feet of space on either side for each moving line.

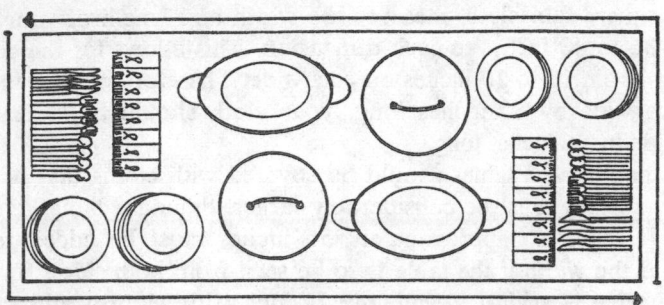

**Dining table capacities** Dining tables come in two shapes: round and straight (oval, square or rectangular). The following chart includes both shapes and also differentiates between full service (a served meal of several courses) and a one-plate buffet (no salad plates, butter plates, etc.).

| STRAIGHT TABLE Guest Capacity | | | ROUND TABLE Guest Capacity | | |
|---|---|---|---|---|---|
| Length and Width | Full Dinner | One-Plate Buffet | Diameter | Full Dinner | One-Plate Buffet |
| 36" × 36" (*card table size*) | 4 | 4 | 24" *or* 30" (*cocktail pedestal*) | 2 | 2–4 |
| 48" × 36" | 6 | 6–8 | 36" | 4 | 6 |
| 60" × 36" | 6–8 | 6–8 | 48" | 4–6 | 6–8 |
| 72" × 36" | 6–8* | 8–10* | 54" | 8 | 8–10 |
| 96" × 36" | 8–10* | 10–12* | 60" | 8–10* | 10–14* |
| | | | 72" | 10–12* | 12–16* |

*\* The first of the figures listed indicates the number of comfortably seated guests, the second the number of tightly seated guests.*

**Available space v. number of guests** If your party is being planned for twenty-four guests seated at round tables, serving a full-course meal at four 48-inch tables will be a little crowded (see chart above), although it is possible. Your guests would be more comfortable at three 54-inch tables. If the 48-inch tables must be used you would be wise to eliminate as much superfluous tableware as possible, such as bread and butter plates, salad plates, unnecessary silver, and dishes of condiments, nuts, and the like.

**Tablecloth dimensions**   To establish the correct width for your rectangular or square tablecloth, measure the width and length of your table and add 36 to 40 inches to each dimension. This allows for the correct overhang—from 18 to 20 inches on each side. Therefore, if your table is 36 inches wide by 60 inches long, your cloth should be at least 72 inches wide by 96 inches long.

Buffet and service tables should be covered with cloths that hang to the floor, so they must be considerably larger. Standard table height is 28 or 29 inches, so approximately 56 inches must be added to the length and the width if the table is to be seen from both sides. If, however, the table is against a wall, the 72-inch wide cloth would suffice, since it could be dropped to the floor in front and still leave an 8-inch overhang at the back.

Round table cloths are more difficult to figure out; here is a chart to assist you:

### LINEN SIZES FOR ROUND TABLES
*(Floor length and knee drape)*

| Table diameter | Linen diameter |
|---|---|
| 36" round | 72" knee |
|  | 90" floor |
| 48" round | 84" knee |
|  | 100" floor |
| 54" round | 90" knee |
|  | 110" floor |
| 60" round | 96" knee |
|  | 120" floor |
| 72" round* | 108" knee |
|  | 136" floor |

*\* The 72-inch table is the largest standard round table manufactured. Accordingly, it may be difficult to find a floor-length cloth for this size table.*

**The bar area**   The most important rule about a bar area is that there must be ample unencumbered space in front of the bar. If at all possible, there should be at least 10 by 10 feet of cleared space in front of a bar serving twenty-five to forty people at a cocktail party.

**Dance floor space**   Dance floor space can be calculated on the following scale. Note that the numbers are for individuals, not couples.

| Size of area in feet | "Slow" dancers | "Fast" dancers |
|---|---|---|
| 9 × 9 | 8 | 5 |
| 9 × 18 | 16 | 10 |
| 12 × 12 | 14 | 9 |
| 12 × 24 | 28 | 17 |
| 15 × 15 | 22 | 15 |
| 15 × 30 | 44 | 29 |
| 18 × 18 | 32 | 20 |
| 18 × 36 | 64 | 40 |
| 21 × 21 | 50 | 30 |
| 21 × 42 | 88 | 60 |

Other suggestions to keep in mind:

Keep the bar away from entrances, coat check areas, food serving or preparation areas, or any other traffic centers. Use the bar to make people move; it can be the attraction that will fill a dead space or relieve the crowding in one room.

Put the bar in a place that is easy for both access *and* exit, for purposes of stocking as well as serving.

If you have a built-in bar, remove all stools and chairs before a large party. However, for a small dinner party the built-in bar with stools can provide a comfortable center for all or part of the group.

### What You Need and Where to Get It

A careful check of your chairs, tables, and other equipment, plus some simple arithmetic, will enable you to arrive at a clear picture of what you already have and what you must obtain. Your first question may well be: Where can I find the additional things I need? We will try to answer that question.

**Chairs and tables** Traditionally, local funeral parlors, for public relations purposes, have made it a policy to lend folding chairs in quantity to members of families they have served in the past. This may be still true in some areas, but in the city this good-neighbor policy is a thing of the past. Table and chair rental businesses now flourish, though, to fill this need. Renting tables and chairs can be very difficult at certain times —at holiday seasons and throughout May and June because of graduations and weddings. Therefore, if you plan to rent at those times, try to place your order as far ahead as possible.

Often you can turn to family friends and neighbors to borrow folding chairs that are perfectly adequate and will save you the rental fee. Try to pick them up well in advance to give you a chance to rent extras if some of the borrowed ones turn out to be unusable. It's better to stay away from beach and lawn chairs because they are built low to the ground and do not serve well for dining.

When borrowing folding chairs from friends, remember that they are likely to be dusty if they've been in storage. And if you have borrowed from several people, be sure to put labels with the names of the lenders on each chair.

If you entertain regularly and wish to have a number of folding chairs available, don't wait for a party as an excuse to buy them. Chair rental businesses or caterers periodically sell off their inventories at very reasonable prices, so you should watch for such sales. A new coat of paint and a few tightened bolts will refurbish most tables and chairs sold in stock clearances.

As a rule, chairs with aluminum frames and plastic seats are best out-doors, as these frames adjust to uneven ground surfaces better than do wooden frames. Although it is all right to use the aluminum frame chairs indoors, their appearance is not as formal as wooden chairs.

Extra tables are likely to be more difficult to borrow than extra chairs. If you're planning a buffet and your menu is made up of easy-to-eat foods such as casseroles or sandwiches, you can probably use your couches and chairs for seating and a combination of available table top surfaces should provide all the service area necessary: counters, side-boards, dining room tables, etc. But a menu that includes foods that spill easily or are hard to cut requires table space for each guest, and you may need to obtain additional tables.

For a large seated dinner at home, a group of tables seating four to eight each is the most satisfactory arrangement. Try to stick to all round or all square tables, with the exception of your dining room table. A combination of square and round tables creates a disjointed appearance, to say the least.

If your budget makes borrowing a must, plan on more folding picnic tables and card tables than anything else. Large folding round tables and portable rectangular tables are likely to be available only from the rental agencies, not from your friends.

The hostess who entertains frequently would do well to buy several sturdy card tables and buy, or have made, round plywood covers that fit securely over the card tables and provide enough table surface space to serve six to eight people. These covers can be hinged to fold in half for easy storage.

**China, crystal, and silverware** To help you decide what you may need in the way of silver, crystal, and china, we have supplied a check list at the end of this chapter. Be sure to go through this list and check off the items that you will need for your party. It is no longer considered necessary to have a full formal setting at each place. You need to have only those forks, knives, spoons, glasses, and plates that will actually make dining comfortable for your guests and the table attractive to look at. For example, if you are serving wine, you do not need to put out water goblets. However, the thoughtful hostess may ask her guests if they would like ice water as well.

The correct placement of all the items in a setting is described in the next chapter (Setting Your Table).

Very few hostesses own more than two or three dozen place settings of anything, yet for many parties paper or plastic is totally inappropriate. To borrow stemware, and perhaps twenty or thirty plates, knives, and forks, is asking for trouble. Therefore, it is best to rent additional table service when needed. To keep costs down, you may want to do away with or combine certain courses. For example, instead of renting vegetable dishes, serve the vegetables surrounding the roast, or incorporated in a stew or pot roast. You may also combine your own china, silver, and crystal with rented equivalents because most rented service comes in simple patterns or uniform colors.

There is usually no difficulty in differentiating your own china from rented china; however, we suggest that you keep an accurate count of your silverware. It can easily get mixed up with rented silver and may get lost in the return.

**Linen** Linen is so easily damaged that renting it is expensive. Therefore, instead of renting all the linen you will need for entertaining, it is more practical to buy the pieces that hold up the best and are easiest to wash and/or replace, namely napkins. To increase your supply, and to allow for replacement of those pieces that are stained or worn, you might purchase just a few extra each time you entertain. Avoid buying too many exotic shades, which limits your decorating scheme. Ecru, white, and pale yellow are versatile and "safe," and at least half of your linen napkins should be in those colors.

One large white tablecloth is invaluable, as well as several smaller ones if you sometimes use a number of small tables for seating your guests. Additional colors and sizes can always be rented. If, for instance, you own four 90-inch round white cloths, you could rent four 54-inch colored square cloths to create a layered look and protect your own linen. Or, you could alternate white and colored cloths on several small tables.

If you have the time and the ability, the best alternative to buying or renting linen is, of course, to make it. You do not need to be a skilled seamstress to cut material into squares and make a narrow hem. One of the most colorful and economical sources is the wide array of printed or solid color permanent press sheets. Solid napkins combined with a printed tablecloth, or vice versa, makes a beautiful set when chosen to go with the rest of your decorating scheme. These, too, may be combined with your basic white linen supply.

One note of caution, however. If you do make a tablecloth from material as thin as sheeting, you will also need a thin flannel pad cut to the size of your table to go under it. Otherwise the cloth will be slippery and appear to be flimsy.

**Serving pieces** Very few households contain more than one or two large chafing dishes. But you can undoubtedly think of several friends, each of whom have one and would be willing to lend it to you. Other relatives and friends may also be able to provide you with extra silver platters and vegetable dishes, punch bowls, big coffee urns, serving trays, and any other equipment you may need for a large party. Using a mixture of silver patterns is perfectly acceptable, but if you do borrow silver, be sure to be meticulous in your record keeping. If you aren't, three weeks after your party you may end up with two extra pieces of silver and not know to whom they belong. Or a friend may call to ask for her missing chafing dish, which has been delivered to someone else. If you label all the large pieces and keep an accurate list of the small ones, you will avoid any embarrassment.

Most rental serving dishes come in stainless steel; only a few places rent silver or silver plate. Too often, the hostess uses her best china and silver, and then finds herself serving her beef stroganoff from a stainless steel chafing dish. Before settling for that, shop around a little and see if you can locate a rental agency that might have some silver plate.

**Pertinent questions about equipment rental** Does the quoted price include delivery, installation (if necessary) and removal? If not, what are the additional charges for those services?

Can rented items be delivered the day before the party at no extra charge?

What length of time does the rental charge cover?

What is the liability for loss, theft or damage to rented goods?

Do dishes and flatware have to be returned clean?

Are there any savings or discounts for labor you supply yourself—cleaning, pickup and return, installation, etc.?

## Outdoor Entertaining

**Tents, marquees, and other coverings** Almost everything we do indoors, we also do outdoors, and party giving is no exception. In the past twenty years, the equipment that has been devised to protect, shade, and frame outdoor parties has become very sophisticated. There are five basic coverings that are used for outdoor parties: tents, marquees, canopies, awnings, and umbrellas. Each has a specific use and appearance and may be used in combination with the other four.

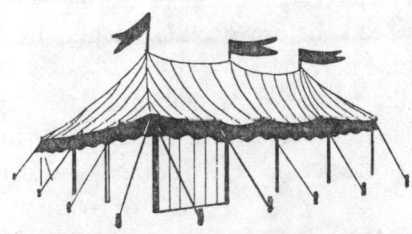

The term "tent" is often misused. The professionals define a tent as a covering of canvas or synthetic fabric suspended and rigged from poles of at least 14 to 21 feet high. A marquee performs the same function as a tent and may have the same perimeter size, but it is usually not as high and often comes without center supports.

Awnings are marquees suspended from a wall or frame. They're most often used to cover reception lines, serving tables, and work areas that are situated near a wall.

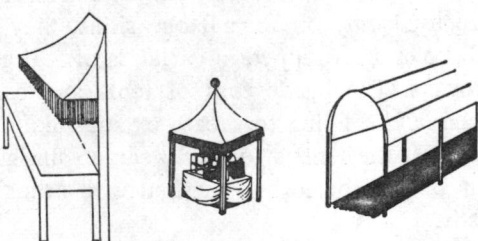

A canopy is a running, vaulted covering of 6 to 8 feet in width with side supports. It is used to connect tents and marquees to each other, to buildings, and to other areas. It can also be used to shelter buffet tables, reception lines, and the paths of predetermined processions in weddings and other formal functions. "Red carpet" events are often covered with a canopy. Small square canopies or marquees (10 by 10 feet) are used in some religious ceremonies or to shelter wedding cakes, gift tables, and reception lines.

Standard umbrellas of 8 feet in diameter cover 42-inch round tables and the six guests around them. They do not provide the same protection as tents, so they should be used only when the chances for good weather are 80–20 in your favor.

Tents are definitely not the most economical solution to at-home party entertaining. For example, to hold a party for 200 to 300 beneath a tent, the necessary 3,000 square feet of tenting would rival food and beverage costs per head. Before deciding definitely on using tents or canopies, consider the following:

*Cost.*   What is the total cost of all tent-related expenses and how much does that come to per guest? If it costs $900 for a tent covering only 60 people, the cost per head is $15 and would alter your budget drastically.

*Space.*   Do you have a surface that is big enough and flat enough, free from obstructions above and around as well as within the area? If guy wires and anchors are needed, there must be either sufficient additional space for wires or substantial surface for anchoring, such as trees and sides of buildings.

If a portable dance floor is to be used (often supplied at additional cost by canopy companies) it must be on a flat surface or leveled with a support structure, and the latter can be very expensive. In short, don't count on using a tent until you've received professional advice.

*Decorating.*   How much decorating will be necessary? Since tents and canopies are used only on formal occasions, they are often elegantly decorated. Poles are wrapped in garlands of real greens or paper or with fresh flowers. The inside tops of tents and canopies can be dressed with swags and draping to create exciting color combinations and lighting effects. If the tent is located near an unsightly or muddy area, this area must be carpeted and masked with artificial turf. All of the above are costly.

*Fire.*   When tents are used near or over open flames, such as torches or candles, certain fire regulations must be observed. Local ordinances should be checked with your fire department.

*Permits.*   Some municipalities require permits for tent erection. Check with the company renting to you or with the town or city hall.

## TENT SIZES AND CAPACITIES

| Size | Number of guests | Size | Number of guests |
|---|---|---|---|
| 20′ × 20′ | 35–40 | 40′ × 40′ | 175 |
| 20′ × 30′ | 60 | 40′ × 50′ | 200–220 |
| 20′ × 40′ | 80 | 40′ × 60′ | 240–260 |
| 30′ × 30′ | 90–100 | 40′ × 70′ | 280–300 |
| 30′ × 40′ | 125–135 | *50′ × 50′ | 250–275 |
| 30′ × 50′ | 150 | 50′ × 60′ | 300–325 |
| 30′ × 60′ | 180–200 | 50′ × 70′ | 350–400 |

* *50-foot tents are the largest tents used with a single line of center poles. 60-foot tents require three rows of poles in the center, which cuts into the space.*

*Weather problems.* The season for tent usage in most of the country starts in April or May and ends in October. The temperature should be between 55 and 85 degrees (F).

To protect the guests from getting wet feet, try to have your tent or canopy in an elevated area and "gutter" the connections between the tent and buildings. Tent gutters are pieces of plastic that create a gutter between the tent and the surrounding area so that water drains off.

The number of heating units required to heat a tent is, of course, determined by the size of the area. Your tent man will advise you about this. Since electrically operated heaters are likely to overload standard fuse boxes, plan the distribution of electrical wiring in advance. You may find that the tent you need will be too large to use electric heat; heating units are also available that are operated by gas or Sterno.

If you are planning an outdoor party to be held during the fall, whether you are using a tent or not, remember this is the season for falling leaves and twigs, so prune all overhanging branches in advance.

**Insects** The most dreaded guests to crash an outdoor party are the mosquitoes. They can spoil your event quicker than any other pest. There are numerous means of dealing with these intruders. Citronella candles are good for repelling them as well as for suppling illumination. Certain torches and sprays are effective in controlling flying insects. Here are some important pointers to keep in mind when using insect repellent:

• Consider the length of time of protection; if advance spraying is in order, do so just before the guests arrive, but also before the food is brought out.

- If you choose to use torches or flame burning agents, consider wind conditions so that the smoke will not blow toward guests.
- Avoid placing eating and cooking areas near damp areas such as ponds, thickets, and hedges where insects congregate.
- Electronic devices for killing bugs are effective. They can be used in conjunction with light spraying and/or additional burning devices.

**Lighting** The sun goes down late in summertime, so try to plan lighting that goes from daylight to dark. There are many attractive and safe temporary lighting fixtures on the market. Make sure your light increases as darkness falls. The light from overhead strings of lanterns or tall torches is enhanced by lower tabletop candles, which must, of course, be protected from the wind. Simply place inexpensive glass chimneys over your candlesticks, or you may buy complete hurricane lamps for the tables. Floodlights high in a tree shine through the foliage and make beautiful patterns. A different but equally glamorous effect is created by placing floodlights on the ground shining up at the foliage. However, it is extremely important in both cases to be sure that the lights do *not* shine directly toward the guests, as they can be blinding if one looks into the glare.

**Paper and plastic** Paper and plastic tableware are generally accepted for outdoor parties because they eliminate the danger of breakage. This, of course, is especially true when your party is held on a stone patio, a driveway, or on the area surrounding a swimming pool. If, however, the tables are on a lawn (at a wedding reception, for example) or you carpet an area with outdoor-indoor carpeting, real china and glassware are preferable. There is no question that the use of plastic lends an air of informality to a party.

Good quality plastic plates and glasses as well as paper napkins come in very attractive patterns and are certainly highly recommended for most outdoor entertaining. Paper tablecloths, however, tend to blow in the wind and they rip very easily. Unless your party area is well protected, you would be wise to use heavier plastic cloths, or cotton or linen cloths if you prefer.

## Party Equipment Check List

When you are thinking about your next party, run through this check list. You will find it an invaluable aid in planning what you will need, and in avoiding any unpleasant last-minute surprises. In each category, the most basic and important items are listed first.

### China

Soup plates or cups
Dinner plates
Salad plates
Dessert plates
Coffee cups and saucers

Butter plates
Demitasse cups and saucers
Mugs
Creamers and sugar bowls
Service plates

### Bar Glassware

Highball glasses
On-the-rocks glasses
Old Fashioned glasses
Stemmed cocktail glasses
Punch bowl and cups
Beer mugs

Liqueur glasses
Brandy snifters
Water pitcher
Cocktail shaker
Martini pitcher

### Table Glassware

Water goblets
Wine glasses (red and white)
Champagne glasses
Sherbet glasses

Dessert bowls (for ice cream,
  fruit, etc.)
Parfait glasses

### Silverware

Dinner forks
Dinner knives
Seafood cocktail forks
Salad forks
Teaspoons
Bouillon spoons
Soup spoons
Serrated knives

Dessert spoons and forks
Butter knives
Demitasse spoons
Serving spoons and forks
Carving set
Salad servers
Ladles and condiment spoons
Cake or pie servers

### Serving Dishes

Platters
Vegetable dishes
Casseroles
Chafing dishes
Coffee urn or large pot
Salad bowls
Bread baskets
Hors d'oeuvre servers
Creamers and sugars

Wine coolers
Soup tureens
Pie or cake plates
Gravy boats or bowls
Tea service
Condiment dishes
Trays
Pitchers
Fondue pots and forks

## *Bar Equipment (other than glasses)*

Ice containers                           Measurer
Bottle opener                            Spoons
Ice pick or breaker                      Strainer
Corkscrew                                Can opener
Knife                                    Towels and sponges

## Linen

Round tablecloths                        Square tablecloths
Rectangular tablecloths                  Napkins

## Chairs

Dining room chairs
Folding chairs
Lawn chairs

## Tables

Dining tables (permanent and             Buffet or serving tables
  temporary)                             Bar tables
Card tables

## Miscellaneous

Ashtrays                                 Silent butlers or table crumbers
Coasters                                 Coat racks
Candlesticks and/or candelabra           Charcoal briquets for barbecues
Electric hot plates                      Ice cream scoop
Bun or roll warmers                      Extension cords

---

*\* These are the necessary items. Other equipment that is helpful but not essential is listed in chapter 1, p. 11.*

# 3

# *Setting Your Table*

Possibly the most important single feature of your party decorations is the way in which you set your table. With the choice of colors, your creativity in designing the centerpiece or floral arrangements, and your combination of utensils and decorative items, you can set the mood for a dinner party, as well as providing a visual treat.

## Color Coordinating

For many, many years white was the standard color for table decoration, and there can be no doubt that all white creates an air of crispness, freshness and a definite sense of formality. However, current taste in table decor and color encourages the use of *any* appropriate color. Because color is such a personal consideration, there are no steadfast rules about using it. Some hostesses prefer to use pastels, for example, while others lean toward the strength of darker colors. Still others opt for a more imaginative use of color, such as light blue on medium blue or pink on red. Grading color from its lightest tones to its darkest is another popular variation, and if you would like to try this scheme, you might select a floor-length tablecloth of forest or hunter (dark) green, overlaid with a smaller square of lighter moss green. With the napkins or a center runner you could introduce a still lighter shade of green. These colors could contrast with your china or continue the color-on-color theme using various patterns of green plates.

In addition to an unlimited range of solid color linens, there are a number of patterns such as florals, plaids, stripes, and checks available. Almost invariably, a patterned cloth is best with either matching nap-

kins or solid color napkins that pick up one of the colors in the pattern.

There are occasions when the food can inspire your choice of color. Certain ethnic menus suggest specific color combinations—red checked cloths with a spaghetti dinner, for example. A more sophisticated Italian menu would look better with more subtle Roman colors, such as terra-cotta and green.

Food should always look attractive and appealing against your color selection. If a certain dish simply does not appeal to you against your linen or on your dishes—beet salad on a brown plate, for instance—then follow your instincts and choose a different color for that course.

**Using color as a party motivation**   "Think Pink" on a Valentine party invitation, or "Come in green" on St. Patrick's day can help to set the stage for a party even before it begins. By coordinating what the partygoers will be wearing, the hostess has taken the use of color to a new dimension. Usually such parties are tied to a symbolic or traditional celebration, such as the Saint Patrick's Day celebration with "the wearing of the green."

An example of a more contemporary party where one color sets the theme is a summertime "White Party." Here the use of color is not only decorative, but lends a touch of cooling to the party. It also allows your guests to show off their summer tans. The effect can be best achieved, naturally, if you have a room that can be easily converted into a basically white setting. If you don't, simply design as much of your party decoration and equipment in white as possible. Linen, flowers, candles, balloons, pillows, etc., can all be used to provide accents of white.

Although an all white menu is not impossible, it is unappetizing. While you might arrange your basic dishes to be white, you will want to do things like adding chives to vichyssoise, watercress to surround the potato salad and strawberries to top the vanilla ice cream to inject the necessary touches of color.

## The Table Covering

As you begin to set your table, you will need to consider what it will be covered with. It is not necessary to cover the table completely, in fact a highly polished table may be perfect for your place setting. Generally speaking, however, there are few occasions when there is not at least a place mat, doily, or cloth between the dish and the table.

Tablecloth dimensions and shapes have already been discussed in the previous chapter. For informal functions—luncheons, outdoor parties, and the like—place mats, with or without runners, are more often used. A runner is simply a strip of fabric, matching the place mats, that runs lengthwise in the center of the table.

Place mats come in any number of materials and in every conceivable color and pattern. They are also quite easy to make since a set is usually a consistent shape. Fabric and woven-fiber mats are often laminated to protect their finish and color and to allow them to be easily cleaned.

Place mats may also be used in conjunction with tablecloths. The combination can create interesting patterns and color combinations and may serve to protect your tablecloth. However, for more formal settings, you will probably want to stay in the traditional mode and cover the table with a linen, lace, or damask cloth. Except when using a lace cloth, which is prettier when the dark wood shows through, you should use a table pad. These can be purchased in standard table sizes, or cut to the size of your table. If you don't have one, you may use a regular sheet or lightweight blanket folded to the size of the table. This protects the table, deadens sound and creates a softer feel—a cushioning effect—to the table top.

Before progressing to the place setting, be sure to view your cloth from every side and see that it hangs evenly. This is also the time to iron out any wrinkles and correct any minor defects.

## The Place Setting

The place setting described below is for the maximum number of courses. For anything less, simply eliminate the items that you do not need, but follow the text and the drawing for the correct placement of each article you use.

If you are going to use service plates (very fine china plates that hold the containers for the first course), space them evenly around the table. The silver is then put in place, starting from the outside in, in order of its use. Forks are on the left of the plate: the fish fork (if there is to be a fish course) to the far left, the dinner fork next, and the salad fork next to the plate. However, if you plan to serve salad before the entrée, the salad fork would be placed to the left of the dinner fork. The knives are placed on the right, the one to be used first farthest from the plate, with the sharp edges toward the plate. The soup spoon goes to the right of the knives. Dessert spoons and forks may be placed horizontally above the place setting, or may be brought in on the dessert plates. The butter plate is on the left above the forks and the butter knife is placed diagonally across the butter plate, from upper left to lower right, with blade toward the left. If coffee is to be served with the meal, the cup and saucer are placed to the right of the setting and the coffee spoon goes on the saucer. If a shellfish (or oyster) fork is needed, it is placed to the right of the spoons—the *only* fork that is ever found on the right.

No more than three of any implement is ever put on the table, so if a fourth fork is necessary (as for dessert), it should be brought in when the dessert is served.

The water goblet is placed above the knives and the wine glass or glasses arranged to the right of it. The glasses may be grouped with one slightly behind and to one side of another, or they may be placed in a straight line, descending in height from the goblet.

Whether you use one, two, or three forks, or nothing more than one wine glass and a paper napkin, the setting should be in exactly the same order. If your table is set correctly it will eliminate any confusion on your guests' part, because they will be using the appropriate utensil when they go "from the outside in."

## Napkins

The napkin at a formal dinner is placed on the service plate. At a less formal setting it may be in the center of the setting or, if a first course is on the table when the diners sit down, to the left of the forks.

Large dinner napkins are folded in one of two ways. They may be folded into a large square and the sides are then folded in to form a loose rectangle one third the width of its height, or, the square may be folded in half diagonally and the two long points folded under. Small luncheon napkins and paper napkins that are already folded into a square when purchased may simply be folded once again to form a rectangle, or diagonally to form a triangle. The sharp corners may be tucked in slightly or not, as you wish.

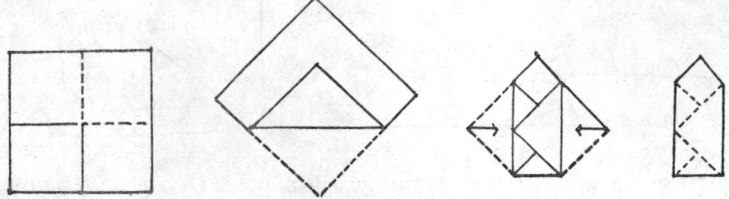

BASIC FOLD. *Fold the napkin in half, and in half again, to form a square. Turn up the folded corner three-quarters. Overlap the right and left side points. Turn napkin over and adjust the sides until they are even.*

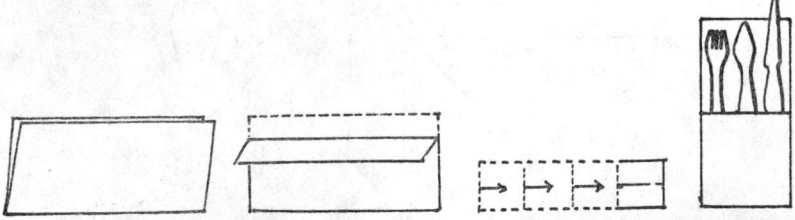

BUFFET SERVICE. *Fold the napkin in half with open ends at the top. Fold down one open side to the middle of the fold. Turn the napkin over—face down—and fold over four times from left to right. Turn the napkin face up and place silverware in the pocket.*

While fancy napkin folds are not appropriate at very formal dinners, when you would probably be using monogrammed napkins, on other, less formal occasions, exotic napkin folding gives you an opportunity to be truly creative. Whether you're doing a fancy bird of paradise, a lotus leaf, or an elegant oriental fan, the unusual way you fold your napkins can add a fascinating touch to a table setting. Each napkin fold will create a different effect, so consider which fold will look best with your china and your other table decorations. Very fine linens, unstarched linen, many synthetics, and napkins smaller than 17 × 17 inches do not lend themselves to novelty folds, so if you wish to try some unusual folds, be sure the napkins you have are suitable. (You will find several exotic napkin folds illustrated in chapter 10, Chinese New Year's Dinner, pp. 123–126.)

You may choose not to *fold* napkins but rather to put them in rings. Although some of the enameled, pottery, or china rings available are

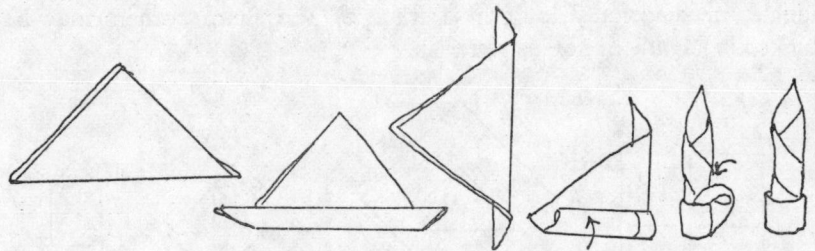

**CANDLESTICK OR CONE.** *Fold the napkin into a large triangle with the point facing the top. Turn the bottom edge up one and one-half inches. Turn the napkin on its side. Roll the napkin as shown. Tuck the end in, to hold the fold. Stand upright and, for added effect, decorate with ornaments, greens or ribbon.*

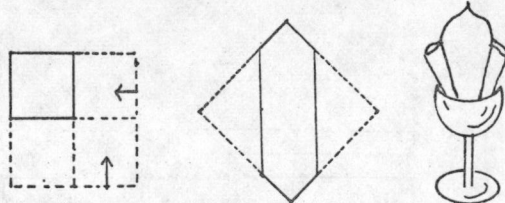

**LILY NAPKIN FOLD FOR GLASSES.** *Right side down, fold into quarters. Turn over and, if ornamented, face point up. Fold back left and right corners. Make soft pleats, folding napkin evenly, shaping it to glass. Place the folded napkin in the glass.*

beautiful, you may prefer simply to glue a sprig of holly or a crêpe paper flower onto plain napkin rings to dress them up for the occasion. Or you might tie the napkin with a large satin ribbon two inches wide.

## Candles

Probably the surest way to create a dramatic lighting effect is with candlelight. Candles may be part of a floral arrangement, stand individually, in clusters, or be part of a candelabra with from three to five branches. The commonest candles are made from bees' wax or paraffin. These candles burn the slowest, are smokeless, sometimes dripless, and can be found in many shapes and sizes. The standard candle forms are straight-sided or tapered.

Dipped candles are manufactured to "burn straight," into the hollowed interior, and are good because they are dripless.

Votive candles are another good choice because they burn for so long. The length of time depends on the dimensions, from ten hours for a $1\frac{1}{2} \times 1\frac{3}{4}$-inch candle, to fifty hours for a $2\frac{1}{2} \times 4$-inch candle. They are usually burned in clear or colored glass containers. Votive candles may be placed around a centerpiece, in front of each guest, and/or scattered throughout the area of the party to create a magical glow.

Unprotected candles, that is those that stand in holders without globes or glass, should not be placed in locations other than the dining table. The unprotected candles are difficult to keep an eye on and they drip messily because of the drafts created by people moving about. Instead, votive candles or candles in glass chimneys are a better option.

Candles on the dinner table should be either lower or higher than eye level and should pick up the party's color theme, whether white or colored. Candles in candelabra are taller, of couse, but guests can look across the table *below* the candelabra and the added height gives a graceful formal effect.

Tapers are lovely additions to the table, placed either in groups or spaced individually. These are long, very thin candles (thickness varies from $\frac{1}{4}$ to $\frac{1}{2}$ inch). Tapers tend to burn very quickly and somewhat messily, and they need special holders, because regular candleholders are too wide.

Candles made into special shapes, covered with sand or shells, scented or unscented, are usually made more for their appearance than for light. Remember that a big candle may not necessarily burn brighter than three or four smaller candles.

In addition to store-bought candleholders, there are a number of homemade options you may wish to consider. The tops of pineapples and artichokes (with their bottoms flattened) make beautiful natural candleholders. There are also a number of ordinary items that lend themselves to holding candles or to masking holders: ashtrays, statuettes, and objets d'art, as well as greenery, flowers, mosses, and the like.

Floating candles have become very popular and are an interesting alternative to more traditional candle displays. The delicate interplay of light and water gives a very sophisticated effect. Floating candles burn two and a half to three hours, and come in a variety of popular shapes: white semispheres, lilies (white with yellow centers), green lily pads with a green turtle on them, and so on.

## Other Lighting

To create special or different lighting effects, consider the dining room or setting as it will be seen at the time of the party. If the event will be held during the evening, then you should make your decisions about lighting when it is dark. To soften a room's lighting, try using smaller wattage bulbs—replace 100-watt bulbs with 40-watt bulbs, and if there are three bulbs in an overhead fixture, use only two with decreased wattage.

Bounce indirect lights off the ceiling, or place a spotlight behind a large house plant to make interesting patterns above the table. You may also use a spotlight to accent a sideboard floral display or perhaps the centerpiece or main dish on a buffet table.

You must, of course, leave plenty of light in work areas such as the kitchen and pantry. However, try to avoid fluorescent kitchen lighting from spilling over into the dining area, perhaps by the use of a screen to hide the door into the kitchen.

A rheostat or light dimmer is an invaluable accessory over a dining table. Since installing a dimmer is a relatively inexpensive and one-time-only expense, you might consider putting one in your dining room and on certain permanent fixtures in your most often used party rooms.

# 4

# *Decorating with Flowers*

Whatever the occasion, the importance of fresh flowers in the home cannot be overemphasized. As an integral part of home decoration, especially when you're entertaining, flowers give a lift to the spirit by adding color and warmth. A beautiful centerpiece, for example, greatly enhances the enjoyment of dining with friends.

The trend in flower arranging is toward personal expression. It is no longer necessary to follow strict rules of color, shape, height, and so on. Imagination and creative flair are the goals of good floral design.

The first decision you need to make regarding flowers for your party is whether to buy the flowers and arrange them yourself, or to have them done by a professional florist. The type of party, the number of guests and tables, the amount of time you have to spend, and your budget must all be taken into consideration.

The range of choices is wide—from a simple centerpiece consisting of a few individual flowers placed with a well-chosen accessory or two, to elaborate decorations that transform your home into an exotic floral fantasy. Both simple and elaborate arrangements take imagination and practice, and experience will be your best teacher. In either case, you will probably have to buy the flowers unless your own garden is able to supply your needs.

## Using a Florist

Selecting a florist is almost as important as choosing your caterer or bakery. But once you have developed a continuing relationship with one florist, he or she will come to know a great deal about your personal needs, likes and dislikes. You will find that your florist can become an invaluable ally and resource. Do not hesitate to praise his work, and to sing his praises to your friends. At the same time, do not hesitate to voice any valid complaints. A conscientious florist will appreciate knowing what is not right, as long as your criticisms are honest and appropriate.

Take the time to visit your florist as soon as the invitations to your party are sent—usually two to three weeks in advance. Try to take along a list of information that will aid him, as well as a list of questions that you will want him to answer.

## Information to give the florist

- Date, time, and place of party.
- Number of guests.
- Number and sizes of tables that will require centerpieces.
- Formality of party.
- Theme or occasion for party.
- Additional arrangements needed for placement on buffet table, sideboard, mantel, coffee table, entrance hall, or powder room.
- Style and color of decor.
- Color of table linen and china.
- Number and type of containers you have available.
- How many personal flowers, if required (corsages, boutonnieres, etc.)

## Questions to ask the florist

Can he help you to plan a theme?

Can he add to the theme by providing additional decorations or props (balloons, ribbons, trellises, baskets, candles, etc.)?

What fresh flowers will be available at the time of your party?

What sizes and shapes of arrangements does he suggest?

Does he wish to see your home in advance? (If you use the same florist regularly, he will undoubtedly wish to keep information about your room sizes and decor on file so that he need not visit before each party.)

Can he provide:

Skirting for buffet tables?

Chandelier festooning?

Swagging for tents or canopies?

Stanchions?

What does his estimate cover? Be absolutely sure that every item is listed, including labor and delivery costs.

Ask him to show you pictures of parties he has decorated. Although your party should be handled entirely differently from any other, photos of his work can serve as a useful guide.

## Equipment for Doing Flowers Yourself

For economic reasons, as well as for the sheer pleasure of arranging flowers, many people prefer to do their own floral decorating.

**Supplies, materials, and tools** Before you can begin to create floral works of art you must have at hand certain tools and materials. There are also rules to be followed, not only to make the arrangements attractive, but also to make them last longer. Here is a complete check list of the materials you need, although you will not use all of them every time you arrange flowers. All the items are available at your florist's or a hardware store.

| | |
|---|---|
| Sharp knife | Flower holders |
| Wire cutters | Moss |
| Pruning shears | Waterproof adhesive tape |
| Florist wire for supporting | Floratape |
| stems | Vaporizer |
| Chicken wire | Pebbles, marbles, gravel |
| Styrofoam | Florist putty |
| Oasis | |

**Liners and containers** Almost anything can be used as a container for flowers as long as it will hold water. If you are the least bit uncertain as to whether it is leakproof, use a liner to prevent possible damage to table surfaces. Any waterproof container that will fit into another container without showing can be used as a liner. With the insertion of a liner, you could use a fine antique porcelain vase that might get damaged by water, or a china pitcher with a crack in it. All containers that cannot hold water, such as wooden boxes and bowls or terra cotta pots require the use of liners.

Disposable aluminum pans, available in most grocery or dime stores, work well as liners for shallow containers. So do many types of plastic refrigerator storage containers, which are somewhat flexible and can be cut down in height. Heavy duty aluminum foil can be used in several thicknesses, but you must be sure that it is pressed tight into the container and does not show. Even plastic bags, if used in double thickness, are helpful for hard-to-fit containers.

Here is a list of articles you may have in your home that can be used as containers.

Vases (all sizes, shapes and materials)
Urns
Decorative bowls (porcelain, glass, wooden, copper, pewter, silver, etc.)
Mugs, cups, and drinking glasses
Kitchen utensils (tea kettle, casserole, copper mold, etc.)
Baskets
Garden pots (terra cotta, not plastic)
Trays with raised sides
Large sea shells
Sturdy boxes (Christmas gift boxes, for example)

## Selection and Care of Flowers

Your choice of flowers will be based partly on color, size and shape; but the most important consideration is freshness. Just as in buying vegetables, one must be guided by the eye. Examine the heads of flowers for discoloration or bruised petals. The leaves should be strong and firm and stems should be all of one color. Dark discoloration at the base indicates the flower has been in water for some time. Very tight buds are unlikely to open. On the other hand, overly mature flowers are likely to drop their petals or to droop by the time of the party.

Ask your florist about seasonal changes, when new and often unfamiliar blooms are available. Ask for the names of flowers you don't recognize, and about their care and life expectancy. Some of the most delicate or exotic blooms are very fragile and last only a short time, yet the pleasure they give may compensate for their brief life.

To prepare the flowers for arranging, use a very sharp knife to cut an inch off each stem on a sharp diagonal. This exposes more open surface and allows the flower to take water more freely. If the stems are hard or woody, such as pussy willows or flowering crab apples, use heavy pruning shears. It is also beneficial to slit these woody stems up an inch or two, or to crush the ends with a hammer.

Pull off all lower leaves—especially any foliage that will be under water—as these leaves will rot and cause discoloration and an unpleasant odor.

To keep the flowers until you are ready to arrange them, place them in a large bucket or a tall pitcher of fresh cool water, filled two-thirds up the height of the stems. Keep them in a cool, shaded place.

Fresh water and clean containers are the two most important features in keeping cut flowers beautiful and fresh. Be sure that the bucket you store flowers in, or the container you use for the arrangement, is full.

Change the water daily if possible; if not, add fresh water to keep the level high. Several products are available to help keep flowers alive (Floralife is one). Most come in individual packets of powder. An aspirin dropped in the water is helpful, and a small piece of charcoal keeps the water clear. A copper penny or two added to an arrangement of tulips prolongs their life.

Flowers that droop can sometimes be revived. Submerge the stems in very warm water and, while they are still under the water, cut off an inch. Let the stems soak in the warm water for twenty minutes and plunge them into a deep container of cool water. Be sure the head of the flower is supported and is not in the water. Wrapping a weak stem in a wet piece of paper can help support it.

## Making Your Own Flower Arrangements

**Advance preparations** Two or three weeks before your party, you should start to deal with the following items:

- Decide where flower arrangements will be needed.
- Check supplies and tools; buy whatever you are lacking.
- Select containers you would like to use.
- Plan your work space. You'll need an area that provides room for both storage and assembly.
- Place your order with your florist. The flowers should be picked up or delivered the day before the party, which is the best time to arrange them. You will not feel pressured, and you can put the arrangements in place with time to make final adjustments. Add a blossom, cut a stem a little shorter, turn a bloom slightly so that the arrangement fits the setting.

**Holders**

*Chicken wire* is the very simplest holder when trimmed and fitted to the shape of the vase. With wire cutters, cut a piece of chicken wire approximately two inches larger on each side than the container into which it is to be placed. Press it into shape, making sure that the pointed ends are all facing downward so you will not snag the flowers or your hand. Secure it in place with waterproof adhesive tape pressed to the edge of the container and looped through the wire. Do this in several directions so that the tape makes one or more X's. After the flowers have been placed be sure the wire does not show above the top of the vase.

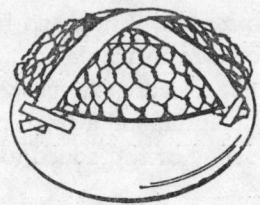

*Pinpoint holders* come in all sizes and shapes: round, oval, square, and rectangular. The base is heavy metal or lead with bristles or sharp points. The weight helps to keep the holder at the bottom of the container, but it is wise to affix it with florist putty.

*Frog holders* also come in various shapes and resemble glass paperweights with holes. They may also be made of metal in various shapes, looped or cut out to form the necessary holes. Like pinpoint holders, they must be secured to the bottom of the container with florist putty.

Both pinpoint holders and frogs are indispensable for arrangements in low bowls where chicken wire and oasis would show. They also serve for Oriental arrangements that are made with just a few flowers.

*Oasis* is by far the easiest and most popular flower holder to use. It comes in various shapes, the most common being brick shaped. Very light when dry, quite heavy when soaked in water, the bricks can be cut to the shape of the container, placed side by side, or stacked one on top of the other.

Determine the depth of your container, and cut the oasis to reach just to the top. Completely submerge the oasis in a pot of water and hold it under until all bubbles top rising. Then place the oasis in the selected container and secure it in place with waterproof (green, if possible) adhesive tape. Since you will fill the container with additional water when you have finished the arrangement, which tends to make the oasis float, the taping down is necessary.

When you're making a large arrangement, or one that will contain many flowers, or branches with heavy stems, a piece of chicken wire should be cut and shaped to cap the oasis. This will prevent the block or blocks from coming apart. It is also helpful to make holes in the oasis with an ice pick before inserting soft-stemmed flowers.

Oasis should never show. It can be covered with natural peat moss that has been saturated with water and pressed into shape, or a base of green foliage can be arranged to cover the taped-in oasis.

*Stones, pebbles, and marbles* are also useful aids in flower arranging.

A glass vase filled with clear marbles not only looks wonderful, but the marbles serve to balance the vase and disguise the flower stems. Shiny black stones covering the base of a pinpoint or frog holder help to hide the mechanics of the arrangement.

Some containers, such as a tall narrow vase, will not need a holder at all.

**Arranging the flowers** Before using flowers that have been cut for a day or two, cut the stems again on a diagonal (as described on p. 50).

The rule for determining the height of your arrangement is that the tallest flower should be approximately one and a half times the height of the container. (This is, however, a rule that can be broken as the style and placement of the container dictate.) Only your tallest flowers need to be that height; other varieties may be shorter.

Start with some green foliage as a base to hide the holder, but leave spaces to insert the stems of the flowers. Then place the largest flowers in groups of two or three so that they make splashes of color. Fill in between the groups with smaller flowers and taller greens. Be sure that all the flowers are not the same height. There should be a feeling of depth and dimension—flowers behind flowers, with ample space between them. Place large open flowers at the outer line of the arrangement rather than in the center. Not all flowers have straight stems, and you can use that fact to your advantage. Turn and twist such flowers before inserting them to achieve the most graceful effect. For ideas on shapes of arrangements, refer to the illustrations on pp. 54–55.

Turn the container constantly as you work, especially if it is to be seen from all sides. Even if it is to be placed against a wall, remember that it can still be seen from the sides and it should never be flat. Pay special attention to the rim of the container. The flowers and foliage should come down over the edge and the arrangement should look as if it were a part of the container, not sitting on top of it. Many types of foliage help to achieve this effect. Ivy, Virginia creeper, and clematis, for example, hang gracefully and can be intertwined around the lower part of the container. If the container is a basket, the vines can be wrapped around the handle.

**Style and placement of flower arrangements** What is known as a romantic arrangement appears to be without plan—a jumble of mixed garden and/or wild flowers. Its success depends on a profusion of well-blended varieties. This is a case of "more is better," but do not overcrowd. The individual blooms should be visible, too.

Just the opposite is true when you are making an Oriental or Japanese arrangement. Here, a linear movement, one of simplicity and restraint, is the goal.

In modern arrangements, the shape and material of the vase will often dictate the kinds of flowers and the number that can be used. The container, more than in any other style, is an integral part of the design.

For any style of arrangement, keep the background colors in mind, picking up the colors in the room for a harmonious effect.

When flowers are used as a centerpiece, the linen and place settings must be considered. The colors of the arrangement must blend well with them, as well as with the surrounding decor. Bushy, solid arrangements should never be more than twelve to fifteen inches high, or the guests will not be able to see each other across the table. However, a container with a pedestal base elevates the flowers effectively and allows low see-through space. Exotic blooms in individual bud vases at each place, rather than a centerpiece, lend a glamorous touch to simple china and crystal.

Book shelves make a good setting. The contrast between the rather severe lines of books and the colorful flowers can be striking. And a large arrangement of flowers or of foliage is ideal for filling an empty fireplace.

Flower arrangements can be used to hide architectural flaws such as pipes, air conditioners, etc., but you must be careful. If the covering is not sufficient it will only call attention to the flaw rather than disguising it.

## BASIC SHAPES OF FLORAL ARRANGEMENTS

Hogarth Line. *Named for the English painter William Hogarth. S-shaped arrangement.*

Rectangle. *Modern design without a single focal point. Not too compact.*

**Sphere.** *Round, solid compact ball of flowers.*

**Asymmetrical.** *Off-balanced either to the right or to the left.*

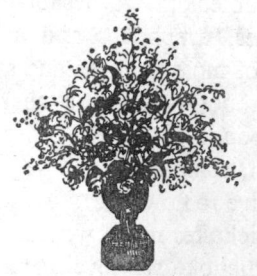

**Circle.** *To be seen from all sides. Round arrangement.*

**Triangle.** *Classic shape. Has many variations.*

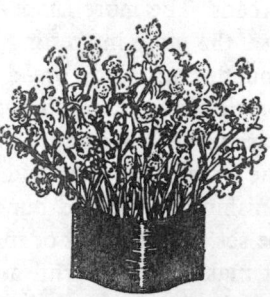

**Vertical Line.** *A more or less unbroken straight line.*

**Diagonal.** *Very similar to Hogarth Line, but not as exaggerated. One group of flowers upward, another downward.*

**Fan Shape.** *Arrangement in the shape of a fan. Can be flat at back.*

Make sure that accessories complement an arrangement and do not fight for attention. Statues or ornaments that are the same size as the arrangement should be moved or put away. But china figurines, marble obelisks, crystal animals, silver swans, or even a beautiful shell, to name just a few, are examples of objets d'art that can be attractively combined with a floral design.

When you have put your arrangement in place, step well back and view it from all sides several times to judge the total effect.

## Using Fruits, Vegetables, and Breads

Vegetables and fruits are a natural combination. An arrangement of eggplant, dark grapes, and plums can be a very dramatic study against a pale tablecloth. A basket of all-green vegetables—beans tied in little bunches, artichokes and avocados, broccoli, and parsley, with little tucks of moss between and strategically placed green and white gingham ribbon bows—makes a charming centerpiece for a midsummer's day luncheon, and the vegetables can be used afterward. For those on a tight budget, using fruits and vegetables for table decoration is a practical alternative to flowers.

Artichokes make wonderful natural candlesticks. Cut off the stem so the artichoke sits level, gently open the center leaves and insert a candle. The same can be done with a pineapple. Select only those pineapples with perfect tops. Separate the center leaves and insert a candle. As a safety measure, place a ring of florist putty at the bottom of the candle.

Another variation on the edible theme is to make an arrangement of breads. The more shapes, sizes, and colors of the breads and rolls you use, the more interesting the arrangement. You might start with a large, round, dark black bread in the center, with thin long loaves of French bread coming out from under it. Surround the center loaf with rolls of various shapes and colors: twists, oblong ryes, and bread sticks. Fasten the breads together with clean wooden skewers and toothpicks. As a finishing touch, add bunches of wheat or dried grasses. All of this can be set on a large wooden cutting board, a tray, or a wooden salad bowl. It makes a wonderful autumn arrangement, as do gourds and squash, which are cheap and plentiful in the fall.

The possibilities are endless and one idea leads to another. Jot down ideas as they come to you and also clip pictures from magazines of centerpieces that appeal to you. Don't be afraid to take chances. When you do something unusual, there's no right or wrong, and no one will know if you made a "mistake."

## The Finishing Touches

After you clean up your work area and put away all the supplies, make a note of how much time you have spent on doing the flowers. This information will be useful to you in the future, and you will learn what you are capable of doing.

When you set out your finished arrangements the day before the party, make sure that every container is filled with water. Then, the following day, check the water level again. You will be surprised how much the flowers have "drunk." Add whatever is necessary.

Check each arrangement for wilted blooms. It is a good idea to keep a few extra flowers in a bucket of deep water so that you can replace dead or dying ones just before the party.

# 5

# *Invitations*

Invitations are important pieces of communication that serve as both a source of information and a "stage-setter" for your party. There are standard forms of address, layout, and folding, as well as technical aspects like printing and embossing that a good hostess should know about.

First of all, invitations should include as much pertinent information as possible, in addition to the type, the time, and the location of the party. For example, "black tie" or "dinner jacket" on invitations to formal occasions, and phrases like "garden reception—bring a wrap or jacket" for less formal events are most helpful to your guests. An invitation is the first inkling that a party is planned. It is the only way you can establish an attitude and a mood *before* the party begins.

The following sections include samples of various kinds of invitations. Most stationers can show you a set of standard samples, from which you can choose the layout, typeface, and other elements you prefer.

## Formal Invitations

**Traditional engraved invitations**   The traditional engraved (formal) invitation is used for official functions, or, socially, for a debut, a dance, a wedding or any very formal entertaining. It is always written in the third person, on conservative-looking paper in equally conservative color and type style. The wording is proscribed and unchangeable. No abbreviations are used except "Mr." "Mrs." and "Dr." Street and state names are written in full. There is no punctuation except a comma between the day and the date, and between the town and the state, and no capitals except where a word is normally capitalized. The time of the party is written as "half after nine" or "half past nine o'clock" rather than "nine thirty." Either R.s.v.p. or R.S.V.P. is correct, although the latter is used mostly in diplomatic circles. "Please reply to" and "The favor of a reply is requested" are permissible, too.

---

*Mr. and Mrs. Franklin Parks*
*request the pleasure of your company*
*at a dance*
*Friday evening, February the third*
*at half after nine*
*Green Grove Country Club*
*Woodland, Texas*

*R.s.v.p.*								*Black Tie*
*1200 Smith Avenue*
*Woodland*
*Texas 00000*

---

The R.s.v.p. and address (no address is necessary if it is the same as the address of the party) is always in the lower left-hand corner, and information such as "Black Tie" or "Dancing" is in the lower right.

When an event is held to honor a person or group of persons, this is made clear on the invitation.

---

*Mr. and Mrs. George Parsons*
*request the pleasure of your company*
*at a dance in honour of their daughter*
*Miss Sarah Parsons*
*etc . . .*

---

Or, the invitation may be printed in the standard form and "In honour of Miss Sarah Parsons" may be written by hand at the top. Note that the word "honour" is always spelled with a "u" on formal invitations.

Wedding invitations are worded slightly differently:

---

*Mr. and Mrs. Howard Storm*
*request the honour of your presence*
*at the marriage of their daughter*
*Penelope*
*to*
*Mr. John Cravens*
*on Saturday, the eighth of March*
*at four o'clock*
*The Church of the Resurrection*
*Byram Way*
*Holyoke, Massachusetts*

---

**Fill-in formal invitations** If you entertain frequently—and formally—you may wish to order a supply of engraved "blanks." The basic, changeless wording is engraved and the pertinent information (underlined in the example below) filled in for each party.

Formal invitations are always mailed at least three weeks in advance of the event.

**Response cards** Since the formal invitation is indicative of an important event, an accurate count of attending guests is crucial, and you may therefore find it necessary to enclose a response card with the invitation. We deplore this practice because it indicates that prospective guests lack the courtesy to send a handwritten response. But since this frequently seems to be the case, and since the widespread use of caterers

> Mr. and Mrs. Harold Storm
> request the pleasure of
> <u>Dr. and Mrs. Kenneth Fayston's</u>
> company at <u>dinner</u>
> on <u>Saturday, the seventh of May</u>
> at <u>eight o'clock</u>
> 110 Kirby Lane
> Harrison, New York 10566
>
> R.s.v.p.

and rented equipment makes it imperative to have an accurate estimate of numbers, the response card is becoming a necessary evil.

Response cards are printed or engraved to match the invitations, and the self-addressed envelopes that accompany them should be stamped. There are two forms generally used and we recommend the first, since it indicates exactly for whom the invitation is intended.

> <u>Mr. and Mrs. John Stock</u> (to be filled in by hostess)
> ☐ accept
> ☐ regret
> Friday, February the third
> Green Grove Country Club

or

> <u>Miss Joan Arthur</u> (to be filled in by guest)
> ☐ accept(s)
> ☐ regret(s)
>
> etc.

The problem with the second form is that guests tend to enlarge the guest list by writing

<u>*Miss Joan Arthur and guest*</u>
or
<u>*Mr. and Mrs. Frederick Stout and son, Robert*</u>

## Informal Invitations

There are many inventive and unusual approaches that can be used in the wording, color, paper, packaging, and even delivery of informal invitations. The following is an example of a somewhat different invitation that might be considered for a Sweet Sixteen party.

---

### *THE SIXTEENTH SEASON*

*Starring* ....................................................................*Janyce Goldstein*
*Matinée* ........................................................*2:00 P.M., Saturday, May 25th*
*Featuring* ..................................................*Luncheon and swimming*
*Scene* ..........................................................................*206 Arch Street*
*Black Point, Connecticut*
*Producers* ...................................................*Janet and Joe Goldstein*


*Please call ticket office*                    *Please bring:*
*555-2222*                                     *bathing suits and towels*

---

If you plan to make your own invitations, any number of ordinary household items such as yarn, ribbon, and colored tape can be used to dress them up. An array of mailing devices—padded envelopes, cardboard folders and mailing tubes—are available and add another dimension in the packaging.

Finally, there is an infinite variety of preprinted invitations available, from the simplest fill-ins that are adaptable to any type of party, to invitations made up specifically for every conceivable occasion.

---

*You are invited* <u>*for cocktails*</u>
*on* <u>*Thursday, January 6*</u>
*at* <u>6 P.M.</u>
*at the home of* <u>*Lib and Bill Post*</u>
*address* <u>*North Hill Farm*</u>
<u>*Waterbury Center*</u>

*R.s.v.p. 000-1111*

<u>*(regrets only)*</u>

---

or

---

*A Kitchen Shower*
*for* <u>*Susan Bell*</u>
*date* <u>*Saturday, Oct. 6*</u>
*time* <u>5 P.M.</u>
*at* <u>*Nell Marton's*</u>
<u>*6 Overlook Dr.*</u>

*R.s.v.p.*                    <u>*Red and white*</u>

---

Telephone invitations are perfectly acceptable for informal parties. Just be sure that you include all the necessary information. Verbal invitations are particularly satisfactory when appropriate because you usually receive an immediate acceptance or refusal.

## Reminder Cards

When invitations have been telephoned or extended in person, or if they have been sent out several weeks in advance, it is a good idea to follow them up with a reminder card. This used to be done on the hostess's "informals," but these small cards do not meet the current size requirements of the United States Post Office, so they must be written on a post card or personal note paper. All they need say is:

---

*To remind you*
*Saturday, the 6th—7 P.M.*
*at Mary and Jack's*

---

or

---

*Dear Fran,*
   *Just to remind you that we are expecting*
*you and Herb on the 23rd at 6:30.*
                                          *Muriel*

---

### Ordering Your Invitations

There are certain occasions when it is not appropriate to use ready-made, fill-in invitations, so you must order your invitations through your local stationer. If he is not equipped to deal with your order you can, as long as you know exactly what you want, go directly to a printer. Real engraved invitations must be ordered through your stationer or jewelry store, but today the less expensive thermographed invitations are acceptable, and many printers can do that process right on their own premises.

You will want to order invitations when:
  • The invitation is to be very formal.
  • The number required exceeds the number you have time to write by hand.
  • You want a special color stock or print.
  • The copy requires more than one type style.
  • You want a special effect such as embossing or die-cutting.

If you go directly to a printer, there are certain questions you should be sure to ask him.

Is the stock you select immediately available, and if not, how long will it take him to get it?

Can he guarantee delivery by a specified date?

Does he have equipment on the premises to do thermography, engraving, embossing, special colors, etc., or must he send out the work? If he plans to subcontract, it might be cheaper or more satisfactory to check with another printer.

Will he show you proofs for your approval?

Does his quoted price include the stock; special colors; the plates (if engraving is used); scoring and folding; delivery; taxes?

# 6

# Temporary Help

There is no such thing as a party where there isn't at least some pressure on the hostess. Whether it's a small gathering or your big entertaining event of the year, you must plan and execute any number of details. In order to relieve yourself of some of the burden, you'd be well advised to consider obtaining extra help when you entertain more than casually.

## Determining If You Need Help

The time to get help is not at the last moment. Running through the party step by step as you make your plans will give you some idea about the amount of work involved, and this information, along with the total number of guests and the amount of food to be served, will help you to determine whether you need help and, if so, how much and for what purpose(s).

For a cocktail party of fifty to eighty, for example, you may need only one or two bartenders. Or if a buffet for forty is planned and the only liquor to be served is wine, you may not need a bartender at all but only someone to help clean up.

Accordingly, asking yourself "Who's going to do this?" will help you determine the jobs you want to delegate to temporary help. Here are some situations in which you may find that you do need that help.

**Food considerations**

• When the menu requires constant attention to foods in the process of being cooked (soufflés, broiled dishes, etc.).

• When the menu features courses that need to be carved or especially prepared for serving.

• When you're having a formal dinner for more than ten or twelve at one table, or more than sixteen at three or four tables.

• When the hostess is pressed for time before the party (especially in the case of working hostesses).

• When the hostess is not very well organized and fears she will be tied to the kitchen during the party.

**Drink considerations**

• When a cocktail party is larger than forty people.

• When a dinner party is formal enough (or large enough) that you don't want guests to mix their own drinks.

**Space, equipment and time considerations**

• When the area of food preparation is an inconvenient distance from the area in which it is to be served and consumed—patios far removed from kitchens, entertainment rooms in basements, or upper floors that are accessible only by stairways.

• When it is essential to the success of the party that it begin and/or end at a specific time, such as progressive dinners, pretheater or opera parties, and so on.

• When equipment to be used is complicated, or dangerous or time-consuming to operate, such as the playing of recorded music for disco parties, cooking with pressure cookers, gas rotisseries, and so forth.

• When more than one or two days are needed for yard clean-up, heavy housework, painting, etc. Of course this depends on your own stamina and the amount of time you're willing and able to devote to such chores.

## Kinds of Help and What They Do

*Waiters and waitresses* generally assemble and serve food, clear dishes and tables, clean food areas and wash utensils. But these duties vary according to locale, type of party, and labor regulations.

*Bartenders* serve drinks, maintain and clean up the bar area, and handle the supplies. Most bartenders do not bring any equipment, but some do, and if you are in need of extra glasses, shakers, etc., be sure to discuss this in advance. If he has no equipment himself it's a good idea to ask his advice on where to obtain it.

*Temporary cooks,* unlike caterers, work almost exclusively in your own kitchen and only on the preparation of the food. Their concern is not with service, tableware, or wines. Often a cook will work hand in hand with a hostess throughout the preparation of intricate meals.

*Hostess helpers* provide the extra pair of hands in the kitchen you've always wished for. They sometimes serve, usually clear tables, and always wash up. Remember that young people who are not of drinking age cannot legally serve liquor in many states, so do not ask your high school hostess helper to pass cocktails or tend bar without checking on the regulations. There is no problem, however, about their removing glasses and washing them. For hostesses who entertain regularly, training the same hostess helper throughout a number of parties may produce a valuable and trusted assistant and is well worth the time spent. Hostess helpers are usually available through your local high school placement office.

*Cleaning women* who regularly work for you can be a valuable source for extra party help. Since your cleaning woman is aware of the day to day working of your home, specifically the kitchen and eating facilities, she will save you considerable time in explaining to temporary party help where things are. She can also provide extra help for pre-party cleaning projects. And even if your cleaning woman is not available for the night of the party, she may well be able to help with the cleanup the morning after.

*Baby-sitters* are a necessity for hostesses with young children. The excitement of party preparation is bound to get to youngsters and, because they want to be a part of it, they are constantly in the way. Furthermore, if you have small children who must be fed and put to bed while the party is going on, and you don't want to leave your guests for that long, there is no alternative. You should plan to have a baby-sitter throughout the party and, if possible, throughout the time when you're busy with preparations. If you have invited guests who are bringing their children, you should arrange in advance for your baby-sitter to supervise these children as well as your own. If one baby-sitter won't do, get additional help, or your party may become a disaster.

*Yard cleaning services and painters* are, of course, listed in the yellow pages, but you can sometimes have these chores done more economically through high school and college service associations as well as urban programs such as Rent-a-Kid.

*Bouncers* are sometimes a necessity. If you are planning a party for a number of high school students, for example, there is a strong possibility that there will be gate-crashers, and the presence of a big, burly bouncer at the door is very discouraging to them. The best source for providing a bouncer is your local police department. An off-duty policeman is usually happy to make a few dollars and just the sight of his badge is generally enough to keep youngsters from sneaking a drink from your liquor supply or smoking pot. To make him less conspicuous, the bouncer may be put in charge of the beer keg or the soft drink bar.

*Traffic directors* are necessary when there will be more cars than your driveway or parking area can accommodate. They are responsible for directing people to areas where there is parking space, and seeing that the cars are parked properly so that no one is hemmed in and there can be a free flow of traffic when the guests begin to leave.

Some municipalities require that parties over a certain size be attended by a uniformed police officer. There is always a charge for this service, whether the municipality sends him or you make the arrangement yourself.

## How to Get Help

Having a stranger come into your home is not something to be handled lightly and finding the right person is not always an easy task. It is most important that you check personal references, or, if you go through an agency, make sure that it is a reliable and well-known organization.

A telephone call is the most effective way to check a reference. It is all too easy for someone who is in need of work to forge their own written reference, saying that the "signer" has left town or is not available for checking. When you hire temporary help from an agency, the agency's recommendation is supposed to be sufficient reference, but you should feel free to ask the person you are hiring for the names of people he has worked for before.

Because it *is* a risky business, the best possible way to get temporary help is to hire someone you know (or whose family you know), or someone who has worked for one of your friends or for a respected member of the community such as the principal of the high school. When help is obtained in this way, the word of the former employer is sufficient reference.

If, however, you are new in a community, have not hired help before and don't know anyone who has, you must resort to other means. The following methods of finding help, if executed with the above-mentioned safeguards, are the most practical.

**Advertisements** Once you determine exactly what sort of help you will need, look for advertised help. The most logical place to obtain leads is in the yellow pages of the telephone book. Try looking under such headings as:

Employment contractors—temporary help
Personnel consultants
Caterers

Organizations providing temporary help sometimes advertise on local community bulletin boards, in churches and supermarkets, or through the local chamber of commerce and Better Business Bureaus. They also place ads in local newspapers in the classified section.

On the other hand, if there is not an abundance of advertised help, try advertising *for it* instead. Here again, the community bulletin board is a logical place. Your ad might read as follows:

---

### BARTENDER WANTED

Need experienced, well-mannered
bartender for evening of January 6th
Please reply 555-1212
References required

555-1212 | 555-1212 | 555-1212 | 555-1212 | 555-1212 | 555-1212 | 555-1212 | 555-1212 | 555-1212 | 555-1212 | 555-1212 | 555-1212

---

The tails drawn on the bottom of this sample ad are removable tabs with your telephone number. When someone sees your ad in a store, instead of looking for pencil and paper to write down your phone number, all he needs to do is tear off one of the tabs so he can call you later at his convenience.

You may also wish to advertise in your local classified newspaper sections.

**Agencies** There are two kinds of agencies you can turn to—professional temporary help agencies and student agencies. For the most part, the temporary help agencies are staffed by experienced moonlighters, although they may also have a number of students working for them.

However, they have no school or college affiliation. Temporary help agencies are usually listed in the yellow pages (under "employment"), and also with organizations like the Better Business Bureau.

Student agencies might also be listed in the yellow pages, but they can always be reached by calling the main number of your local college or university.

**Restaurants or private clubs** Teams of waiters, cooks, bartenders, etc., who are used to working together as a group are possibly the most satisfactory type of temporary help. An experienced team that has worked together for a number of years is well equipped to handle almost any party situation.

These teams can sometimes be contacted through a caterer, more often through the manager of a restaurant or hall. Many private clubs have bartenders and waiters who moonlight during their free time.

**Friends and relatives** Asking a friend or relative to help out is a possibility, but it is not always the best solution. There are a number of pitfalls, especially if the person is friendly with the rest of your guests. No one wants to be serving and cooking at someone else's party when she could just as easily be enjoying it as a guest. So when you're asking for help from friends and relatives, try to keep it confined to a brief task. For example, you might ask your sister to help you clear the table, or to empty the ashtrays in the living room while the others are serving themselves at the buffet. It is a good idea to arrange this ahead of time, so that your "helper" is prepared and knows what to do.

### Things You Should Discuss

The first thing to remember about instructing help is be explicit and don't assume anything. If you expect a soup to be served at 7:45, then specify that hour. If the band must play "Here Comes The Bride" at the entrance of the happy couple, then see to it that the bandleader is told. Here is a check list of instructions for the various categories of temporary help:

**People who deal with preparing the food**
- Discuss the complete menu and the recipes.
- Familiarize them with all necessary kitchen/eating area facilities. Labeling the outside of kitchen cabinets is a great help.
- Establish a timetable for preparation and serving.
- Specify duties. Does the contract include cleanup?
- Rehearse specialty service such as dishes en flambé.

**People who deal with the table(s) and service**
- Show location of all tableware and serving equipment.

• Explain exactly which foods will be served in what dishes and platters.

• Set out one place setting as a sample, and specify the number of diners at each table.

• Describe how you want hors d'oeuvre served—whether they should be passed or brought in and left on side tables.

• Specify the time and method for announcing dinner, and signals for passing second helpings, clearing table, etc.

• Discuss other duties—taking guests' coats, clearing living room during dinner hour, washing up, etc.

• Establish places for everything, both clean and dirty. If many of the utensils are rented or borrowed, explain that they should be cleaned and stacked and segregated from your equipment. Note the differences between "yours" and "theirs."

**People who deal with drinks**

• Run through your bar check list with the bartender to insure that the bar is completely stocked.

• Familiarize the bartender with storage and supply areas, cleaning facilities, ice storage and disposal, etc.

• Advise your bartender how you like your drinks fixed, and how many ounces of liquor you want him to put in each drink.

• Establish a policy about tipping and fraternizing.

• Instruct the bartender on how you would like the problem of too much drinking handled and inform him (discreetly) about any potential problems you may be aware of.

• Encourage his suggestions and advice.

**People who supply other services**

• Outline the responsibilities for each service fully and describe how you wish it executed.

## Show Your Appreciation

In the rush of events, we often overlook the niceties like "please" and "thank you." But the best performances come from people who feel comfortable, so take a few minutes to encourage your helpers and to let them know that you appreciate their work. Remember, without them, you do it alone.

A more tangible evidence of your appreciation is always appreciated, too. Even though you have established an hourly rate of pay beforehand, an extra $5 or so "because you've done such a great job!" will help to insure enthusiastic help for your next party.

# 7

# *Entertainment*

When the guests are compatible, the food and drink ample and good, and the hostess relaxed and in charge, there is no need for any entertainment at all at the average cocktail or dinner party. Good conversation, an opportunity to talk to interesting people and listen to different viewpoints or amusing stories is all the entertainment one needs.

However, there are many parties that are given specifically for a particular type of entertainment—dances, bridge parties, disco parties, parties where guests come to hear a singer or to have their palms read and so on. There are also occasions when the hostess must entertain people who she feels will not be able to keep the conversational ball rolling well enough, so she plans on some kind of entertainment to keep the party alive.

Naturally, the final choice of the type of entertainment you want is up to you. What we will try to do here is to supply you with as much information as we can to help you make that choice.

## Entertainment Options

It would be impossible to list all the entertainment options, so we have compiled a list of those that are most readily available and popular. Unless you know some well-trained and experienced amateurs, you will be wise to hire professionals to do the entertaining. Accordingly, their remuneration should reflect payment for professional service—not necessarily at the level of a headliner's salary, but don't expect a "bargain."

**Musicians**

*Instrumentalists* These include pianists (when they sing as well they are called piano-vocalists), guitarists, violinists, and accordianists. Instrumentalists require the least amount of space and preparation. They can provide either background or focal entertainment. However, the subtleties of, let us say, a violinist may be lost at large noisy parties. It's perhaps best to hire instrumentalists to serve as roving entertainers unless the party is small enough so that your guests are willing to sit and listen to their performance.

*Combos* are usually made up of three pieces—rhythm or drum, string, and piano. A combo may feature a vocalist but that is the exception rather than the rule. It is ideal for background or intermittent entertainment and can fill in while a larger band is taking a break. A good combo can also provide the dance music if the room is not too large.

*Groups* are larger and more flexible than combos. They vary from six to eight members, including vocalists. Some perform choreographed routines or comic bits or skits.

Both groups and combos provide their own material, props, and instruments. The host is responsible for other facilities such as lighting, sound amplification, and chairs, if needed.

*Dance bands* vary greatly in size. The average these days is a five-piece band with one keyboard (piano) man, a drummer, guitarist, saxophonist, and a trumpet player. Bands with full sound include sections with as many as three to five similar pieces (for instance, a brass section or a string section).

While rock-'n'-roll bands require intricate lighting and sound amplification, other bands do not. They do, however, require a good deal of space and good acoustics. Remember to ask if they will need a piano. This is the one instrument you may be expected to supply.

When hiring a band, inquire about the breaks—how frequently they come and how long they last. And will the band stay on if the party is so successful that you wish to extend it? What would the rates for this be?

Make sure the band plays the kind of music you want, and mention any specific pieces you will want played so that they can get the music and practice it if it is not already in their repertoire.

If it is a disco or rock-'n'-roll band you are hiring, determine whether they bring their own lighting and sound equipment. If they require rented equipment, ask them to specify their needs and suggest suppliers. If they offer to obtain the equipment themselves, get a price quote in advance. It is assumed that standard equipment is included in the band's price, but special effects and techniques are additional costs.

**Magicians, mimes, and comedians** Professional magicians, mimes and comedians are usually represented by agencies or unions that set standard prices and guidelines for their performance at private parties. They are great fun for parties with a limited space when after-dinner entertainment is in order. Often a comedian will ask you ahead of time for some innocuous information about your guests that he may incorporate into his routine.

If you have doubts about how to choose the right performer, make arrangements to see his act if he's appearing somewhere nearby, or request references. But remember that asking for a private audition, unless he can supply a tape, is asking for two performances for the price of one.

**Character actors** These actors can be hired to mingle with the guests and supply spontaneous, ongoing entertainment. The most familiar character actor is the hired Santa Claus. Another is the Easter Bunny, or a Walt Disney character. Although character actors are perhaps most often used at children's parties, you might want to have an actor portray President Lincoln at a political fundraiser, or hire one to perform as a dancing tiger at a Princeton reunion.

Be sure that the amount of time these actors will be performing is spelled out, and that such items as costumes and props are included in their fees.

**Disk jockeys** Often disk jockeys from local radio stations can be hired if they are not on the air at the time of your party. And you can add novelty to your party by having a disk jockey there to supply the music just as he does on the radio. Again, arrangements must be made with the disk jockey concerning the equipment he will need, the choice of tapes or records, etc.

Disk jockeys are the ideal solution for the hostess who can't afford to hire a dance band but wants plenty of music and a variety of it for her party.

**Clairvoyants, palm readers and hypnotists** Finding performers in these categories would not be possible in some rural parts of the country, but if you live in a city where they practice or advertise their skills, they can provide unusual and provocative entertainment for your guests.

Clairvoyants and palm readers may, like the comedian, ask ahead of time for a little information about your friends. Be careful not to give out any gossip that could embarrass or distress anyone.

Hypnotists provide fascinating entertainment, but be sure to check their references or otherwise establish that they are reputable, because hypnotism is a tricky business, and can even cause emotional damage if not practiced by an expert.

## Entertainment Sources

Entertainers, bands, theatrical agencies and unions are listed in the telephone directory's yellow pages. Try looking under the following listings:

Musicians
Orchestras and bands
Theatrical agencies
Entertainment bureaus
Recorders—sound equipment and supplies

**Unions** Singers, dancers, musicians, and many other entertainers are usually represented by unions that, for the benefit of their members, post notices of work available on their bulletin boards. When you call the union headquarters, explain your needs to the person who answers and ask his advice. You'll probably find he has a number of interesting people available.

**Theatrical agencies** The agent business is strictly one of representation. In most cases an agency will represent similar clients—some agencies may specialize in rock bands, for example, others in folk dancing groups. Still others handle any kind of performer they think they can place. You deal entirely through the agency when you hire this way. They supply all the information you want: references, what the performer will or will not do, length of time of his performance, and availability for overtime. Agents' fees are paid by the performer; very seldom is the client asked to pay anything directly to the agency.

**Theater groups** Theater groups can be a good source for obtaining entertainment. If they do not offer a set piece that serves your purpose, the group itself or a member of it may create one for you.

Theater groups can be found in a number of places: high schools, colleges, religious and community organizations, as well as local independent groups. And getting members of the chorus from a local production of a well-known musical to sing a medley of Cole Porter or Rodgers and Hart is a sure-fire entertainment treat.

**Newspapers and magazines and radio** Often the entertainment or living section of local newspapers and magazines features stories, reviews, profiles, etc., on local entertainers and groups as well as carrying their advertisements. If you are planning a party, keep an eye on these sections to get an idea of what entertainment will be available.

Television listings, too, may offer unexpectedly appropriate programming for entertaining your guests. Since nostalgia is so fashionable today, a re-broadcast of famous old movies such as Our Gang, or Laurel and Hardy is an inexpensive means of entertainment.

Check your newspaper listings of what entertainers are in town, what they're doing and where they are. If your entertainment budget is a healthy one, you may be interested in hiring one or more well-known entertainers who are appearing locally. Attend their performance and if they seem to be what you want, send a note or card to their dressing room and ask them to join you at your table. In discussing their fee, be sure to make clear what you would expect of them and provide for them in the way of food, transportation, etc.

**Community bulletin board** In smaller towns and rural areas, the community bulletin board at supermarkets, general stores, etc., may be your best and only source of information. It may be the last resort in the city but elsewhere it is still a valid option and should not be overlooked.

### Doing It Yourself

In most cases, there is no better way to amuse your guests than with each other. Don't be mistaken—it is not the lazy way out. On the contrary, planning successful entertainment without the services of a professional requires time and commitment. Don't wait until the last moment to coordinate the details.

**Games** There are, of course, hundreds of party games. Among my favorites for the active are carpet bowls, table tennis, and bumper pool (equipment for the latter two can be rented); bridge or poker for the card-minded; crossword puzzle contests or dictionary games for the intellectuals; and scavenger or treasure hunts for the outdoor group. I cannot possibly describe all of them, or enumerate the many other possibilities, but you will find several excellent sources of information in the bibliography.

**Dancing** Getting people to dance is another matter. You must know your guests and you must provide the necessary ingredients that are conducive to dancing. In most cases, if there's a good band, a good dance surface, and ample space, people *will* dance. It also helps if the host and hostess start dancing—often people don't want to be the first on the dance floor, and all they need is someone to follow.

Square dancing parties make a great hit if you can find a caller competent enough to make it fun for a group with a wide range of skills. Even the greenest novice can quickly learn the basic steps, and you can always have a few sets just for the more experienced.

**Movies and tapes**  For casual entertaining, or for guests with similar interests, rented movies and video tapes that can be shown on a home video machine attached to your television set are viable entertainment options. If you already have most of the equipment, the rental of the films or tapes is not necessarily expensive, but if you have to rent projectors, a video-recorder set, and so on, the costs can add up quickly.

Home movies are another possibility, but they must be of excellent quality and severely edited. The tendency of all amateur moviemakers is to take too much of a cute or unusual subject, and this can be a dreadful bore to your friends. But a well made (with sound if possible) film of your African safari or your fishing trip to Alaska can be a real treat for an interested audience.

Renting video equipment to record a special event to be played back later at the party—perhaps the Kentucky Derby, a football game or a New Year's Eve countdown—will provide great entertainment for the right group.

**Gambling**  Whether you have eight or twelve people in for poker or bridge, or forty people for a bingo game or a Las Vegas night, gambling is always a lively source of entertainment. If you are reluctant to have your guests gamble for real money, you can always add up the total points or chips at the end of the evening and give out prizes instead.

Card games of various kinds are the most common means of gambling at home. Several books on the subject are listed in the bibliography. To make a bridge or poker party successful, the rules or method of play should be made very clear, and if your group is large enough to require several tables, a mimeographed copy of the rules should be at each table. If you know that there will be some very slow players present, it is a good idea to set time limits for each rubber of bridge, hand of Scrabble, etc., with penalties for delay.

Board games, such as Scrabble, checkers, or backgammon provide exciting competition for a small group. The winner of each game moves on to challenge the loser at the next table, and each player keeps an individual point total for himself.

**Spectator sports**  For good friends with similar interests, a sports event such as a high school, college, or professional football game provides a fine excuse for a party. If you live in the city where the game is being played, a luncheon before the game or a celebration or wake afterward are the logical choices. A betting pool is usually part of the fun.

If, however, you and your friends will be driving to the game, you can organize a station wagon tailgate picnic. Although you can provide all the food if you wish, more often each carload brings ample food and drinks, and then everyone shares or passes around their contributions. Just be sure that everyone arrives well ahead of game time (at least one and one-half hours) and knows exactly where the meeting place is; otherwise some of the prospective picnickers will get lost in the crowd.

**Outdoor games** Outdoor games can provide the entertainment only if you have the space and the facilities, or can rent or reserve them. It is perfectly possible, for example, to reserve two or three courts at your club or the local public facility in order to have a round-robin tennis party. All you need is a big yard or an open field in a park to organize a touch football or softball game. Volleyball, croquet, and the like require space and equipment, but are easy to set up in a level area and are lots of fun for an outdoor-loving crowd. The rules should be simple and clearly explained at the start.

The hostess at this kind of event is responsible for having plenty of cool drinks available during the play. Beer and soft drinks are the usual choices. Although it is not strictly necessary, she usually has a get-together afterward, serving sandwiches or salad in summer, a chowder or fondue in the fall. If she wishes, the menu can be substantial enough to serve as dinner, but often these outdoor games parties end late in the afternoon and the guests go elsewhere for dinner.

**Using "work" as entertainment** For groups of friends who are especially close, there are a number of ways to make a worthwhile project the source of party entertainment. The classic examples of this were the barn raising and harvesting parties of old. For groups of friends who party together often, using a common activity such as sewing or cooking as a source of entertainment is a refreshing change.

Banding together to help out a friend or neighbor in need can turn a tedious job into fun for everyone. The "party" where guests spend a Saturday together cleaning up a vacant lot in the neighborhood or painting the house of an elderly neighbor requires some clever manipulation on the part of the hostess to get it all together. But if you can convince people of the need and offer ample reward in food, drink, and conviviality, you can create an event that will be long remembered as something special.

For the more commercially minded, the concept of using work as entertainment took on a new twist when the Tupperware party was introduced. Since then the products, devices, and services marketed through parties have mushroomed. At functions such as these, the party fare is usually not too elaborate. Coffee and light sandwiches provide the refreshment, and the presentation of the product is the only entertainment. However, the basic facts remain: If the sandwiches are not good, the wares not attractively displayed, and the hostess not gracious and well-organized, the party will flop—both commercially and socially.

# 8

# *The Big Event*

Family and religious celebrations are the milestones of one's life—births, confirmations, marriages, anniversaries. They are often the occasions for the big party, one for 150 or more guests. However, some hostesses simply like to combine all their party giving for the year into one major affair—a big costume ball, the large Christmas open house, a lawn party.

The traditional *big* wedding, which saw a decline in the 1960s, is very much back in style again. It has become less formal, and some of the frills have been eliminated (little white boxes of cake for the guests to take home, for instance) to keep down the cost, but small, outdoor weddings on the beach or a hilltop are being replaced by a church service followed by a big reception at a hall or in the home. The buffet reception has increased in popularity, as it is less expensive and easier to arrange than a sit-down meal. If the difference between buffet and sit-down is $8 per head, simple arithmetic shows that for a wedding with 250 guests, the savings are dramatic.

Aside from the traditions and particular characteristics of the events, there are more similarities than differences among a big anniversary, a big wedding, or a big Christmas party. The difficulty in their execution lies in their *bigness*.

When you're inviting more than 150 people, there are a number of special considerations that will make the event unlike any smaller party you have given. The greatest danger is that you will be so intimidated by the numbers that your ability to organize becomes impaired. The important thing is to stay cool and give your attention to the tasks at hand, one at a time. There is probably no more appropriate time to keep copious notes than when you're planning a large function.

## The Guest List

Making up the guest list for a big party is somewhat of a chore. The sheer weight of the number of names, addresses, and zip codes tends to be overwhelming. Make a tentative list first—all the people you would *like* to invite, followed by the people you *should* invite. Once this number has been reviewed, you can determine whether it is within your budget. If not, this is the time to trim some names from your *should* list, but keep them handy in case you receive some early refusals and have time to send out a few additional invitations.

Your final list should be organized in as neat and orderly a way as possible. Some hostesses make several duplicates of the list—one for acceptances and regrets, one for a seating plan, one for keeping a record of gifts and thank you's, and so on. Other people prefer to keep a card index with a card for each guest (or couple). Although this is a little harder to look through, the cards provide space for all the information necessary for each person, and the index is useful for future parties.

Your decision about what type of party to give may also be influenced by the length of your guest list. For example, the cost of a cocktail party is far less than a seated dinner, so a hostess who has a long *should* list and a limited budget will find the cocktail party the best alternative.

## Food and Service

The timing of the food service is an important consideration. If an event is to begin at 6 P.M., for example, one would expect cocktails and hors d'oeuvre to be served first, and then a meal between 7:30 and 8:30. A party beginning at 8 P.M. requires that hors d'oeuvre and snacks be available throughout the evening, and something more substantial served around midnight. That late supper might consist of scrambled eggs and sausage, eggs benedict, pizzas, hamburgers—or whatever is appropriate to the type of party and the taste of your guests. The afternoon open house, which falls between meal hours, is an easy way to avoid full meal service, thereby cutting down on service and food costs.
**Food and serving tips**
Service will be simpler if you:
Don't serve foods that must be piping hot.
Don't serve foods that require a number of accompaniments.
Don't serve dishes that need a lot of last-minute preparation.

Don't select a menu that must be served at an exact moment—soufflés, for example.

Try to plan a main course of no more than three items, and combine these items so that no more than two dishes have to be passed. You can do this by:

Surrounding the sliced steak or roast with potatoes.

Arranging potato salad within a ring of sliced tomatoes and cucumbers, spears of asparagus, etc.

Serving a ragout or stew that combines the vegetables and potatoes with the meat.

Obviously, the fewer dishes that need to be passed, the quicker the service and hotter (or colder) the food.

Focus attention on the main attractions. For example, at a low-budget wedding reception where only cake and champagne are served, the focus is on those two items. They should be presented as perfectly as possible to minimize the lack of a more substantial menu. Use real crystal, wrap the champagne bottles in white napkins and be sure the cake is perfectly decorated and impeccably served.

The manner of serving the food is a crucial consideration. There is nothing more disastrous than a big party with too few in staff: the food gets cold, the guests get restless, and tempers flare in the kitchen. So be sure that there will be enough waiters and waitresses. The following chart should serve as a good indication of your needs.

| Number of guests | Bartenders | Servers for Sit-down | Servers for Buffet |
| --- | --- | --- | --- |
| 150–250 | 3–5 | 5–8 | 4–5 |
| 260–350 | 5–7 | 8–10 | 5–6 |
| 360–450 | 7–8 | 10–12 | 6–8 |

## Entertainment

Some big parties follow traditional entertainment patterns such as caroling at Christmas parties and the bridal dance at weddings. The costume ball, too, can be counted on to create an electric party atmosphere and the theme becomes the basis for the entertainment.

Dancing is undoubtedly one of the best entertainments for a big crowd, and various forms of group dancing, too, can work well at a large function. Having a bandleader or master of ceremonies can insure that the action will get started and be sustained. For other entertainment suggestions, refer to the preceding chapter.

## Space and Movement

Contributing to the success of a big party is the space in which it is held. Aside from good lighting and appropriate decor, a big party obviously needs *lots* of space—whether in one large room, tent, or hall, or a number of connected rooms, tents, etc.

When several hundred people begin to dance or eat simultaneously, they will move to the designated area *en masse*. To forestall a massive traffic jam, try to avoid connecting rooms with stairs, tight hallways, dark passageways, steep inclines, etc., and never situate food and drink areas near entrances, coat checks or entertainment areas.

You should also be aware that large halls often have substandard public address systems. Communicating with a crowd is not easy, and a good P.A. is essential. Check this well ahead of time.

To control temperature in a huge room or a number of joined areas is difficult. Make sure that there are adequate means of heating or cooling the party areas.

## Special Services

Several hundred guests in winter are bound to mean several hundred overcoats, umbrellas, boots, hats, and gloves. You can imagine the problem they could create if you're not prepared. Most large banquet halls and hotels do have coatrooms, but the availability of attendants and general policy will vary with each. For example, in some cases the attendant's fee is added to the bill and in others tip dishes must be put out for gratuities.

For parties held in your house or in a tent, prepare a space slightly away from the main party area for coats and hats. Clothing racks can be rented, but be certain that hangers are included and that there are sufficient racks. (One six-foot rack will hold approximately thirty heavy winter coats.)

If your at-home party will be attended by as many as 100 couples, encourage a number of them to share rides to cut down on the number of cars to be parked, as well as to conserve gas. To handle more than forty or fifty cars, either a valet service or someone to direct guests where to park is essential. (For further information, see chapter 6, "Temporary Help.")

## Special Equipment

Large crowds at sit-down meals and at buffets produce a great deal of dirty *everything*. Accordingly, you must plan on extra space to accommodate 150 or more sets of dirty china, glasses, linen, silver, serving trays, and so on. That means ample counter or table space in the kitchen and serving area. You will need up to 100 square feet of tabletop to hold the used tableware and serving equipment for 100 guests.

**Obtaining extra equipment** Few households are equipped to keep large amounts of food cold or hot. If you plan to rent extra equipment to do this, try the yellow pages under "Caterer Supplies—rental." In urban areas, you may be able to rent a portable ice maker, a refrigerator, and electric hot trays or hot plates, but they are not available in many rural locations. The alternative would be to borrow the necessary equipment from friends. In any event, be sure (if necessary, check with an electrician) that you do not overload your circuits with the additional appliances.

As another alternative, big plastic laundry baskets and garbage pails filled with ice can serve as "refrigerators," and if it is wintertime, many dishes as well as wines can be kept chilled in covered containers in the snow or simply outside the kitchen door.

Should your big event be a cookout, an above-ground pit of cinderblocks 2 feet wide by 10 feet long and 30 inches high, covered with a grill and filled with charcoal, provides enough cooking space for four to five chefs who can serve 200 to 300 guests.

## The Hostess and the Master of Ceremonies

Supervising the mechanics of a large party is not the function of the hostess. Keeping the food, band, guests, and bartenders organized is a full-time job that no hostess should ever assume. For this responsibility she must depend on the caterer or the bandleader. If she has neither, there are alternatives. She can hire a maître d' from a local hotel or restaurant, or a captain/hostess from a temporary help agency to do the behind-the-scenes organizing. Even then, she would be well advised to hire an M.C. as well.

The hostess should meet with the M.C. at least once before the event. It will help if she gives him notes on what is expected, who will be in charge of what, where things are located, and so on. The objective of the M.C. is to keep the party moving without having to bother the hostess.

It should be the M.C.'s duty to coordinate the help and to supervise the entertainment, receiving line, and traditional ceremonies. Be certain to run through the event yourself *before* meeting with the caterer or M.C. so you can tell them what *you* want and not let them take over the show.

If pictures are to be taken at the party, a family member or friend should be asked to accompany the photographer to get the names and addresses for any copies that may be ordered, and also to identify special guests who must not be overlooked.

## The Receiving Line

The receiving line at weddings, anniversaries, bar mitzvahs, and many other large receptions is obligatory. The space where the line is set up should be comfortable for the honorees, and accessible to the guests. There should be an entrance and an exit on opposite sides of the room or a large open space at either end of the line so that people waiting to pass through the line and those who have already done so will not bump into each other. If people are already seated when the line forms, it helps if the M.C. or the caterer announces that "the receiving line will be called by table number." This keeps people from standing too long in line.

## Seating Guests by Table

Random seating is fine for open houses and buffets, but it is far from ideal for large sit-down dinners. However, it can be very difficult for a guest to find his or her place when there are a number of tables. At a very large dinner it is best to identify the tables in some way and distribute the place cards, with the table and seat number on them, at the entrance to the dining area. Some hostesses prefer to assign tables only, and then let the diners at each table select their own seats. The tables may have large numbers on them, or they might be identified by different colored cloths, or different flowers in the center. The place cards would read:

> *Allen Fairlee*
> *Table No. 2 (or Red Table, or Rose Table)*
> *Seat 4*

A diagram of the seat and table numbers should be clearly displayed behind the table where guests will pick up their place cards.

The cards should be arranged alphabetically on one or more card tables covered with pretty cloths. If you have more than one place-card table, label them clearly, A–M, N–Z. These tables should be removed after everyone is seated.

# 9

# *The Hostess and Guests*

### The Requisites for Success

Until now we have dealt mainly with the technical aspects of entertaining—the equipment, the space, the mechanics of preparation, and so on. These things are important, of course, but none can compare in importance with the graciousness and warmth of the hostess. As mentioned in the introduction, the key to being able to entertain your guests as if it were the greatest pleasure in the world (and it *should* be) and as if you have little to do but to enjoy their company (and you *should*) is advance preparation. Careful planning and doing all that can be done well ahead of time will insure that you will be relaxed, self-confident and rested when your party begins. Probably nothing can ruin a party more quickly than a nervous hostess. Try not to worry about possible disasters. Usually they don't happen, and when they do, the chances are the guests won't notice them anyway. Remember that it is far less important to have matching silverware or twelve plates of the same pattern than it is to make your guests feel welcome and comfortable.

Whatever the size of your party, the requisites for success are the same:

Congenial guests
An attractive dining table or tables
Well-prepared food and plenty of beverages
A menu that is well suited to your guests' tastes
Competent, pleasant servants (if help is needed)
A gracious hostess and/or a cordial host

## Making Up the Guest List

When making up your guest list, try to invite people you think will be interesting to each other. You may secretly consider your new neighbor who is the football coach at the high school a bit of a bore, but your friend Amy, whose son is an aspiring quarterback, may find him absolutely fascinating.

Try to mix your guests. Invite a few who know each other well but include two or three new faces. One of the greatest pleasures in going out to dinner is the opportunity to meet new people. However, don't ask *all* strangers who may not turn out to be congenial at all. And don't ask *one* stranger in a group of intimate friends, because the outsider will only feel like a fish out of water.

Unless there is a particular reason to do so (celebrating the signing of a big contract, for example), don't restrict your list to people who work in the same office, play on the same team, or live in the same neighborhood. The conversation will inevitably center on the same old topic that is discussed every day—very dull for the spouses or others who are not involved.

Whenever it seems appropriate, invite members of different generations. In many countries, family members of all ages (within reason) are invited to the same parties, but Americans seem unintentionally to foster the generation gap by keeping parents and children in their own little cubbyholes. Try inviting your friends' teenage or young married children when your own children can be present. Don't isolate them; seat them between the older guests, and I'll guarantee you'll have one of the liveliest parties you've ever had!

Finally, don't leave out your single friends, especially women. Dinner parties don't have to be dating or mating affairs, nor is it necessary to have an even number of men and women. Single men are generally much in demand to "even up" dinner parties, but just because a woman is single, widowed, or divorced is no reason that she can't be a delightful and interesting dinner companion—with or without a "date."

**Last-minute invitations** When you have planned three tables of bridge, or your dinner seating plan is just right for eight couples, and your friend Sue calls at the last moment to say that she and Jim have been suddenly called out of town, what can you do? You can, and you should, call a close friend and ask if she and her husband could possibly fill in, or call a single friend and tell her (or him) to bring a date. Don't call someone you don't know well—it will look like an afterthought. But any good friends, rather than being insulted at such a last-minute invitation, should be complimented that you feel free to ask them to come to your rescue.

## Greetings and Introductions

The hostess's place when any party, large or small, begins is near, or accessible to, the door. At a very large party, she and the host should both stay in the entrance area, greeting the guests as they arrive. At a smaller, more casual dinner, she may stay in the living room with early arrivals, but each time the bell rings or someone comes in, she should go immediately to greet them. If there is a servant to take coats in the hall, the host and hostess may stay just inside the living room door, but they should always be the first people to see and welcome new arrivals.

If a party is small, strangers are naturally introduced to each of the other guests. At a big cocktail party or buffet, however, the hostess need only introduce the strangers to two or three people and then leave them to take care of themselves. The hope is that the few guests they have met will in turn introduce them to others, and they should also feel free to introduce themselves to anyone they wish.

In introducing two (or more) people, it is helpful to identify them to each other as well as to give their names. It makes it far easier for them to get a conversation under way if you say something like: "John, this is Mary Spring. Mary is the new director of the Marly clinic," or "Alice, I've been wanting you to meet Sarah Pond for so long. She is a member of the garden club, and I've told her about your beautiful garden."

Even at a large party the thoughtful hostess checks every so often to see that no one has been left completely alone. If the shy stranger has been stranded by the first people she introduced him to, she should take him over to another group and try to get him started again. She may even enlist the aid of a convivial friend: "Henry, our new neighbor seems to be a little shy—would you do me a favor and take him in tow for a few minutes and see that he gets to meet a few more people?"

**The late arrival** The question is often asked: How long should I hold dinner for a guest who is late? The answer depends on your local customs, and on the type of party.

If, for example, you are serving cocktails before dinner, you should plan to start eating approximately one hour after most of the guests have arrived. If one guest or couple has not appeared by that time, you should announce dinner without delay, for the benefit of all the others.

If it is not your custom to serve drinks before dinner, you should plan on eating fifteen minutes after the hour on the invitation. This allows time for such emergencies as a traffic jam or a ringing telephone just as your guest is leaving his house. But to delay more than fifteen minutes, or twenty at the most, would be rude to those who did arrive on time.

When a guest arrives after the meal has begun, the hostess excuses herself to greet him and quickly brings him to the table. He is served whatever course is being enjoyed at the moment, unless of course it is dessert, and then the hostess or the waitress would prepare a plate with a helping of the main course.

## When It's Time for Dinner

**Going in to dinner** If you have help in the kitchen, it is only fair that your guests sit down to eat as soon as dinner is announced. It is up to you to decide on the dinner hour and to see that cocktails are not served for fifteen minutes before that hour, so that everyone will have finished his last drink and be ready for the meal. No self-respecting cook—whether permanent or hired for the evening—will work for you for long if his meals are ruined by having to wait until they are cold or overcooked.

Even when you have prepared the meal yourself you will not want the roast too well-done, or the casserole dried out, so it is very important to get people to eat at the hour you have planned. To do this some hostesses (and this is a good idea) announce, "Dinner will be ready in about 15 minutes, so would anyone like one more drink?"

Another method, if several guests still have half-filled glasses, is to suggest that they take their drinks in to dinner. However, if the hostess prefers that the guests drink the wine she has planned to serve, she should not make the suggestion.

If the guests are enjoying the cocktail hour so much that they refuse to budge, as sometimes happens, the host or hostess may enlist the aid of a friend or two by asking them to lead the way, and others will surely follow.

When there are place cards on the table, the guests look for their own seats, although at a very large party the hostess may help by saying "Janie, I think you're at the table in the corner," or "Jim, you're on my right at that end of the table." When there are no place cards the hostess should indicate where she would like each person to sit, referring to a written table plan if necessary. At a seated buffet, she stands at the end of the serving table and tells the guests where to sit when they have filled their plates and are ready to sit down.

**Who sits by whom?**   At informal, casual gatherings of good friends, there are only two rules that are important: men and women should be alternated, insofar as possible, and husbands and wives should not be seated next to each other. They can talk to each other every other night of the week, but on the night of the party they should have the opportunity to enjoy someone else's company.

At big parties, where some of the guests do not know each other well (or at all) there are further considerations. Avoid seating two brilliant talkers next to each other. Each one would prefer a listener beside him, and conversely the shy, quiet guest would enjoy being next to someone who would keep the conversational ball rolling.

Don't avoid a little controversy. It isn't wise to seat two really bitter political adversaries together, because a nasty argument can ruin the party, but opposing views, within limits, add zest and interest to the table talk. If an argument does get out of hand, the hostess should introduce another subject, if necessary saying, "Oh, simmer down, Jim— let's talk about something else. What did you think of the . . ."

Try not to put Susie Smith, who talks about nothing but her baby's accomplishments or the sitter problem, next to Professor Groves, who isn't married and is only interested in entomology and tennis. In short, try to seat people who have something in common next to each other.

Finally, unless you know that each one is looking for a new interest, don't seat a newly divorced woman and a single man next to each other. It *might* work, but far more often they feel that you are matchmaking, and they run the other way. Having them both at the same party is introduction enough, and they'll follow it up after dinner if they're interested.

**The seating plan**   There is no problem in seating parties of six, ten, or fourteen. The hostess sits at one end of the table, and the host at the other, with men and women alternating on either side. That does not work, however, with eight, twelve, or sixteen—the host and hostess cannot sit opposite each other unless they seat two men or two women together at some point. Therefore, when there is a multiple of four guests, the hostess should move one seat to the left and seat a man in her usual place at the end of the table.

When your guests are to be seated at two or more tables, the host should sit at one and the hostess at another. A good friend who can be relied upon to act as a surrogate host and see that wine is poured or plates refilled should be seated at each of the other tables.

**Place cards and menus** Place cards are certainly not necessary for informal dinners where the hostess can just say, "John, why don't you sit over there, and Kathy, you sit next to him." But for the large dinner parties they are invaluable. A good hostess has thought carefully about who will enjoy sitting by whom and, if there are no place cards, some of her guests will surely have grabbed seats before she can tell them where she wants them. Place cards are the only way to insure that her seating plan is adhered to.

The cards measure about 3½ x 2 inches unfolded, or 3½ x 1 inch folded lengthwise. If unfolded, they are slipped into a place card holder; if folded, they sit on the service plate or directly above the place setting. They may be plain white with a gold or colored border, or have a motif appropriate to the occasion, such as a turkey on a Thanksgiving place card. Place cards are available in stationery or party-goods stores, and the holders are found in gift shops.

You may also use your own artistry to create original place cards. For example, for a festive holiday table you might buy gold Christmas tree balls, write your guests' names on them with clear-drying glue and then shake blue, green or red glitter over them. The glitter adheres to the glue when you shake off the excess, leaving the name clearly written.

Place cards are printed or engraved only for the most formal official dinners. At all other times the hostess writes the name in her best handwriting. She uses only first names for informal parties, or the first name and last initial if several Johns or Marys are present. On formal occasions, the title and last name are used: "Mrs. Jenkins" or "Dr. Gordon." If there are two Dr. Gordons at the party, she writes "Dr. Joan Gordon" and "Dr. Robert Gordon."

## Serving the Meal

**The help-to-guest ratio** You should not try to serve more than eight people at a sitdown meal (unless it is family style) without help. You can cook the meal for as many as you wish (as long as your menu can be prepared in advance) but to serve more than eight quickly and efficiently you need help. For sixteen or more you should have two in help; one to pass drinks and hors d'oeuvre and to serve dinner, the other to cook and prepare the food for serving. For very large parties, you should plan on one waiter or waitress for every eight to ten guests.
**Expert service** Unless you have hired the same people before, don't ever assume that your temporary help knows all about serving. If you

want your dinner to be expertly served, remind your waiter or waitress of the following:

Plates are put down in front of the guests and serving dishes are passed to them from their *left*. When practical, plates are removed from the right, but this may be forgotten if it is awkward.

Water glasses and wine glasses are filled from the diner's right, with the glass remaining on the table.

Dinner plates should be brought from the kitchen or side table one at a time, since the server will need his other hand to remove the service plate or empty first-course plate.

Dinner plates are never stacked for removal. However, if the party is not very formal, the butter plate may be placed on the dinner plate to expedite the clearing of the table.

Bread or crackers are passed during the soup course and again during the main course. At informal meals the bread basket is often left on the table and the diners pass it around themselves.

When the main course is over, salad plates, butter plates, salts and peppers, and condiment dishes, as well as the dinner plates, are removed. Only the glasses and dessert silver are left. The table should be crumbed before dessert is brought in.

If you are using finger bowls, they should be brought in on the dessert plate with a small doily under the bowl, and the dessert fork and spoon on either side. The diner sets the bowl and the doily above the place setting, and the fork on the left and the spoon on the right of the plate. Few of us use finger bowls (unfortunately) today, except perhaps after a lobster dinner, so the dessert spoon and fork are brought in alone on the plate and placed in the same way.

After-dinner coffee is sometimes served at the table, but more often (and more correctly) it is served in the living room. It may be passed around on a tray, the cups already filled, or the empty cups may be passed to the guests who hold them in their hands while the waitress (or hostess) pours the coffee.

**Order of service**   At a formal dinner, the lady seated on the host's right is considered to be the guest of honor, and she is always served first. The service then continues counterclockwise around the table, with the host served last. Some hostesses prefer that they be skipped and served last, but this results in the waiter doubling back and forth and is totally unnecessary. When a single woman is hostess, the woman guest sitting at the right of the man seated opposite the hostess or at the end of the table is served first.

The one cardinal rule is that the hostess should never be served first.

The only exception might be if she were giving her guests a very hard-to-serve dish, in which case she might say, "I asked John to serve me first so that I could get the first wedge out and make it easier for you to help yourselves."

**With one maid** One maid cannot possibly do all the preparation and serving of a large dinner party, but she can do a great deal to help the hostess and allow her more time with her guests. Although the service is basically the same, there are practical shortcuts to make it run smoothly.

The maid can do last-minute cooking and warming, and prepare the food for serving during the cocktail hour, so that the hostess can be with her guests.

The first course (if there is one) can be already on the table and the water glasses filled when the guests sit down.

The maid can pass the serving dishes one at a time, first the meat and then the vegetables. Or the host or hostess can fill the plates at the table and let the maid pass them around, starting with the woman on his right. After three or four people have their food in front of them, a good hostess says, "Please begin—I don't want your dinner to get cold."

Condiments, bread, and sauces are on the table to be passed around by the diners. Butter pats or balls are put on the butter plates just before dinner.

Divided vegetable dishes are a great help as the maid can serve the potatoes and peas at the same time.

If you have a large electric hot plate or other warming device, the serving dishes may be left on a sideboard or side table until they are passed for second helpings. Otherwise, the maid takes them to the kitchen to keep warm.

While the guests are eating, the maid cleans out the ashtrays and generally neatens up the living room or area where cocktails were served.

She clears the table for dessert. If there are several tables, the hostess sometimes rises to help to expedite the process. Dessert may be brought in already served—fruit compote in chilled stemmed glasses, for example—or it may be placed in front of the hostess and served in the same way as the main course.

The maid brings the after-dinner coffee to the living room and the hostess pours and serves it. Liqueurs and after-dinner drinks are served by the host or hostess, leaving the maid free to clean up the dining room and wash the dishes.

**With no help** Far more parties are given without help than with it. A clever hostess can take the necessary shortcuts and eliminate the frills so smoothly that her guests hardly realize that she has done or is doing all the work alone.

Although buffet service is the easiest solution without help, some party givers prefer that their guests be seated and served at a table or tables. To do this graciously, the hostess slips away a few minutes before she plans to serve dinner and fills the water glasses, lights the candles, and puts a stack of plates and the dishes of food in front of her place or her husband's.

She dispenses with a formal first course, serving instead substantial hors d'oeuvre with cocktails, or even serving an easy-to-eat first course such as clams on the half shell or jellied madrilène in the living room.

The hostess may fill the plates in the kitchen and bring them in two at a time, but that leaves the guests no choice of white or dark meat, rare or well-done and so on. I feel it is preferable to have the host serve the meat and vegetables from his seat, and hand them to the guest on his right to send on around the table counterclockwise. If there is a real guest of honor—a much older or very important guest—on the host's right, that person should be urged to keep the first plate. The next is passed down the right side and kept by the person at the far right corner, then the plates are sent down the left side. The hostess's plate is filled next to the last and passed down either side to her, and finally the host serves himself. As he fills each plate, he may ask his friends how they like their meat, and if they want gravy on the meat or on the rice, etc., since they do not have the option of serving themselves. Again, the hostess should urge her guests to start eating when three or four have received their plates.

The salad is passed from guest to guest, counterclockwise, and, if the table is crowded, each diner should hold the bowl while the person on his right helps himself. Vegetables may be passed in this way, too, but it is less complicated if the host serves them along with the meat.

When the hostess rises to clear the table, some of her friends will probably offer to help. She should politely refuse, unless she has a relative or very close friend at the table who knows where things go and how the kitchen functions. The plates may be removed two at a time, but not stacked. Salts, peppers, and condiment dishes should be taken away, but it is not necessary to crumb the table. Neither is it necessary to remove the empty dessert dishes if the party moves to the living room for after-dinner coffee.

**When guests offer to help**   After dinner one or several of the women will surely offer to wash the dishes. If it is just an informal gathering of close friends, you might allow them to scrape the plates and get one load into the dishwasher. But at all other, even slightly formal dinners, you *must* refuse. You invite people to your home to give them a chance to relax and get away from household chores—not to do yours for you. You can say "No, honestly—the dishes will be here tomorrow and you won't and I'd rather enjoy your company now and do the dishes later." Or you may just flatly refuse with a polite "Thanks for the offer, but no."

**Buffet service without help**    The duties of a hostess serving a buffet dinner without help are far lighter. She must still leave her guests for a few minutes before dinner to light candles, open the wine, and put the chafing dishes or platters of food on the buffet. She then tells her guests that dinner is ready, and they form a line and fill their plates. She stands at the end of the buffet table, seeing that they get some of everything they want, and telling them where to sit if it is a seated buffet. She and her husband fill their own plates last, and then join their guests. They may join forces to remove the empty plates or the guests may put them on a side table when they go to get dessert. Before the dessert is brought in, the hostess must, of course, clear away the serving dishes from the buffet. If the dining room or serving area can be closed off, dessert plates and serving bowls may be left on the tables, but if the area is part of the living room, the dirty dishes should be taken to the kitchen or put out of sight in a sink or on a concealed counter.

## The Smoking Problem

More and more people are giving up smoking every day, and they are becoming more and more openly critical of those who still smoke. To those prospective hostesses who want to know if they have to allow people to smoke in their homes, we can only say this: A hostess's first duty is to make her *guests* happy. If they are miserable going through an evening without a cigarette at her insistence, she is not being a good hostess. If you or some of your friends are rabidly against smoking, you should not invite those who do smoke until summer, when you can entertain them outdoors.

You should provide ashtrays when smokers will be present, but you need not offer cigarettes. And you need not suffer their smoking at the table. If you do not put ashtrays on the dinner table, that is a clear indication that you do not want people to smoke during the meal, and your guests should take the hint. If they ask if they may light up after the main course you may say, "Cigarette smoke especially bothers some of us while we are eating."

## The Drug Problem

Another problem that many hostesses face today is that of the guests who want to smoke marijuana. If the hostess approves of the practice and is untroubled by the fact that it is illegal, of course she has no problem. But if she does not approve and is concerned about people breaking the law in her home, she should say so firmly. The moment she sees the first joint being lighted or passed around she should tell her guests that she's sorry if she's being a spoilsport, but she doesn't want people smoking in her home where she would be held responsible if the illegal use of marijuana were detected. Then, rather than letting the group continue to sit and chat, she should get some lively games or activities under way to distract them.

## The Lingering Guest

The very last and possibly the worst problem you will encounter are the guests who won't go home. There is no ideal way to get rid of them, but there are a few things you can do to help speed them on their way.

First, and most important, close the bar. Stop offering them refills, and, if necessary, openly put the liquor away.

Glance at your watch occasionally, and stifle a yawn or two, not too inconspicuously.

Empty ashtrays and take used glasses to the kitchen.

If none of these subtle hints has any effect, come right out with the truth: "Jim and Nancy, I'm exhausted, and I have a tennis game at 8:30 tomorrow. We'll see you soon, but this party's over for now."

When a cocktail party is dragging on through the dinner hour, and closing the bar hasn't gotten rid of the lingerers, you can always say, "I'd love to offer you another drink, but we're meeting friends at Sloppy Joe's for dinner and we're late now." Or, if you wish, you can say, "I'm famished—why don't we all go down to the Hash House for a bite to eat?"

# part two

# Parties, Parties, Parties

# 10

# *Seasonal Parties*

This section of the book is devoted to helping you plan your parties in advance, and to suggesting the way to carry out that plan. As I mentioned in the introduction, the key to successful entertaining is having as much as possible done ahead of time in order to be relaxed and well-organized at the time of the party, and to be able to devote most of your time to your guests, rather than to the cooking.

I have selected occasions throughout the year that are natural times to think of entertaining, and suggested specific parties that would be appropriate at those times. Naturally, any one of these parties could be given at any other time you choose—to celebrate a birthday or an anniversary or for no reason at all other than that you feel like entertaining your friends. Some of the parties are, of course, especially appropriate to the season in which I have placed them—a clambake, for example, is almost always a summertime party—but even a clambake can be adapted to other times of the year, and might, if you do so, create even more of a sensation. The Chinese New Year's Dinner certainly need not be held only on Chinese New Year's, and of course the Kentucky Derby Cocktail Party—minus the betting devices—could be given any time at all.

The suggested timetables are approximate. Your working schedule, for example, may make it impossible to make and freeze a casserole at the recommended time. But that makes no difference. Do it two or three days or two weeks sooner, and it won't suffer in the least. The schedule should, however, suggest the *order* in which things should be done, and help you to think each chore through ahead of time.

The menus, too, are intended as guides, and you will certainly want to vary them according to your taste and that of your guests. If you substitute, do try to select dishes of a similar type so that the preparation times are approximately the same and the change does not affect the balance of the total menu.

The inspiration for this whole section of the book was a magazine article I saw several years ago describing a party step by step in the same way I have done here. I followed it faithfully, and the result was one of the most successful parties I have ever given. Whether you are an inexperienced hostess or a veteran partygiver, I think you will find, as I did, that having a timetable to adhere to, and to use as a check list, is an invaluable aid. I hope you will use it as it is intended—as a source of ideas for menus, recipes, and decorations, and also as a ready-made organizer to take some of the worry and the work out of your entertaining.

---

## New Year's Day Brunch for Sixteen

---

Whether we like it or not, New Year's Eve means drinking to most people. No matter if you spend it at an elegant dinner party at a friend's home, dancing in a disco or a hotel ballroom, reveling in Times Square, or square-dancing in the country, you can be sure that there will be plenty of liquor consumed. If you intend to enter into the spirit in that way yourself, I would not recommend that you entertain on New Year's Day. You simply will not feel up to it. But if you are among the many who prefer to spend a quieter New Year's Eve and are content to watch the revelry in Times Square on television, then New Year's Day is a wonderful time to entertain. An early morning breakfast can provide a great last stop for those friends who really made a night of it, and need to taper off slowly. Even more popular is the midmorning brunch, which satisfies those who need a little of the "hair of the dog" that bit them as well as those who did not celebrate the night before at all.

In fact, brunches are a delightful form of entertaining at any time of the year. After church during the winter, or as a cheerful prelude to an afternoon of tennis or sailing in the summer, the brunch is a relaxed, informal way of bringing people together. To me, it is one of the best parties of all.

## *Menu*

*Rum fizz, Bloody Marys*
*Pink grapefruit with strawberry sauce*
*Chicken livers in wine*
*Eggs hollandaise on artichoke bottoms*
*Sausage casserole*
*Corn bread*
*Toasted herb rolls*
*Raspberry ring and/or pastries*
*Coffee*

## SHOPPING LIST

*Ingredients for herb rolls and sausage casserole*

2 loaves white bread (a thin, soft bread such as Hollywood Diet is recommended)
1 pound butter or margarine
2 pounds sausage meat
2 green peppers
½ pound mushrooms
Flour
1 quart milk (for corn bread also)
Savory
Basil
Chives
Curry powder
Bread crumbs (or make your own in a blender or food processor)
Grated Parmesan cheese
Toothpicks

*Remaining recipe ingredients*

2 pounds chicken livers
1 bag large yellow onions
1 pound mushrooms
1 pound bacon, or slice of processed ham
1 can chicken broth
1 bottle inexpensive red wine
8 pink grapefruit
3 pints fresh strawberries, or 3 boxes frozen sliced berries

2  pounds sugar
3  cartons orange juice
2  dozen eggs
1  pound butter
   Cayenne pepper
3  cans artichoke bottoms
3  lemons
2  10-ounce packages frozen raspberries
4  3-ounce packages raspberry gelatin
   Fresh or dry-frozen blueberries or raspberries to
   fill rings
2  pints vanilla ice cream
2  6-ounce cans frozen lemonade
6  oranges
2  quarts ginger ale
2  quarts V-8 juice
4  cans beef bouillon
1  bottle unsweetened lemon juice
   Celery salt
   Worcestershire sauce
   Tabasco sauce
   Celery (for celery sticks in Bloody Mary glasses)
   Coarse salt for rims of glasses
   Regular and decaffeinated coffee
½  pint cream

*If you plan to make your own corn bread*

1  box yellow corn meal
   Baking powder

*Liquor*

2  quarts vodka
2  quarts rum
1  six-pack of ginger ale (in addition to ginger ale for
   rum fizzes)
1  six-pack of cola

# TIMETABLE

*Party Day Minus 3 Weeks*
Send invitations
Plan the menu

*Party Day Minus 2 Weeks*
Check china, crystal, bar equipment, etc.
Rent or buy any equipment necessary
Order pastries and corn bread

*Party Day Minus 5 Days*
Buy or order special New Year's decorations and
flowers
Purchase ingredients for toasted herb rolls and sausage
casserole and prepare and freeze these dishes

*Party Day Minus 2 Days*
Polish silver, shine glasses, etc.
Purchase ingredients for all remaining dishes
Buy liquor, soft drinks, and mixes

*Party Day Minus 1 Day*
Pick up pastries and corn bread
Set the buffet table and arrange furniture in the dining
or living room
Prepare chicken livers, pink grapefruit, hollandaise,
raspberry ring
Slice oranges for rum fizzes
Precook bacon for eggs and artichoke bottoms
Take sausage casserole and toasted herb rolls from
freezer and put into refrigerator when thawed

*Party Day Early*
Set up bar and make Bloody Marys
Heat chicken livers, herb rolls, artichoke bottoms,
sausage casserole
Heat the bacon
If you make your own corn bread, do it now, or heat
corn bread from the bakery
Prepare coffee

*Party Time*
Serve grapefruit halves with strawberry sauce
Heat other prepared dishes and set out
Unmold raspberry ring and fill with fresh berries
Poach eggs and assemble dish

## Party Day Minus 3 Weeks

You know your friends and what they would like better than anyone
else, so you must decide the best time to schedule your party for. But
whether you decide on a 6 A.M. "tapering-off" party, or a midmorning

brunch to welcome the New Year, many of the ingredients will be the same. Even those who managed to have a few hours sleep before your party may be suffering from the aftereffects of the night before, and will need to be treated with the same tender loving care as those who might be just on their way home if you choose to give an early breakfast.

**Send invitations** Because New Year's Day is such a popular party day, your invitations should go out well ahead of time. You may have them printed if you opt for a formal brunch, you may write the bare essentials on note paper or you may buy the commercial fill-in invitations made especially for such occasions. Allow two weeks for printing invitations, three to four weeks for engraving. But whatever you do, don't telephone. At this season of the year, a reminder is a must, and your written invitation serves as that reminder.

A formal printed or engraved invitation for brunch might read:

---

*Mr. and Mrs. Joseph VanHorn*
*cordially invite you to a*
*Ring-in-the-New-Year Brunch*
*on Sunday, January first*
*at 11:30 o'clock*
*(address)*

*R.s.v.p.*

---

For an early breakfast, an informal or fill-in would be more appropriate.

---

*Sunday, January 1*
*on your way home*
*breakfast at 7 A.M.*
*(name and address)*

*Regrets only—TA. 8-2427*

---

Your invitations may be open-ended like those above, or, if you are afraid that your party will last all day, you may say "from 11:30 to 2," or "breakfast from 7 to 9." If you do this, however, your guests may arrive at any time between the stated hours, and you will have to have food ready all the time. Whereas, if you simply give an arrival time, you may serve your dishes all at once, half an hour to an hour after the stated time.

**Plan the menu** The menu I have selected is diversified, out-of-the-ordinary, and easy to prepare. But breakfasts and brunches are wonderful occasions to use your imagination. Aside from the dishes described in this chapter, many, many others are appropriate and interesting.

At an early breakfast, it is safe to assume that your guests will not have eaten before their arrival, and they will be hungry! Accordingly, your menu may lean toward quite filling kinds of food—filling but not heavy. Various egg dishes—omelets, quiches, scrambled eggs—are staple fare. Fish is a welcome change—kippered herring, trout fillets, crabmeat mornay, or lobster thermidor served on waffles. Sausage and bacon, though not unusual, go well at this hour. Fried or grilled tomatoes are an ideal vegetable, as are mushrooms and peppers, perhaps added to the eggs. Cheeses should be light and mild flavored. The sharp tangy varieties have a tendency to be slightly overpowering at breakfast. Fruit or fruit juice, muffins, popovers, or biscuits with the appropriate jams, jellies and preserves round off a satisfying breakfast menu.

Webster defines the brunch as a late breakfast, an early lunch, or a combination of the two. Therefore, the above suggestions are appropriate for brunch as well as for breakfast. However, the brunch is usually slightly more formal and calls for an even more varied menu. Foods served at this hour (anywhere from 10:30 A.M. to 2:30 P.M.) should be more substantial than breakfast since they also serve as lunch. Eggs are often served at this hour, but you may want to introduce some other main dishes such as beef stroganoff, lamb chops, chicken legs or wings, turkey hash, or shellfish in a casserole. Various vegetable dishes may also be added to your table. Cold vegetables are crowd pleasers because they are not too heavy, yet still have substance.

Sandwiches, which many people associate with lunch, are just not appropriate for brunch, particularly on such an important holiday as New Year's. Although there are elaborate and delicious sandwiches, for most of us the sandwich is just too ordinary to be considered sufficiently special for this occasion.

To provide a finishing touch for those with a sweet tooth, offer a finger pastry—éclairs, tiny cream puffs, or little fruit tarts. And, of course, fruit cakes, stollen, strudels, and other traditional holiday favorites are perfect at this time, the end of the holiday season and the beginning of the New Year.

## Party Day Minus 2 Weeks

**Check your equipment**   Rent or borrow whatever is needed because the days between Christmas and New Year's are likely to be busy ones. It is a good idea to check your equipment well ahead of time so you can acquire whatever you don't have on hand. Since our party is planned for only sixteen, you may well have all the china and glassware you need. It is never necessary to have everything of one pattern. In fact, it makes a more interesting buffet table to mix several colors and patterns, as long as you are careful, of course, that colors do not clash and that the patterns do not overpower each other.

The trend in breakfast entertaining, and to an even greater extent brunch entertaining, is toward the slightly formal. Somehow, egg soufflés and delicately browned Canadian bacon just don't seem as good on white paper plates. This party is a perfect opportunity to use your best china and finest Irish linen.

On New Year's Day, you will want your buffet table to be all aglitter, so use your silver chafing dishes. Because this is such a special day, if you don't own a silver chafing dish try to rent one. There is nothing more festive and elegant than silver.

You will not need a punch bowl for your breakfast or brunch, but you will need a number of highball and large Old Fashioned glasses. If you don't have enough, look over the supermarket stock. They often have very presentable glasses at extremely moderate prices. Buy or borrow, but *don't,* for this occasion, resort to plastic glasses.

The best plan for a breakfast/brunch—especially on New Year's Day —is to keep your guest list down to a manageable number of close friends and to have an informal seating arrangement. The living room near a fireplace (and, of course, the patio or lawn in warmer climates) is the perfect breakfast or brunch setting.

However, don't force your guests to hold their plates on their laps or, worse yet, to eat standing up. Whatever you must do to get table space —rearrange your furniture and borrow tables from friends or rent them —do it! Make sure that every guest has a seat and a small table or section of a larger table for his plate. And do it *now,* not when stores are closed or out of rental stock, or your neighbors are out of town for the holidays!

**Order pastries and corn bread**   Because of the rush of orders during the holiday season, you would be wise to order your pastries now. Be sure to get a written copy of your order, to insure that you can check on it by number and that it will be exactly what you want when you pick it up. Because homemade corn bread should be made shortly before it is served, you may want to order it from the bakery now rather than taking the time to prepare it the morning of the party.

## Party Day Minus 5 Days

**Buy decorations and order flowers** Ordinarily, I would say "Party day minus 1 week," but that would be Christmas Day and you will be otherwise occupied! So, a day or two after Christmas it will be time to buy your New Year's decorations. The Christmas decorations will be off the shelves and the New Year's equipment will be out—fresh and plentiful.

Actually, the balloons and streamers of New Year's Eve are no longer necessary on New Year's Day. A special centerpiece (again available at party stores) for the table, and flower arrangements or plants to brighten up the dark winter day are all that are necessary. Of course, your Chirstmas decorations may still be up, and, with a quick sprucing up, they will add to the festivity. However, it is the atmosphere you create that is important. On New Year's Day, the weather in most places is usually brisk, if not actually snowy and icy. A successful breakfast or brunch is certain to please, regardless of budget, if the atmosphere is warm and cozy. A good fire, hot foods, and tasty drinks will relax your guests, and relaxation is very important for this kind of party.

**Purchase ingredients and prepare dishes to be frozen** The following two dishes may be prepared ahead and frozen. See the shopping list on pp. 103–104 for the ingredients to purchase for these dishes.

### Toasted Herb Rolls

2 sticks butter or margarine at room temperature
1 teaspoon savory
1 teaspoon basil
4 tablespoons chopped chives
2 loaves soft white bread, sliced

Thoroughly mix the softened butter with the savory, basil, and chives. Remove the crusts from the bread slices and spread each slice with the herbed butter. Roll and secure with a toothpick. Bake in a 350-degree oven for 30 minutes. Check frequently and, if necessary, turn to brown evenly. When completely cool, wrap in foil and freeze.

### *Sausage Casserole*

---

2   pounds sausage meat
2   green peppers, chopped
½   pound mushrooms, sliced
2   tablespoons butter or margarine
2   tablespoons flour
2   teaspoons curry powder
1½  cups milk
    Salt and pepper
    Bread crumbs
    Grated Parmesan cheese

Cook the sausage meat in a frying pan, separating the meat with a fork so that it cooks evenly. Drain well. Add the green pepper and mushrooms and mix well.

In a saucepan, melt the butter or margarine and blend in the flour and curry powder. When smooth, add the milk gradually. Cook, stirring, until thickened. Add salt and pepper to taste.

Mix the sausage and the sauce and pour into a shallow casserole. Sprinkle the top with bread crumbs and grated Parmesan. Bake in a 350-degree oven for 30 minutes. Cool, then cover with foil and freeze.

## Party Day Minus 2 Days

**Check condition of equipment**   This is the time to be sure that your silver is clean, the glasses glistening, and linens spotless. If your good dishes have been stored away, run them through the dishwasher, or if they are too delicate, wash them in hot sudsy water. Wash any spare glasses you have bought or rented for the occasion. If you are using chafing dishes, be sure to have plenty of Sterno on hand.

**Purchase ingredients for all remaining dishes**   Check the shopping list carefully and list the provisions you still need. Also, go through your staples to be sure that your supply of such things as coffee, salt, sugar, and milk is adequate.

Make your purchases and store them in such a way that they will be conveniently at hand when you start to prepare the food. Caution your children that these supplies are taboo for their snacks. Buy liquor, soft drinks, and mixes.

### Party Day Minus 1 Day

Early in the morning, pick up the pastries you ordered so that you can devote the remainder of the day to preparing your meal. Set the buffet table and arrange the furniture in the dining or living room area to provide the extra table space you will need.

Remove the sausage casserole and the herb rolls from the freezer. When thcy arc thawcd, store them in the refrigerator.

Slice the 6 oranges for the rum fizzes and refrigerate.

**Prepare the following dishes**

#### Chicken Livers in Wine

2 pounds chicken livers, about 24
½ cup plus 1 tablespoon seasoned flour
2 large onions, chopped
4 tablespoons butter or margarine
1 pound mushrooms, sliced
1 cup chopped cooked bacon or ham
1 cup chicken broth
1 cup red wine

Remove tough membranes from the chicken livers and cut them in half. Roll them in ½ cup seasoned flour. Sauté the onion in the butter until wilted. Add the chicken livers to the onion and cook for about 3 minutes. Add the mushrooms and bacon or ham and sauté briefly. Stir in the 1 tablespoon seasoned flour and cook, stirring, until slightly browned. Add the chicken broth and wine and cook gently for 3 minutes. Cool and refrigerate.

#### Pink Grapefruit with Strawberry Sauce

8 pink grapefruit
3 pints fresh strawberries, sliced, or 3 boxes frozen sliced berries

1½  cups sugar
 1  cup orange juice

Halve the grapefruit, remove the seeds and section them carefully.
Cover the halves tightly with foil and store in the refrigerator.
   Put the strawberries, sugar, and orange juice in a saucepan and heat,
stirring, until the sugar is dissolved and strawberries soften. Chill.

## Hollandaise Sauce for Eggs on Artichoke Bottoms

2  sticks butter
3  tablespoons lemon juice
6  egg yolks, lightly beaten
¼  teaspoon salt
   Dash of cayenne

In a small pan, heat the butter and lemon juice. Meanwhile, heat the
water in the bottom of a double boiler and bring water to boil in a kettle. Put the egg yolks in the top of the double boiler and place over the
boiling water, stirring constantly for a moment. Add 8 tablespoons boiling water from the kettle, one at a time, stirring hard after each addition. Remove the top of the double boiler from the heat and pour in the
hot butter-lemon mixture in a thin stream, stirring constantly. As the
sauce thickens, add the salt and cayenne. Cool and store in the refrigerator.

## Bacon for Eggs on Artichoke Bottoms

Precook 4 slices bacon for 15 minutes on the broiling pan in a 350-de-
gree oven. Cool, crumble and store in a jar in the refrigerator.

## Raspberry Ring

2  10-ounce packages frozen raspberries
4  3-ounce packages raspberry gelatin
2  pints softened vanilla ice cream

**2 6-ounce cans frozen lemonade, thawed**
   **Blueberries or raspberries for garnish**

Thaw the raspberries and drain, reserving the syrup. Dissolve the gelatin in 4 cups boiling water. Add the ice cream by spoonfuls. When thoroughly melted, stir in the lemonade and reserved raspberry syrup. Chill. When partly set, add the thawed raspberries and pour into two 6-cup ring molds. Return to the refrigerator. When unmolded the day of the party, the rings may be filled with blueberries or fresh raspberries.

## Party Day Early

**Set up the bar**   In addition to setting out the necessary glasses and ingredients for the drinks, our menu calls for two special preparations. A quantity of ice should be cracked fine or put through an ice crusher for the rum fizzes. It should be kept in a separate cooler. The orange slices should be taken from the refrigerator and placed in a convenient spot on the bar.

Celery stalks for the Bloody Marys should be placed on the bar, along with a plate of coarse salt and a shallow bowl of water. The rims of the glasses are dipped into the water and then the salt, making an attractive and tasty frosting on the glasses.

Plenty of soft drinks should be available, as well as a choice of another liquor or two for those who do not care for rum or Bloody Marys.

The necessary ingredients should be set out to complete the rum fizz and the Bloody Mary recipes.

### *Rum Fizz*

**¼ cup light rum**
**¼ cup orange juice**
   **Ginger ale**
   **Orange slices**

Fill each highball glass approximately three-quarters full with cracked or crushed ice. Add the rum and orange juice and fill the glass with ginger ale. Garnish with an orange slice.

*Bloody Mary*

1 quart V-8 juice
2 cans beef bouillon
1 teaspoon celery salt
¼ cup lemon juice
¼ teaspoon Tabasco sauce
2 tablespoons Worcestershire sauce
2 teaspoons salt
2 cups vodka
  Celery sticks

In a large pitcher, mix all ingredients well. Before serving, dip the rim of each glass in water, then coarse salt. Fill with ice and pour the mix in. Insert one celery stick in each glass.

Make two batches at the same time and keep one in the refrigerator until it is needed.

**Prepare coffee**   You will want to have plenty of coffee ready, whether you are having a breakfast or a brunch. If you have a forty-cup coffee urn, use it, even though you will only be sixteen people.

If you are using percolators or other coffee makers, be sure to get them started so that the coffee will be ready. Make decaffeinated as well as regular coffee in the same way.

If you are making instant coffee, measure the coffee and the water into coffeepots or other containers and bring to a boil, rather than making it in individual cups. It has far more flavor prepared in that way.

**Heat prepared dishes**   Remove hollandaise sauce from the refrigerator and warm it slowly on an electric hot plate.

If you have two ovens, you will have no problem heating all the dishes at once. If you have only one, heat them in two stages.

Heat the chicken livers in a 325-degree oven for 20 to 30 minutes.

Put herb rolls and the artichoke bottoms in the oven for the last 15 minutes. Keep all three dishes hot on an electric hot plate.

Turn the oven up to 425 degrees and heat the sausage casserole for 20 minutes. Warm up the pre-cooked bacon, and if you make your own corn bread, bake it at the same time, or heat the bakery corn bread.

Turn the oven off when the corn bread is finished, leave the door ajar and return the sausage casserole and bacon to keep warm with the corn bread.

## Corn Bread

---

```
    2  cups flour
    7  teaspoons baking powder
1½  teaspoons salt
    6  tablespoons sugar
    2  cups yellow corn meal
    2  eggs, lightly beaten
    2  cups milk
    ½  cup melted and cooled butter
```

Sift the flour and add the baking powder, salt, and sugar. Resift and add the corn meal. Combine the eggs with the milk and butter. Mix with the flour and stir until moist. Turn into two 8-by-8-inch pans. Bake in a 425-degree oven for 40 minutes.

### Party Time

Barring the final assembly, all your dishes are now ready except for the poached eggs. If you plan to serve your breakfast/brunch 45 minutes or an hour after your guests arrive, you will have plenty of time for your last-minute preparations, and you will not even have to leave your guests for too long a time.

Shortly before serving the main dishes, pour the strawberry sauce over the grapefruit halves and set them out on your buffet table. While everyone is enjoying them as a first course, you can quickly put the finishing touches on the other dishes.

Unmold the raspberry ring and fill with fresh berries.

Put the chicken livers into a chafing dish and light the Sterno.

Cut the corn bread into squares and set out in a bread or roll dish covered with a napkin. Arrange the herb rolls on a warm plate, also covered.

Place the sausage casserole on the buffet table, preferably on a hot plate or other warming device.

Put a plate of butter balls or slices on the table for the corn bread.

Finally, prepare the Poached Eggs on Artichoke Bottoms.

Poach 16 eggs until firm, but still soft. Arrange 16 warm artichoke bottoms on a hot platter. Place one egg carefully on each artichoke bottom. Spoon 2 tablespoons hollandaise sauce over each egg. Sprinkle tops with crumbled bacon.

Call your guests in to enjoy the feast, and remove the grapefruit halves to the kitchen while they are serving themselves from the buffet.

When everyone has had their fill, ask someone to clear the main-course plates while you serve the raspberry rings, pastries, and coffee. Put cream and sugar on the table.

## Hangover Headaches

This brunch or breakfast may, of course, be served at any time of the year. However, I have suggested it as a splendid way to celebrate New Year's, and in case you choose to do it at that time I would like to suggest several special offerings for those who might be suffering from a little overindulgence the night before. In addition to the drinks described above, the following concoctions are reputedly effective for hangovers, and might be a worthwhile addition to your bar menu.

*Bullshot*   Consommé with lemon juice, drops of Worcestershire sauce, Tabasco, salt, pepper, and vodka

*Eggnog*   or any milk drink

*Prairie Oyster*   Tomato juice, raw egg, teaspoon of Worcestershire sauce, Tabasco, salt, and pepper

*Las Vegas Remedy*   Three fourths glass of tomato juice, 2 table-spoons cream, 1 raw egg, 3 ounces of beer and dash of nutmeg

*Morning Fizz*   One jigger of rye, 2 ounces of Pernod, juice of ½ lemon, and teaspoon of sugar

*Black Velvet*   One half stout and one half champagne

## Drinking and Driving

One further word about drinking. If your party is a breakfast and your guests will be coming by after a night of revelry, some may well have had more to drink than they should. You, unwittingly, may serve them the drink that sets them reeling. If that should happen, or if their earlier drinks suddenly rise up and hit them (as can easily happen), *don't let them drive home*. Ask a friend to take them, call a taxi, offer them a bed for a recuperative nap, steal their car keys if necessary, but *don't let them drive*.

## Chinese New Year's Dinner for Twelve

Chinese New Year provides a wonderful background for a winter celebration. It is steeped in traditions that go back many thousands of years, making Saint Patrick's or Saint Valentine's days seem like youngsters in comparison. The New Year's celebration, which begins on a different day each year, usually falls between January 21 and February 19, and the holiday lasts for four days. Each Chinese year is symbolized by a specific animal, and you may want to use that animal as the basis for your decorating and accessories. The Chinese year 4678 (our year 1980) is the year of the monkey. Upcoming (in chronological order) are the years of the rooster, dog, pig, rat, ox, tiger, hare, dragon, snake, horse, and finally, the year of the sheep (1991).

In any year, a key symbol of Chinese New Year is the dragon, signifying good, protection, fertility, and ancestor worship. Masks, kites, and costumes utilizing the dragon motif are very popular at this time.

The traditions of Chinese New Year are indivisible from the ancient cooking traditions of the Chinese culture. Food is as important to this celebration as it is to Passover and European Easter celebrations. How better, then, could one combine the rudiments of a formal dinner with an unusual, exotic gourmet menu? For our party, I have selected a varied menu of delicious dishes that can be prepared over a period of time.

### *Menu*

*Shrimp puffs        Canton spring rolls*
*Chinese noodle soup*
*Lamb with scallions*
*Chicken with bean sprouts*
*Spicy chang (pork with brown bean sauce)*
*Rice*
*Watermelon bowl*
*Fortune cookies and Tea*

## *SHOPPING LIST*

If you live in a city where there is a Chinatown, or in a town that boasts an Oriental market, you will be able to purchase the ingredients for your menu any time you wish. If, however, you live in a small town or in the country, you will have to take advantage of an occasional trip to the city to replenish your supply of Chinese staples. To be able to complete the menu described in this chapter, you need the following ingredients on your shelf.

*Chinese staples*

> **Soy sauce**
> **Canned bean curd**
> **Hoisin sauce**
> **Brown bean sauce**
> **Dried mushrooms**
> **Sesame oil**
> **Chinese tea**

*Other staples*

> **Cornstarch**
> **Sugar**
> **Salt**
> **Pepper (black and white)**
> **Butter or margarine**
> **Garlic**
> **Monosodium glutamate**
> **Eggs**
> **Peanut or corn oil (about 2 quarts)**
> **All-purpose flour**
> **Thyme**

*Ingredients for shrimp puffs and spring rolls*

> 1 **loaf thinly sliced white bread**
> 1¾ **pounds raw, shelled shrimp**
> ½ **pound bacon or pork fat**
> ¾ **pound lean ground pork**
> 1 **bottle dry sherry**
> 1 **ginger root**
> ¾ **pound fresh bean sprouts, or 1 can**

    1 bunch celery
    1 pound fresh mushrooms

*Ingredients for spicy chang*

    ½ pound dried mushrooms
    1½ pounds boneless pork
    3 green peppers
    1 can red bean curd
    ½ cup brown bean sauce
    1 can bamboo shoots

*Remaining nonperishable ingredients*

    1 box long-grain rice
    ½ pound thin egg noodles
    1 pound Smithfield ham (or similar smoky ham)
    3 13¾-ounce cans chicken broth
    1 pint white vinegar
    1 bottle sesame oil
    Hot mustard (dry English or bottled)
    Bottled sweet sauce
    2 cans bean sprouts
    1 package frozen snow peas
    3 cans litchis
    2 cans preserved kumquats
    2 cans mandarin orange slices
    Fortune cookies

*Perishable items*

    4 whole boned chicken breasts
    1 bunch watercress
    1½ pounds boneless lamb, preferably from the leg
    4 bunches scallions
    1 large watermelon
    Fresh mint

*Optional*

    1 honeydew melon, seedless grapes, canned apricots

*Liquor (if you wish to offer cocktails before dinner)*

    1 quart vodka
    1 quart Bourbon or blended whiskey
    1 quart gin
    1 bottle vermouth
    Wine or beer

## TIMETABLE

Whenever you are near a Chinese (or specialty) market, purchase Chinese staples, and cooking and serving equipment (including chopsticks and decorations).

*Party Day Minus 3 Weeks*
**Make and send invitations**
**Plan the menu**
**Plan the table settings**
**Consider help and service**

*Party Day Minus 2 Weeks*
**Plan your decorations and purchase materials (except for fresh flowers)**
**Practice napkin folding**
**Design and make place cards**
**Rent, buy, or borrow equipment you do not already have**
**Check food staples**
**Purchase ingredients for shrimp puffs and Canton spring rolls and prepare and freeze these dishes**

*Party Day Minus 1 Week*
**Purchase ingredients for spicy chang, prepare and refrigerate**
**Buy all other nonperishable ingredients**
**Buy liquor, soft drinks, and mixes**

*Party Day Minus 2 Days*
**Buy all remaining (perishable) ingredients—meat, poultry, fruits, and vegetables**
**Hang lanterns, clean house**

*Party Day Minus 1 Day*
**Set table and/or buffet table**
**Buy fresh flowers and make arrangements**
**Make noodle soup and refrigerate**
**Prepare and refrigerate melon bowl**

*Party Day Morning*
**Remove shrimp puffs and spring rolls from freezer**
**Prepare ingredients for lamb with scallions and chicken with bean sprouts**

*Party Day, Final Preparations*
**Set out soup bowls, chafing dishes, and dessert plates**
**Heat shrimp puffs and spring rolls**
**Heat spicy chang and chicken with bean sprouts**
**Heat soup**
**Prepare rice**
**Stir-fry lamb and scallions**
**Make tea**
**Arrange fortune cookies on platter**

*Party Time*
**Pour soup in warm bowls**
**Put chafing dishes, casseroles, and rice on table**

## Party Day Minus 3 Weeks

In the ordinary kitchen, or without a staff of Chinese chefs, it is impossible to serve a Chinese dinner for more than twelve people. It is a simple matter of cooking space and time. Therefore, I highly recommend that you keep your guest list down to twelve.

**Make and send invitations** A Chinese New Year celebration is a splendid time to do something different with invitations. For example:

---

*IN HONOR OF THE CAT*
*Who Will Supply Our Needs Purrrrfectly*
*Throughout This*
*FOUR THOUSAND SIX HUNDRED AND NINETY-FIFTH YEAR*

*Mr. and Mrs. George Greco*
*request the pleasure of your*
*most honorable company*
*At half past the seventh hour*
*on Wednesday, February 18*

*Please call:*                    *Black Tie (optional)*
*899-8914*

---

If you have time, draw or cut out some simple cat figures, make a stencil from them, and decorate the corners of your invitations with playful kittens (or monkeys, roosters, dogs, etc., whatever is the appropriate animal symbol for the year you are celebrating).

**Plan the menu** In planning your menu, stick to dishes that are not too complicated, that you have done before, or that you recognize by the instructions as something you can do. Also, since the usual Chinese menu involves a great number of dishes, select several that can be prepared ahead and frozen. Do not choose too many stir-fry or last-minute dishes because you will spend too much time in the kitchen and not be able to produce the main-course selections simultaneously.

Although I do suggest that your dinner be Chinese-formal, don't forget that some of your friends may be intimidated by too much exoticism, and by surroundings that are unnatural to them. Inviting people to share new and exciting food is one thing; making them uncomfortable with chopsticks and sugarless Chinese tea is another. If your friends are not "into" chopsticks, bird's nest soup and pickled squid, compromise with a fork at each place, a clear chicken broth, and more mundane alternatives to the squid.

**Plan the table setting(s)** Formal dinner tables, with their array of wine glasses, ashtrays, nut dishes, etc., have a tendency to get crowded, to say the least. If you want to serve in the traditional Chinese style of putting all the dishes for each course on the table at once, and having everyone help himself, you must leave off such things as butter plates (no bread is served anyway), salts and peppers (not used with Chinese food), and a centerpiece (the dishes offered serve as the centerpiece). You will naturally want to use your loveliest, gayest linen and china for this party. But there will be certain things that the normal household does not have, and you should start to look for them now because they may be hard to find: small individual rice bowls; little sauce dishes for hot and sweet sauces—two for each guest; small cups without handles for the Chinese tea; chopsticks (should be at every place, even though guests may prefer to use their forks); cruet for soy sauce; two or three chafing dishes.

If your dining room table is not large enough to accommodate your guests *and* the serving dishes of food, the best alternative is to serve the meal buffet-style from a sideboard or side table.

**Outside help** Many Chinese restaurants provide catering service. If you plan on a party of twenty-four instead of twelve, you will be well advised to use this service. However, even for a smaller party you may wish to get temporary help. Chinese waiters who can help with the last-minute preparations, who know how to serve Chinese dishes and can also clear away and wash up, are invaluable. But if they are not available, we would suggest that your helpers be restricted to bartending, some serving and cleaning up, because Chinese food served "American style" by an uneducated waiter can be a disaster. If you decide to have help for the evening, make the arrangements now, so that you have time to compare and select the very best help you can find.

## Party Day Minus 2 Weeks

**Plan the decorations** The ancient Oriental art of origami is the inspiration for napkin-folding, and beautifully folded napkins can add wonderful touches to your table settings. If you are not already an expert, a week or two before the party you should refer to a book on origami (see Bibliography) and practice and perfect the folds. When you are satisfied, the folded napkins may be carefully put away—ready to be put on the table at the last moment.

There are some twenty traditional napkin folds, including the fan, the bird of paradise, the lotus, as well as several styles of sailing ships and cones. Their uses vary as do their decorative possibilities. The lotus, for example, is better used for finger bowls and condiment mats; the bird of paradise looks best against a glass; the fan is made to be placed on a plate.

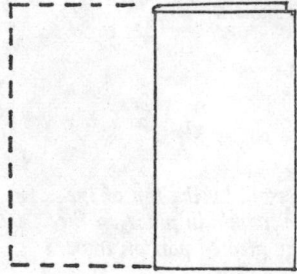

ORIENTAL FAN. *Fold a square napkin in half.*

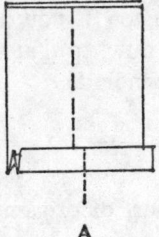

Accordion pleat the napkin from one end until slightly more than half is pleated. Fold the napkin in half on line A with the accordion pleats on the outside.

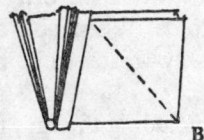

Keeping the open end up, fold the corner with the three loose points along line B.

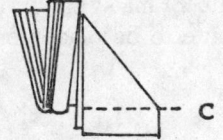

If the napkin has been folded properly, there will be a slight portion of the end that must be folded under line C as shown.

Holding the napkin upright by the top of the pleated section, set the napkin in place on the table or dish, facing the pleated portion toward the end of the table.

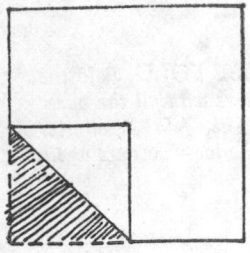

**LOTUS FOLD.** *Fold the corners of a square napkin to the center.*

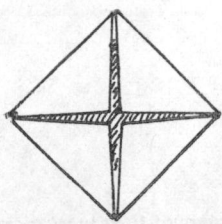

*Fold the four corners to the center again.*

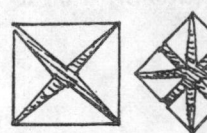

*Fold the four corners again. This is the third time folds have been made on this side. Turn the napkin over and fold the four corners in to the center. This makes the fourth time the corners have been folded. Hold the folded napkin firmly in the center. Reach under each of the corners, pulling up and out the loose point. Do this to all four corners, and when that is completed, reach beneath the space between the corners pulling up and out yet another four points. Finally, reach beneath the folded napkin for the third set of points. These four points are the original corner points. Be careful not to pull too much and to hold the center firmly throughout the process. The third set of points locks the fold in place. The lotus is perfect for a nut dish or for holding a favor or placecard.*

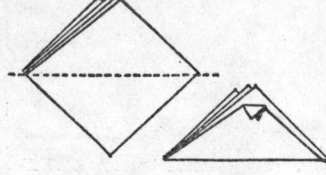

**BIRD OF PARADISE FOLD.** *Fold the napkin into four quarters with all the open points facing the top. Then fold the quartered napkin in half, with the loose corners at the top of this triangle.*

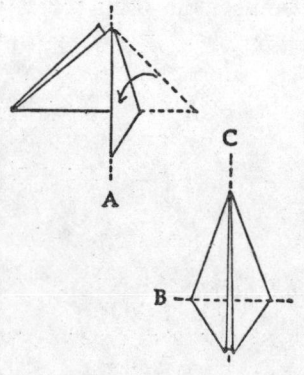

*Fold the two bottom corners so they meet along line A. Tuck the bottom points underneath line B and then fold napkin in half along line C. This exposes the four loose corners at the top.*

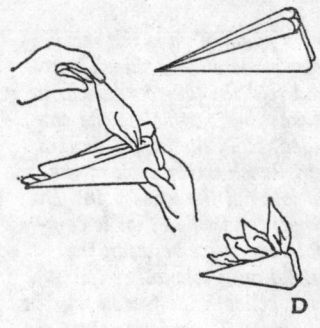

*These two folds result in a wedge-shaped napkin. Holding the widest end of the napkin, pull the points up one at a time. The points lock as each is pulled up. The result is a birdlike fold. This napkin looks great with a stemmed glass nestled against point D.*

Table decorations for a traditional Chinese New Year celebration may include noise makers, masks, streamers, snappers, confetti, and candy, all usually available in Chinese or Oriental stores. You may incorporate any of these traditions, or none of them. Although you may not *think* your guests would use noise makers, if they find them at their places they may just be enticed into the full spirit of the occasion.

The Chinese New Year comes at the coldest time of winter in most regions of the country and certain flowers are not always readily available. Flowers should be used, however, only as accents. Oriental arrangements have always been noted for the drama of their symmetry and simplicity. Heavy arrangements are not appropriate. More important than the volume of flowers is their relationship to their surroundings. If there is room, you may have flowers on the dining table, but in general, Oriental floral arrangements are better used to dress the entry hall, sideboards, living room, and bath. Keep the styles consistent throughout.

**Place cards**   Place cards are *always* written by hand, and one's artistic talents can be exercised in executing appropriate cards. Two weeks before the party, the final guest list should be completed, and you may begin making the cards. If lack of time or talent precludes your doing them yourself, try to find a calligrapher or professional letterer by asking at the better stationers or posting a notice on the bulletin boards of art supply stores and/or college art departments.

The cards may be folded in tent fold or used flat. When they are flat they are displayed on a dish, in a frame or on a stand. Certain napkin folds will also hold place cards.

**Equipment and staples**   Make a final check of your equipment, and arrange to buy, rent, or borrow whatever you do not have. Substitution for hard-to-find articles is perfectly acceptable. For example, if you cannot find Chinese sauce dishes, pyrex custard cups will do nicely, and a heavy frying pan can take the place of a wok. But if you allow plenty of time to find the authentic things, your party will be remembered as very special, rather than as a run-of-the-mill Chinese imitation.

The same is true of staples. You can use fresh mushrooms instead of dried, regular tea instead of Oriental, but you will not achieve quite the same authentic effect.

**Purchase ingredients and prepare dishes to be frozen**   The following two dishes may be prepared ahead and frozen. See the shopping list on pp. 118–119 for the ingredients to purchase.

*Shrimp Puffs*

---

1   **pound raw, shelled shrimp**
¼   **cup pork fat or fatty part of bacon**
2   **egg whites**
1   **tablespoon cornstarch**

    Dash of white pepper
  1 tablespoon dry sherry
1½-inch cube fresh ginger, peeled and minced
 10 thin slices white bread
    Peanut oil for deep frying

Grind the shrimp and pork separately with the fine blade of a meat grinder. Beat the egg whites until foamy. Add the gound pork and beat for 2 minutes. Add the ground shrimp, cornstarch, pepper, sherry, and ginger. Mix well and beat for 2 more minutes.

Remove the crusts from the bread and cut each slice into 4 triangles. Spread each triangle with a heaping teaspoon of the shrimp paste. Heat the oil and cook the triangles, 3 or 4 at a time, until golden. Drain on paper towels. Cool and freeze in foil.

## *Canton Spring Rolls*

*The wrappers*

  3 cups all-purpose flour
  ¾ teaspoon salt
  2 small eggs
  ¾ cup water

*The filling*

  ¾ pound fresh or canned bean sprouts
  5 tablespoons peanut oil
  ¾ pound ground pork
1½ tablespoon sherry
1½ tablespoon soy sauce
  ¾ teaspoon sugar
  ¾ pound raw, shelled shrimp, diced
  6 cups chopped celery
  ¾ cup chopped fresh mushrooms
  3 teaspoons salt
  ½ teaspoon monosodium glutamate

*For final preparation*

  2 cups peanut oil
  1 egg, beaten

In a large bowl, mix the flour and salt. Mix the eggs and water and add all at once to the flour. Stir and mix thoroughly. Knead until dough is smooth. Cover lightly and let sit for 15 to 20 minutes. Divide dough in half. On a floured board, roll out dough as thin as you possibly can, making a square approximately 16 by 24 inches. Cut dough into 4-inch squares. Flour lightly, stack, and cover with a clean cloth.

Rinse the bean sprouts, drain well and set aside. Heat 1 tablespoon oil in a wok or heavy frying pan. Add the pork and stir for 2 minutes. When it loses its pink color, add the sherry, soy sauce, sugar, and shrimp. Remove from the wok and set aside.

Reheat the wok with 2 tablespoons oil and stir-fry the celery for 5 minutes, until dry. Add the mushrooms and bean sprouts and stir for 2 minutes. Add the salt and monosodium glutamate and mix well. Stir in the shrimp and pork mixture and mix thoroughly. If there is liquid, drain. Remove from the wok and cool.

To fill the wrappers, place one piece of dough with a point toward you. Put 1 heaping tablespoon of filling close to the point nearest you. Roll until point is under filling. Brush other edges with beaten egg. Roll toward middle of square. Turn 2 side points in and press gently. Then roll to far point. The egg will make edges and points stick.

Heat the oil in a wok or deep fry pot. Test fat by dropping a piece of bread in. If it starts to brown lightly at once, the fat is ready. Drop 4 or 5 spring rolls at a time into the fat. Cook 5 or 6 minutes, until rolls are crisp and golden. Remove and drain on paper towels. Cool and freeze in foil.

## Party Day Minus 1 Week

Purchase the ingredients for spicy chang and other nonperishable ingredients. Make the spicy chang dish and store in the refrigerator.

### *Spicy Chang (Pork with brown bean sauce)*

9 dried mushrooms
6 tablespoons peanut oil
1½ pounds boneless pork, cut into ¼-inch dice
1½ tablespoons dry sherry
½ cup brown bean sauce
1 tablespoon sugar
¾ cup bamboo shoots, diced

3  **green peppers, seeded and diced**
3  **pieces bean curd, diced**

Rinse the mushrooms and soak in warm water for 30 minutes. Drain and save ½ cup of the soaking water. Remove stems and dice mushrooms.

Heat 3 tablespoons oil in a wok or heavy frying pan and add the pork. Stir until it loses its pink color. Add the sherry and the mushrooms and cook 1 minute. Add the bean sauce and sugar and cook 1 minute more, stirring. Remove from the wok.

Reheat the wok and add 3 tablespoons oil. Add the bamboo shoots and peppers and cook 3 to 4 minutes. Add bean curd, mushroom and pork mixture, and reserved mushroom water. Cover and cook over low heat 10 minutes, stirring once or twice to be sure it is not sticking.

Cool and store in refrigerator in covered chafing dish or oven-proof casserole.

(This dish may be kept up to two weeks if you wish to prepare it sooner.)

Buy liquor, soft drinks, and mixes, if you plan to serve cocktails. However, you will not want your guests' palates to be dulled by too much liquor, so limit the cocktails to two at most.

## Party Day Minus 2 Days

It is now time to buy all remaining ingredients. As long as they are fresh in the store they will be fine until the day of the party. You will have enough to do on party-day morning without having to run to the grocery store.

Except for the fresh flowers, you can do the decorating now. Hang the lanterns, clean the house, and make a list of the chores you will have to do at the very end so that nothing will be forgotten. (I once made a beautiful soup and, in the excitement of serving hors d'oeuvre and preparing the main course, completely forgot to serve it!)

## Party Day Minus 1 Day

In the morning, set the table and/or the buffet table. Remember the folded napkins and the place cards.

Buy fresh flowers and make your flower arrangements.

Polish and clean any accessories that are not already sparkling.

Now it is time to return to the kitchen and make the following dishes.

## Chinese Noodle Soup

8 dried mushrooms
2 whole boned chicken breasts
2 quarts chicken broth
½ teaspoon thyme
½ pound Smithfield ham
1 bunch watercress, approximately 1 cup
½ pound Chinese noodles, or narrow Italian noodles
½ cup bamboo shoots

Soak the mushrooms in warm water for 30 minutes. Drain, remove the stems and cut the caps into quarters.

Meanwhile, simmer the chicken breasts for 10 minutes in 1 quart of the broth seasoned with 1 teaspoon salt and thyme. Drain and reserve the broth.

Slice the chicken and ham into thin strips about 2 inches long and ⅛-inch thick. Cover and refrigerate.

Remove large stems from the watercress.

Bring 4 quarts water to a boil in a large pot and cook the noodles for 4 minutes. Drain and rinse in cold water.

In the same pot, bring the reserved chicken broth and 1 quart additional chicken broth to a boil. Add the mushrooms, bamboo shoots, watercress, noodles, and 2 teaspoons salt. Simmer for 2 or 3 minutes. Cool and refrigerate.

## Watermelon Bowl

1 large watermelon
3 cans litchis, drained
2 cans kumquats, drained
2 cans mandarin oranges, drained

Cut the melon in half lengthwise and scoop out the center, leaving a 1-inch-thick shell. Discard the seeds. Use a melon ball cutter to shape the pulp into balls. Put in a large bowl and add the litchis, kumquats, and mandarin oranges. Mix well. Pour the fruit into the watermelon shell and chill.

(If litchis and kumquats are not available, substitute honeydew melon, canned apricots, or seedless grapes.)

## Party Day Morning

Remove the shrimp puffs and the Canton spring rolls from the freezer. If they defrost quickly, put them in the refrigerator until it is time to heat them.

Prepare the ingredients for lamb with scallions and the chicken with bean sprouts.

### Lamb with Scallions

1½  pounds boneless lamb, preferably from the leg
 4  teaspoons cornstarch
 1  teaspoon sugar
 6  tablespoons soy sauce
 4  bunches scallions
 4  cloves garlic
 2  tablespoons dry sherry
 1  teaspoon white vinegar
 2  teaspoons sesame oil

Slice the lamb into squares, about 2 inches wide and ⅛-inch thick. Marinate the lamb in a mixture of cornstarch, sugar, 4 tablespoons of the soy sauce, and 2 tablespoons water. Cover and refrigerate.

Remove roots and green tips of the scallions. Cut the scallions into 2-inch lengths and shred the lengths. Thinly slice the garlic. Wrap both and refrigerate.

Mix remaining 2 tablespoons soy sauce, sherry, vinegar, and sesame oil in a small bowl. Set aside until the final cooking. You may want to label this sauce so you will remember which dish it is for.

### Chicken with Bean Sprouts

 2  whole boned chicken breasts
 1  egg white
½  teaspoon salt
 6  teaspoons cornstarch

4 cups fresh or canned bean sprouts
1 package frozen snow peas, defrosted
½ pound Smithfield ham
2 tablespoons sherry
1 teaspoon sugar
¼ teaspoon monosodium glutamate
1 cup peanut oil

Cut the chicken into julienne strips about 2 inches long. Mix the egg white, salt, 4 teaspoons cornstarch, and 2 tablespoons cold water and coat the chicken. Refrigerate for 30 minutes.

Soak the bean sprouts in cold water and drain.

Shred enough snow peas to make 6 tablespoons.

Cut the ham into julienne strips about 2 inches long.

Mix the sherry, sugar, and monosodium glutamate in a small bowl.

Heat the oil in a wok or heavy frying pan and add the chicken. Cook until the strips separate and turn white. Strain and reserve the oil.

Reheat wok with 4 tablespoons of reserved oil and add the bean sprouts and snow peas. Stir-fry for 1 minute. Add the ham and chicken and stir well. Add the sherry mixture and stir. Mix remaining 2 teaspoons cornstarch with 4 tablespoons water and add. Stir over high heat until mixture thickens and is coated with a glaze.

Put into the top of a double boiler or chafing dish and set in cool place until ready to reheat.

### Party Day, Final Preparations

Unfortunately, a Chinese dinner requires a certain amount of last-minute work, no matter how well you plan. Therefore, rather than resting and dressing at the last moment, you should plan (if you find it necessary) to get some rest time in after lunch and to be dressed an hour or more before your guests arrive. You can then—carefully aproned—devote the last hour or so to your final preparations.

**One hour ahead** Now is the time to make a last-minute check. Refer to the list you made two days ago.

Arrange the ingredients for the lamb with scallions together close to the stove.

Set out soup bowls, chafing dishes, and dessert plates where they can most conveniently be filled. Be sure that the Sterno cans are in place, and the electric hot plate is plugged in.

**One-half hour ahead of guests' arrival** Preheat the oven to 425 degrees. Just before guests are due, put one-half of the shrimp puffs on a tray and heat them for 7 to 8 minutes. (Heat the second half later to refill the hors d'oeuvre tray.) At the same time, place half the spring rolls directly on the oven rack and heat for 10 minutes. Serve as soon as guests arrive and have their cocktails.

**One-half hour before dinner**   When you have finished heating the hors d'oeuvre, turn the oven down to 350 degrees. If you do not have enough chafing dishes for all your entrées, the spicy chang may be heated, covered, in the oven for 20 minutes.

Bring soup to a simmer. Warm bowls on electric hot plate.

Start the rice. Wash 3 cups long-grain rice in cold water and drain. Bring 5¼ cups cold water to a boil in a large pot. Boil rice for 2 or 3 minutes, until water is reduced and craters appear in rice. Reduce heat to low, cover tightly and cook for 20 minutes. Turn off heat. After 10 minutes, remove cover and fluff rice. Place in warmed serving dish, cover, and keep on hot plate until ready to serve.

Place pot with chicken with bean sprouts over hot water and bring to simmer.

Boil water for tea. Whether using loose leaves or tea bags, brew tea in china pot and serve in Chinese tea cups, without lemon, sugar, or cream.

**Just before dinner**   Now that hors d'oeuvre have been served, and all the other food is heated and ready to serve, it is time to prepare the lamb with scallions:

Heat your wok until very hot and add 6 tablespoons of peanut oil. When oil is heated, add the marinated lamb and the sliced garlic. Stir-fry until lamb loses pink color. Add scallions. Cook 1 minute. Add sauce and cook 1 more minute.

Put into chafing dish for serving.

**Party time**   When your guests have enjoyed a cocktail or two, it is time to serve dinner. Chinese meals are long and leisurely, and should be started at a reasonable hour. Your guests' palates and appetites should not be jaded by too many drinks. So, when the last hors d'oeuvre have been offered, and glasses are almost empty, retire to the kitchen. Arrange the soup in the warm bowls: ladle out noodles and vegetables with a slotted spoon, arrange chicken and ham on top, and carefully pour in liquid. Put the soup bowls on the table and call your guests to dinner.

Arrange ahead of time to have someone remove the soup bowls for you, so that you may get the main courses ready quickly. Transfer the chicken dish to a chafing dish, and bring that and the chafing dish of lamb to the table. Bring out the casserole of spicy chang and the serving dish of rice. Ask the diners to start helping themselves and passing the dishes around as soon as they are brought to the table. While this is going on, empty ashtrays and remove used glasses from the living room. Then pass the tea and leave a pot on the table.

When everyone has eaten his fill and the serving dishes are empty, your helper should again clear the table while you bring in the dessert bowls and the watermelon surrounded with sprigs of mint. Place it in front of you for everyone to admire, and then serve and enjoy it. Pass a platter of fortune cookies, and take turns reading the messages.

Tea takes the place of coffee at a Chinese dinner, and the pot should be refilled frequently. Wine or beer, too, may be served with dinner. Fresh tea, accompanied by liqueurs, should be offered after dinner, and for as long as anyone wishes more.

---

## Kentucky Derby Cocktail Party for Forty

---

Since 1875, the first Saturday in May has always meant excitement and entertainment at Churchill Downs in Louisville, Kentucky. For it was in this year that Kentucky race horse breeders inaugurated the Kentucky Derby, and the mile-and-a-quarter race for three-year-old thoroughbreds was to become the granddaddy of all horse races.

Today, the entertainment has become almost as important as the horse racing itself. It's a tradition that's steeped in Southern hospitality. Since the first of the 106 consecutive runnings of the Derby, much has happened to Derby Day entertaining. As a matter of fact, Derby Day parties have often reflected the trend of the moment, from the flapper parties that surrounded Whisker's victory in 1927, to the disco parties that surrounded the 1978 Alydar/Affirmed royal confrontation. But whatever is "in," from Saturday Night Fever to balls to paddle wheel cruises, Derby Day is still alive and well.

The one consistent element typical of all Derby Day entertainment is good hearty drinking. That's why we've chosen Derby Day as the occasion for a cocktail party.

## *Menu*

*Mint juleps*
*Miniature hot dogs (cooked over Sterno set into cabbages)*
*Smoked turkey on bread rounds*
*Stuffed mushrooms*
*Artichoke hearts in bacon*
*Liver pâté*
*Chili whirls*
*Vegetables with dip*

## SHOPPING LIST

### To order

- 1 whole smoked turkey
- 8 dozen miniature hot dogs
- 8 dozen miniature hot dog rolls

### Nonperishable ingredients

- 2 large Sterno cans
- 1 jar horseradish sauce
- 1 bottle chili sauce
- 1 jar Dijon mustard
- 2 large jars mayonnaise
- 1 bottle dry sherry or Madeira
- 1 small package almonds or pecans (chopped, if available)
- 10 packages frozen artichoke hearts, or 10 cans if frozen not available
- 4 cans chopped mushrooms
- 6 cans Sell's liver pâté
- 1 bottle brandy
- 1 box biscuit mix (Bisquick)
- 3 4-ounce cans hot green chili peppers
- 4 jars dilly beans (pickled green beans)
- 3 boxes of your favorite crackers for liver spread

### Perishable items

- 2 large white cabbages
- 3 loaves thinly sliced white bread

4 pounds mushrooms (medium size)
2 pounds sausage meat
2 pounds butter or margarine
1 bunch parsley
½ pint heavy cream
2 pounds bacon
1 pound hot pork sausage meat
4 boxes cherry tomatoes
4 small to medium zucchini
4 green and/or red sweet peppers
1 bunch carrots
 Lemons

*Staples*

Salt
Pepper
Curry powder
Thyme
Onions
Bread crumbs
Milk
Sage
Toothpicks

*Liquor*

*For Juleps*

8 quarts of bourbon (this will make 128 2-ounce drinks, or 3½ drinks a person. You may have some left over but it will keep indefinitely.)
1 bottle angostura bitters
1 box confectioners' sugar
1 quart sugar syrup (Karo)
 Fresh mint

*Other drinks*

½ gallon gin
½ gallon vodka
1 bottle dry vermouth

*Mixes*

Tonic water, soda water, cola, ginger ale

## *TIMETABLE*

*Party Day Minus 3 Weeks*
Send invitations
Plan menu
Make arrangements with caterer
Arrange for furniture removal
Order hot dogs, miniature rolls, and smoked turkey

*Party Day Minus 1 Week*
Plan use of available space
Clean house
Check equipment
Buy nonperishable menu ingredients
Prepare betting equipment

*Party Day Minus 2 Days*
Buy liquor, soft drinks, mixes
Practice making mint julep
Check staples
Buy all remaining ingredients for menu
Make liver pâté and refrigerate
Make chili whirls and refrigerate

*Party Day Minus 1 Day*
Decorate rooms
Remove excess furniture
Set up bar
Pick up hot dogs, rolls, and smoked turkey
Prepare raw vegetables and dip

*Party Day Morning*
Prepare turkey hors d'oeuvre
Stuff mushrooms
Roll artichoke hearts in bacon
Remove liver pâté from refrigerator
Arrange vegetables and dip
Butter rolls

*Party Time Minus 1 Hour*
Bake chili whirls
Bake mushrooms
Broil artichoke hearts
Warm hot dog rolls

*Party Time*
**Set out hot dogs, rolls, and sauces**
**Set out liver pâté**

## Party Day Minus 3 Weeks

**Send invitations**  The timing for a Derby Day party is easy. It's a calendar-noted event and, accordingly, planning the invitations begins with a simple check of when Derby Day falls. The closer one gets to the heart of bluegrass country, the earlier the invitations should go out, since you could well be competing with other parties set for the same day.

Plan your Derby Day party around the classic themes that make horse racing a rich and exciting event. Any of the following might give you an idea for choosing a motif:

• The names of the horses in the upcoming Derby.

• The colors of the entrants—every horse or stable has a registered set of colors, a list of which can be obtained by writing to: Churchill Downs, 700 Central Avenue, Louisville, Kentucky 40208, Attention: Mr. Bill Rudy.

• Southern themes: bluegrass, antebellum, etc.

Choose one and design your invitations around that motif.

Many stationery stores carry cocktail invitations especially designed for Derby Day, or at least appropriate to the occasion. Check to see what is available—it may save you a great deal of time and effort.

Next, check the starting time of the race and the television channel that will broadcast the Derby in your area to establish the hours for the party. In Eastern time zones, for example, the live coverage of the Derby begins at 4 P.M. However, the Derby itself may not be run until 4:45. Plan to have guests arrive between 3:30 and 4, thus making sure they are in the spirit by Derby time, forty-five minutes later.

Since this is a cocktail party—not a cocktail buffet—your guests should not expect to stay on indefinitely. To make that quite clear on the invitations, give a starting hour *and* a finishing hour—4 to 7 P.M., for example. You need not write R.s.v.p. for a cocktail party, but if you would like some estimate of how many to expect, write "regrets only" and your telephone number at the bottom of the invitation.

**Plan the menu**  At cocktail parties, as opposed to cocktail-buffets, guests do not expect to be given a meal; in fact, most plan on dinner afterward, often going out to a restaurant with a group from the party. Therefore, the food should be plentiful (to provide a sop for the alcohol) but need not be filling; make it as varied and interesting as you can. The above menu fills these qualifications, but you can add your own specialties or substitute anything you know that your friends particularly like.

**Sign up your caterer** You can, of course, do *everything* yourself—prepare the food, serve it, tend bar, run the betting pool, provide the linen, silver, glasses, etc., be an attentive hostess, and then clean it all up. You *can,* but you surely won't enjoy your party if you do!

**Arrange for help and equipment** I strongly recommend that you hire help, at least a bartender and waiter or waitress. You may prepare the food and beverages, but consider renting the glasses, china, linen or silver you require. Since all the food is finger food, you probably can manage by providing serving dishes, small plates and paper cocktail napkins yourself.

Without assistance it is almost impossible to handle such a large party. If you decide to have a caterer do it all, be sure to contact the caterer you want promptly, if you want to avoid settling for second best.

**Arrange for furniture removal** Unless your television area is very large, you may well want to remove some of the furniture for the party. If you have an attic, basement, or garage where the pieces can be stored for a day or two, all you will need will be a couple of good strong friends to help with the moving. But for apartment dwellers, those of you whose furniture is too heavy to handle yourself, a moving company may be the answer. Many companies will bring a van, remove the furniture, and keep it in the van until it is unloaded the day after the party. Investigate this possibility well before Derby Day, and arrange for the return the morning after the party.

**Order hot dogs, rolls, and smoked turkey** Place your orders for the above foods at this time. Your supermarket meat manager or local butcher should have no trouble in getting the baby hot dogs (about one to two inches long), and some bakeries will make little hot dog rolls if given enough warning. The smoked turkey may be more difficult. If there is a specialty or gourmet food shop nearby, they may have it on hand, or can probably order it for you. If there is no such store in your area, wonderful smoked turkey can be ordered from Harrington's of Stowe, Vermont. Order early as this turkey can be kept indefinitely.

### Party Day Minus 1 Week

Now's a good time to chart the space and flow of the party. A room that will accommodate twenty seated may easily, with a little furniture rearrangement, accommodate thirty to forty standing. Furthermore, the crowd need not be limited to one room, and the hall, the den, and the dining room can provide additional space for a cocktail party. The location of the bar is always important at a large cocktail party. It should be easily accessible, of course, but not near the entry or the food table. If possible, it is a good idea to have two bars, which causes people to head in different directions, and greatly reduces congestion.

Don't forget that the location of the television set is all-important. Make sure it is in a room large enough for all the guests to gather; if that is impossible, beg or borrow a second set for another room.

Of course this is the time to plan heavy cleaning projects, especially floor waxing and rug shampoos. They may be executed several days before the party; don't wait until the last minute.

Buy nonperishable menu ingredients.

**Check special equipment** Check on the condition of seldom used equipment or any that may have been stored away, such as long tables, banquet linen, large serving pieces, etc. If you're using your own glasses —a very nice touch—be sure that there is more than one glass for each person. People tend to put drinks down and "lose" them, and there may be some breakage.

**Prepare betting equipment** While drinking may be one element typical of all Derby Day parties, there is another almost as important. That is, betting on the race. There are many ways to do this, but the following is the simplest, and as much fun as any for a private party.

First you will need a large piece of white cardboard on which to list the names of all the entries in the race, the owners, the jockeys, and the probable odds. This last column can be filled in a few days before the party when the projected odds appear on the sports pages. Dress up your chart by using colored pens or crayons and printing the words in the colors of each horse's stable. This chart will help those not "in the know" to decide which horse to bet on.

When this is done, cut out a number of paper tickets. Each ticket can be worth 50 cents or $1 or $5 or whatever you wish, and should carry the name of one of the horses in the race.

Finally, you will need a receptacle for the money paid for the tickets. The most appropriate is, naturally, a facsimile of a horse. Here are two simple ways to make a "horse" to hold the pot.

Cut a large, simplified or stylized horse out of heavy cardboard. Color it pink or blue and make a mane and tail of bright colored yarn. Cut a slot in the horse's side, and attach a big box onto the back side below the slot. As each bettor buys a ticket on his favorite horse, he deposits the money into the slot.

A three-dimensional horse can be made by using an ordinary wooden saw horse with a child's hobby horse attached to one end. A broom or fireplace brush makes a fine tail at the other end. A closed box with a slot in the top may be affixed to the top of the sawhorse, or suspended underneath as a drop for the money.

It's a good idea to go to the bank and get twenty dollars' worth of one-dollar bills in order to be able to make change. Each ticket is worth the same amount, but the bettors can buy as many tickets as they wish at your established price. The pot is simply divided among those who hold tickets on the winning horse. If you wish to spread the take a little further, you can give 75 percent of the pot to those with winning tickets and divide the remaining 25 percent among those with place tickets (those whose horse comes in second). To help you out, you might arrange in advance for one of your friends to be ticket seller and a committee of two or three to apportion the winnings.

## Party Day Minus 2 Days

**Buy liquor, mixes, and soft drinks**  In Louisville on Derby Day, tradition has it that it's either champagne or mint juleps with a strong accent on the latter. A fully stocked bar may also be available, but the old favorites are still featured. At Churchill Downs you can buy mint juleps right in the grandstands.

If you have never made a julep before, we would suggest that you try it a day or two before the party. Also at this time you should start building up a supply of crushed ice in your freezer, as you will need a large quantity on Derby Day.

Two days before the party, buy all of your liquor, mixes, and soft drinks. Even though you plan to feature mint juleps, there will be some drinkers who will want to stick to their favorites, and for their benefit you should have on hand one half-gallon of gin and one half-gallon of vodka. You should also have plenty of tonic water, a bottle of dry vermouth for martini drinkers, and several six-packs of ginger ale and cola for nondrinkers.

For forty people—assuming that at least thirty will want your juleps—you should buy 8 quarts, or 4 half-gallons, of the very finest bonded bourbon you can afford. This allows for three juleps per guest.

Here is the recipe for the juleps, to be tested a day or two beforehand:

Chill a highball glass (if you have silver mugs, or can rent them, that is the perfect serving vessel for juleps) in the refrigerator for 20 to 30 minutes.

Dip a sprig of fresh mint in powdered sugar and crush it in a small bowl or glass. Add 2 teaspoons sugar syrup (light Karo), 6 more mint leaves and a dash of angostura bitters. Blend and stir these ingredients and add a jigger (2 ounces) of bourbon. Stir well.

Pack the chilled highball glass with crushed ice, and strain the bourbon mixture into it. Stir and churn with a long spoon. Add ice to fill the glass almost to the top, and add 1 more ounce of bourbon. Stir until the glass begins to frost. Add a sprig of fresh mint. Enjoy!

Practice this process for an individual serving. With your bartender you can evolve a mass-production system the day of the party. It is one thing to produce *one* perfect mint julep—it is quite another to produce *forty!* The main problem is in keeping the glasses ice cold—preferably frosted. The glasses can be filled with the crushed ice and kept refrigerated, or placed in deep roasting pans and surrounded with ice. An ample supply of the bourbon-sugar-mint mixture should be made in quantity and ready at all times, as well as the opened bottles of bourbon and the prepared sprigs of mint, so that there is a minimum of time between preparing and drinking. Even a small amount of melted ice can change the beautiful julep into an ordinary bourbon and water. The glasses are emptied and refilled with fresh ice for second helpings.

**Buy all remaining menu ingredients** When you have checked your staples carefully, it is time to do your big marketing. Once this is done, you can start to prepare some of your hors d'oeuvre so that you will not be too busy on Derby Day.

The following hors d'oeuvre is simple and not expensive, but has a rich and elegant flavor.

*Liver Pâté*

---

4  cans chopped mushrooms
6  tablespoons butter or margarine
6  cans Sell's liver pâté
¾  cup brandy

Drain the mushrooms and sauté them in the butter. Add the liver pâté and mix thoroughly. Add the brandy and mix well. Smooth into a crock or serving dish, cover, and refrigerate.

## Chili Whirls

- 4 cups biscuit mix
- ½ cup melted butter or margarine
- 1 cup milk
- 1 pound hot pork sausage meat
- 1 pound regular sausage meat
- 1½ cups chopped hot green chili pepper

Mix together the biscuit mix, butter, and milk. Refrigerate for ½ hour. Meanwhile, mix the two sausages with the chili pepper.

Remove dough from the refrigerator and divide in half. Roll out one half into a large rectangle about ¼-inch thick. Spread one half the sausage mixture over the dough and roll tightly. Repeat with the other half of dough and rest of the sausage mixture. Place in the freezer *for one hour only*. Remove from freezer and slice rolls thinly. Return slices to the freezer until ready to cook on day of the party.

## Party Day Minus 1 Day

The morning of the day before the party is the time to decorate your rooms.

As we have noted, your Derby Day motifs should reflect your own tastes and/or current trends. However, whatever you're planning, color is perhaps the most important decor consideration. The color scheme of Churchill Downs—green and white—is a popular choice, but you might prefer to pick a favorite and run with his colors. Although the official entries are not posted until the Thursday before the race, the sports page will no doubt be heralding the favorites for weeks in advance, thereby enabling you to note the top contenders' stables and use the colors the favorites carry.

The center of attraction, at least before the race, will be your chart, your ticket-selling table, and your "horse." A card table draped with the favorite's colors, or covered with a white cloth trimmed with blue, red, and yellow (win, place, and show) rosettes at the corners would be festive and appropriate as a ticket booth. Vases of flowers to carry out your color scheme provide all the decorating necessary, although you can go into banners or balloons with the horses' names on them, or garlands and nosegays to create an Old South atmosphere if you wish.

**Remove excess furniture** This is also the time to remove extra furniture, if it is necessary. If you have made arrangements for a moving company to do it, they will arrive this morning. If you are doing it yourself, have two or three strong-armed friends lined up to help you. Leave plenty of chairs and small tables about, or the rooms will look bleak and unfriendly, but remove large pieces such as sofas, oversized armchairs, desks, etc.

**Set up bar(s)** Even though your bartender will want to make final arrangements to his own liking, you can get your bar set up and ready for him. Whether you are using saw horses with boards across them or a kitchen table, you will want the bar covered with a white cloth. If you are using a good table, be sure to put a sheet of plastic under the linen cloth. Store the liquor and mixes out of sight below the table. Check your ice buckets and coolers to be sure an adequate supply of ice can be maintained at the bar. Set out measuring jiggers, knives, peelers, mixing spoons, sugar bowls, and as many of your own glasses as you intend to use.

**Pick up hot dogs, rolls and smoked turkey** If they have not already been delivered, pick up the items you ordered previously. If they have been delivered, open the bags or boxes and count to be sure you have your full order.

**Prepare raw vegetables and dip** The afternoon of the day before the party you can get more of the hors d'oeuvre well under way. First, the two cabbages may be scooped out until the holes are big enough to hold the two cans of Sterno. Then you may prepare the vegetables for the raw vegetable platter.

Cherry tomatoes: Wash and stem tomatoes. While they are still wet, roll them around in a shallow dish of coarse (kosher) salt. Place in hard plastic refrigerator container.

Dilly beans: Open jars, drain, and put in plastic bag.

Zucchini: Wash and cut in strips, approximately 2 inches long by ½ inch thick. Do not peel. Store in plastic bag.

Carrots: Peel and cut in thin strips. Store in plastic bag.

Green and/or red sweet peppers: Remove tops and cut out seed core. Cut pepper into thin strips, lengthwise, removing white membranes. Put in plastic bag.

Store all vegetables in refrigerator.

To make the dip, mix 2 cups mayonnaise with 2 teaspoons prepared mustard, 1 teaspoon curry powder (or to taste), and 1 tablespoon lemon juice.

Store in covered container in refrigerator.

### Party Day Morning

The morning of the party will be a busy one, but if you have completed all your other tasks according to our schedule, you can easily accomplish the remaining cooking chores in two to three hours.

### *Artichoke Hearts in Bacon*

Remove the frozen artichoke hearts from the freezer and open boxes to thaw. When they are soft, wrap each heart in a strip of bacon and secure with a toothpick. Arrange on a baking sheet or broiler pan, ready to be broiled just before serving.

### *Turkey and Bread Rounds*

If your thin white bread has been in the freezer, remove it to thaw while you carve the smoked turkey. The pieces of turkey should be paper thin, and no more than 1½ inches across. Using a small glass or a cooky cutter, cut 4 rounds out of each slice of bread. Spread the rounds with a thin coat of mayonnaise and top with a piece of the turkey. You need use no other seasoning as it might detract from the superb flavor of this combination. Cover lightly with a damp cloth to prevent drying and refrigerate until ready to serve.

### *Stuffed Mushrooms*

  4 pounds mushrooms (about 120)
½ cup melted butter
  1 pound sausage meat
  2 onions, chopped
½ cup dry sherry or Madeira
  1 cup fine bread crumbs
  2 tablespoons chopped almonds or pecans
  1 teaspoon thyme
½ teaspoon sage
½ teaspoon salt

**2** teaspoons chopped parsley
**4** tablespoons heavy cream

Wash and dry mushrooms. Remove the stems and chop fine. Brush the caps with melted butter and place in buttered baking pans, hollow side up.

Sauté the sausage and onions for 20 minutes. Drain off fat and add the sherry. Cook for 5 minutes and add remaining ingredients (including the chopped stems) except the cream. Cook for 5 minutes longer. Add enough cream to moisten. Fill the caps generously. Cover and set aside.

**Liver pâté, vegetables, and rolls** Remove the liver pâté from the refrigerator, as it has more flavor when it is not too cold. Place container on hors d'oeuvre tray and surround with your favorite crackers.

Arrange the prepared vegetables as prettily as you can on a large round tray or platter. Place the dip in the center. Return to refrigerator.

Butter the little hot dog rolls.

## Party Time Minus 1 Hour

You can now make your final preparations. Your help will have arrived by now, so you will have some assistance. Give the waiters or waitresses a carefully written list of exactly what should be done—how and when the dishes should be heated and served.

You will need an electric hot plate to keep some dishes warm while others are cooked. If you have two ovens you are fortunate; otherwise the hot dishes will have to be done one after another.

First, bake your chili whirls. They need not be defrosted. Bake them for 20 minutes at 400 degrees, and set them, lightly covered, on the hot plate.

Turn the oven down to 375 degrees and bake the mushrooms for 20 minutes. These, too, may be kept warm on the hot plate, lightly covered with a sheet of foil.

When the mushrooms are done, turn the oven to broil. Broil the artichoke hearts, four to five inches from the flame, turning frequently to brown the bacon evenly. This takes little time, and can be done later, just before serving, if you prefer.

In any case, turn the oven to warm, and split and heat the miniature hot dog rolls.

## Party Time

The two cabbages should be set at either end of the hors d'oeuvre table and the Sterno cans lighted. The hot dogs and rolls are divided in half and set beside each cabbage, along with containers of fondue forks and bowls of horseradish sauce, chili sauce, and mustard mayonnaise. The guests braise a hot dog over the Sterno flame, dip it in the sauce of their choice, and place it in a little roll.

The tray containing the liver pâté may be placed in the center of the table, where the guests can spread their own crackers.

As soon as guests start to arrive and have their first drinks in their hands, the trays and platters of turkey, artichoke hearts, mushrooms, and chili whirls should be passed. They should then be left on a table or buffet where the guests can continue to help themselves. The vegetables and dip may be passed or not, depending on the size of the tray. You, or your helpers, should keep a careful eye on these serving dishes to see that they are constantly replenished. Nothing is less attractive than an almost empty, greasy, crumb-filled hors d'oeuvre tray!

During the last minutes before the race and during the race itself, the waiters should not pass food, because it would distract the guests from the business at hand!

As the time for the race approaches, make sure everyone who wants to buy a ticket—place a bet—has done so. Check to see that glasses are full and let everyone settle down in front of the television sets. This is what the party is *for* and the rest of the evening will take care of itself.

---

## Fourth of July Clambake For Twenty

---

Even though recent Federal legislation has moved the observance of other holidays like Washington's Birthday, Columbus Day, and Veterans Day to create three-day weekends, Independence Day continues to be celebrated on the day on which the Fourth of July falls. In most parts of the country, the Independence Day celebration is a large family and/or neighborhood outdoor get-together.

The clambake has become a popular form of summer entertaining all over the country. There are services now that will bring the taste of a New England clambake fresh to you and your guests via airline or escort courier, no matter where you live, if you simply place an order with them ten days to two weeks ahead. For those of us who have more ready access to fresh seafood, the clambake is a perfect opportunity to combine intriguing preparation and heavenly consumption of the best fruits of the sea.

The idea of clam "baking" is that all the food is prepared together from one source of heat, and the traditional image is of the surfside clambake dug into a sandy pit and covered with seaweed. However, all clambakes need not take place on Nantucket or in Malibu. A clambake can just as easily be created in your backyard with a little forethought and some very practical planning. Depending on available space and landscaping, you may decide to dig a pit below ground level, approximately three feet deep, line it with rocks, ready for the white-hot coals. But you will probably prefer the simpler process of cooking the "bake" in large pots over charcoal, or even over the burners on your kitchen stove.

Lobster, clams, mussels and other shellfish in a bake are cooked by the steam created from only a few inches of boiling water or from the seaweed alone. There have long been two schools of thought regarding the status of the lobster before steaming—should it be dead or alive? Many gourmets opt for cooking a lobster while it is still alive, while others, more sensitive to the lobster's suffering, feel it should be quickly killed before cooking. If you agree with the latter group, all you have to do is take each lobster, before you put it into the pit or pot, and insert a very sharp knife between the shell of the main body segment and the tail sections, severing the spinal cord.

Wherever you hold your clambake, be careful not to let your main course sit around uncovered too long. Seafood deteriorates very quickly and the rate of spoilage increases dramatically in hot weather.

### Menu

*Cherrystone and/or littleneck clams*
*Steamed clams with melted butter and clam broth*
*The Bake:*  *Lobster*
*Chicken parts*
*Sweet and white potatoes*
*Corn on the cob*
*Onions*
*Bluefish (optional)*
*Sausages (optional)*
*Watermelons or pies*

## SHOPPING LIST

20  1¼- or 1½-lb lobster (or 10 if too expensive)
160  cherrystone and/or littleneck clams
  2  bottles cocktail sauce
  1  bottle Tabasco
20  dozen steamer clams
30  chicken parts (15 thighs and legs, 15 breasts with
      wings)
15  sweet potatoes
15  white potatoes
40  ears of corn
  4  dozen onions
10  bluefish fillets (optional)
  3  pounds sausages (optional)
  5  pounds butter
  1  dozen lemons
  2  watermelons (or ingredients for 3 pies)
      Coffee
  3  dozen cans of beer
      Soft drinks, tonic, soda water
      Cheesecloth

*Liquor (if you plan to serve cocktails)*

  ½  gallon vodka
  1  quart gin
  1  quart bourbon
  1  quart blended whiskey

## TIMETABLE

*Party Day Minus 2 Weeks*
Check long-range weather forecast—plan rain date or
    alternate indoor site
Choose location in yard or on beach
If required, get permit for beach fire
Plan lighting, purchase necessities
Send out invitations
Order any rental equipment necessary—tables, chairs,
    linen, canopy, tarpaulin to cover bake
Order insect spraying if needed

*Party Day Minus 1 Week*
Order lobster, clams, chicken parts
Purchase all paper and plastic goods
Collect cooking equipment
Wash, paint, and repair yard furniture
Buy nonperishable goods: beverages, charcoal, lighter
  fluid, light bulbs, candles, bug spray, etc.
Borrow additional grills, coffeepots, steamers, etc.
Prepare check list for beach clambake

*Party Day Minus 4 Days*
Bake and freeze pies if you plan pies for dessert
Start to accumulate a big supply of ice cubes

*Party Day Minus 1 Day*
Buy bake ingredients, except for lobster and chicken,
  which would take up too much room in the refrig-
  erator, and the corn, which should be freshly picked,
  if possible. Refrigerate the other shellfish until shortly
  before cooking
    BEACH BAKE
Collect wood for pit fire and bonfire on beach
Dig pit
Collect stones for lining pit and set in place
Set up boards for tables
    PATIO BAKE
Set up tent or canopy if rain threatens
Put tables and chairs in place
Hang outdoor lights, or install torches and floodlights
Arrange cooking area

*Party Day Morning*
Pick up lobster and chicken and purchase fresh corn
  from a farm stand, if possible
    BEACH BAKE
Collect approximately eight bushels of seaweed
Take all equipment to beach
Three hours before starting bake, light fire in pit
    PATIO BAKE
Collect two bushels of seaweed for pots
Set tables
Spray for insects
Assemble all cooking equipment, prepare grills

*Party Time*
Just before guests arrive, take all foods out to beach
  or to patio cooking area

BEACH BAKE

**2½ hours before dinner:**
  Line pit with seaweed and start bake
**1 hour before dinner:**
  Serve clams on half-shell
  Start steaming soft-shell clams and serve
**Zero hour:**
  Open bake and serve

PATIO BAKE

**2 hours before dinner:**
  Light charcoal in grills
**1½ hours before dinner:**
  Line pots with seaweed, put foods in and start
  "bake"
**45 minutes before dinner:**
  Start steamers cooking on kitchen stove
**½ hour before dinner:**
  Serve clams on half-shell and steamers

## Party Day Minus 2 Weeks

Since good weather is all important to a clambake, be sure to check with the Weather Bureau for the long-range forecast. It won't be 100 percent accurate (maybe not even 50 percent) this far ahead, but it may give you some hint as to whether you should plan the bake for the beach, in the garage, or on the lawn. And whether you should select an optional rain date.

**Select the area**  Having gotten the best educated guess possible about the weather, plan your bake site. If it is to be on a public beach, you will undoubtedly have to obtain a permit from the local police station to have a fire. Do this now, before too many other Fourth of July celebrators have applied.

Select a portion of the beach away from the more crowded areas. You will want some privacy, and you will surely *not* want any bake-crashers. If possible, choose a section of beach where there is a supply of seaweed in the water nearby. Also, you will have to have large rocks to line the pit, so it will be a great help if those can be found nearby. Make sure you can drive your car close enough so that you will not have to carry all the equipment too far over soft sand.

A patio clambake is, of course, just that, but the cooking area should be carefully selected. In establishing the outdoor kitchen area, be certain that it is protected from the wind, but choose an area that is neither too closed-in nor confined. If possible, select a hard, flat surface away from the house, bushes and other areas susceptible to scorching and flame.

Here are several other suggestions that apply to any outdoor party including a clambake.

• Avoid seating areas too near low-hanging branches; the same for lighting fixtures and any incendiary devices.

• Tables and chairs should be positioned on the flattest surfaces.

• Choose a grassy or flagstone area that is well-drained.

In short, choose a site that is close enough to enjoy nature but not too close to be a victim of it.

**Lighting preparations** If you purchase (or bring out old) lighting equipment well in advance, you will have plenty of time to try it out and see that it is adequate. Flashlights and three or four kerosene torches are all that are necessary for the beach, as the eating should be finished before dark. But a patio bake may be scheduled for later in the evening, and attractive lighting will add greatly to the atmosphere. Strings of lights or lanterns may be suspended around the cooking and eating areas, or you may prefer floodlights, carefully arranged to shine up into trees and shrubbery, giving a soft and glamorous lighting effect. Torches may also be planted about the area, well dug in so that even a stiff breeze will not blow them over. If bugs are a problem, torches that burn insect repellents are available.

**Order rental equipment and insect spray service** No rental equipment will be necessary for your beach clambake except, if you do not have one, a tarpaulin large enough to cover the bake. But for the patio you will need outdoor tables and chairs, grills, large pots, etc., and you may need to rent these items, or borrow them from friends. If so, now is the time to do it. It is also possible to rent your china, glassware, and linen, and some people prefer to do so, rather than using paper plates, or risking loss and breakage of their own tableware either on the beach or on a patio.

The chances are that you will be able to take care of the insect problem yourself, with hand sprays. However, if you live in a swampy area or close to a pond, you may wish to order professional spraying for the morning of the clambake. It is wise to do this well ahead of time, to insure that the spraying will be at its most effective when you need it.

**Send out invitations** The Fourth of July is a popular time for vacationing and entertaining, so get your invitations out at least three weeks ahead. Some of your prospective guests may be having house guests if the Fourth falls on a weekend, so decide whether you can accommodate a few extras when you are making your plans.

You must also decide whether you wish to include an alternate rain date on your invitations, or whether you can proceed with the clambake in your garage, or perhaps on the kitchen stove if those summer thunderstorms put in an appearance. Frankly, I recommend the latter. The stove-top bake is not, perhaps, as glamorous, but it tastes almost as good!

You can telephone your invitations or buy any one of the attractive commercial cards that appeals to you. Be sure that you make it quite clear that it is an outdoor party so that guests will bring extra sweaters or windbreakers. If your bake is on the beach, you might suggest that they bring bathing suits in case it is a warm afternoon or evening.

Since this is an informal party, put "regrets only" with your telephone number at the bottom of the invitation.

### Party Day Minus 1 Week

**Order the fish and chicken**  Now that you have given your friends a week to call if they're unable to come, you have a good idea of the number to expect, and you can order your lobster, clams, and chicken parts.

In days gone by, it was unthinkable to have less than one lobster per person, and one and one-half was preferred. However, the price of lobster has become so prohibitive that it would be quite understandable for you to plan for half of a 1½-pound lobster for each guest. It will still be costly, but considerably less than ordering one apiece.

You will need six hard-shell clams for each person, and we suggest ordering half littlenecks and half cherrystones to allow people a choice in the size. One dozen steamers apiece is ample when they are served as a first course.

It would probably be possible to purchase your chicken parts right out of the counter, but if you order them ahead you will get just the number of pieces you want, and the desired proportions of white and dark meat. You should have thirty chicken pieces for twenty guests.

When you place your order for fish and chicken, get the name of the person taking the order and check a day or two later to be sure that it is on record.

**Purchase paper and plastic goods**  Although some people prefer to rent china and glassware, or to use their own if they have enough, we personally feel that paper plates of good, strong quality are more appropriate for a clambake. Plastic cups and glasses are far safer than glassware, and the insulated cups are ideal for keeping clam broth or coffee hot in the cool of the evening.

Since you will be very busy the day or two preceding the clambake, you should purchase all your plastic and paper products now. Some stores may also be sold out of the most desirable items as the holiday approaches.

**Collect cooking equipment** If your clambake is to be prepared on the patio, you will need two 10-gallon lobster or clam steamers and four 5- or 6-gallon pots for the bake ingredients. In addition, you will need two slightly smaller kettles for the steamer clams. You will surely need to borrow some of this equipment, or, as previously noted, rent it.

For either patio or beach, you will also need pots for melting butter for the steamed clams and the lobster. An old-fashioned coffeepot is ideal for this purpose. Several large plastic garbage cans for clam shells, lobster carcasses, used plates, glasses, napkins, etc., are a must.

With the exception of the lobster, clambake food is ready to serve when it comes out of the bake, so few serving utensils are necessary. However, two or three sharp knives and lobster claw crackers are essential, as the bake master, with one or two assistants, must split the lobster and crack the claws for every guest.

**Paint and repair outdoor furniture** If it's the site of your party, you will want your patio to look its very best for your clambake, so this is the time to paint old furniture, repair the webbing on folding chairs, and generally spruce up your outdoor living area.

**Buy nonperishable goods** This is also the time to buy your liquor supplies, soft drinks, beer, and mixes. Charcoal, charcoal-lighter fluid, bug bombs or sprays, extra light bulbs, kerosene for torches, should be bought this week.

**Check list** Has there ever been a beach party where something important wasn't left behind—the charcoal, the butter, the umbrella, the matches? We doubt it. To prevent a crisis on the day of your clambake, start making up a check list now, while there is still plenty of time to *think*. This is most important, of course, when it is some distance from your house to the beach, but even the patio bake can profit from a complete check list.

### Check List for the Beach

Plates, cups, napkins, glasses, silverware
Grill for steaming clams
Clam knives (for opening hard-shell clams)
Pot for steamers
Coffeepot (for melting butter)
Large coffeepot (or pots) for coffee
Knives for splitting lobsters

Claw crackers
Matches
Newspaper for starting bonfire
Charcoal for cooking steamers
Charcoal-lighter fluid
Flashlights
Beverages
Coolers full of ice cubes
Fish and meat in ice chests
Lemon juice for clams, lobster
Cocktail sauce and Tabasco for clams
Blankets and beach towels
Tarpaulin to cover bake
Lots of disposable wet towelettes

## Party Day Minus 4 Days

**Prepare food that can be frozen**   Although your guests may be too full
to face a heavy dessert, many people still feel that apple or blueberry
pie is an essential element of a Fourth of July dinner. If you agree, bake
your pies and freeze them now.
**Ice cubes**   You may, of course, buy a supply of ice cubes the day of
the party. However, if you wish to save that expense, start making extra
bags of ice cubes yourself at this time, and day by day fill your freezer
with enough for the party.

## Party Day Minus 1 Day

After a final check with the Weather Bureau, you can start your preparations.
**Beach bake**   The day before the clambake is a very busy one. Chau-
vinistic as it may sound, the duties usually fall into definite male and fe-
male categories. The host, and any helpers he may have, go to the
beach to dig the pit—approximately three feet deep and four or five feet
around. They must then collect the largest rocks they can carry (smaller
stones do not hold the heat long enough) and line the pit carefully so
that the sand is covered with rocks insofar as possible. They must then
collect the wood for the following day. If you are fortunate enough to
be near a deserted beach, this may be driftwood. If, however, vaca-
tioners have cleared the beaches of big, solid pieces of firewood, you
must buy or bring it from your fireplace supply. Again, small limbs and
sticks will not generate enough heat for the bake. Finally, while the men
are on the beach they should set up a long table for serving the food

and another smaller one for the bar. These tables may simply be two or three rough boards laid across smooth rocks or other boards or crates.

**The patio bake** The men's duties are far less arduous if the bake is to be held at home (unless, of course, you plan to dig the pit in your backyard or field). But there are still a number of heavy chores to be taken care of. Tables and chairs must be collected—possibly picked up from the rental agency—and set in place. The outdoor lights should be hung, or the torches set solidly into the ground. You may also need to install floodlights, being sure that wires, switches, etc., are the heavy-duty, outdoor variety. The grills that friends and relatives have agreed to lend you must be collected and set up in the cooking area and the bags of charcoal placed close by. Don't fill the grills until the following day, in case of heavy dew or rain. The big steamers and pots may also be collected at the same time, and put out beside the grills. At this time, you will be able to see the relative size of the pots and grills and determine whether you have enough cooking area to accommodate the necessary pots. Two or even three pots may be heated on the kitchen stove if available grill space is not adequate.

So far we have assumed that the weather forecast is good. If it is not, and you have not set an alternate date, you must make provisions for a rainy day. You can rent one tent or canopy to cover the cooking area and another for the seating area, or the food may be cooked and served under a canopy, but taken inside to be enjoyed. Or, if you have a large two-car garage, it may be cleared out and cleaned the day before the party, and the grills set up there. This should never be done, however, unless there is plenty of cross ventilation, and even then, fans in the windows to help circulate the air will prevent accumulation of noxious fumes from the charcoal.

**Purchase and store food** Meanwhile the hostess and her helpers will need to go to town to buy all the food for the bake, except lobster, chicken, and corn. Nonperishable ingredients should be packed into baskets and boxes, ready to transport to the beach. The potatoes should be washed, and put into several cheesecloth or net bags. The onions can be peeled, but they should be kept in cold water until the next morning when they, too, are put into mesh bags.

### Party Day Morning

Pick up lobster and chicken and store in coolers with bags of ice around them. The corn should be bought and partly husked—removing the outer layers but leaving the kernels well covered with inner leaves.

**Beach bake** The worst of the heavy work is already done, but the seaweed (which should be rockweed—the brown leathery weed with oblong bubbles all over it) must be collected. This is fun for everyone, especially if it is a hot day, and children are expert helpers. For the beach bake you must collect approximately eight bushels of weed. Pile it beside the pit, covering it with your tarpaulin to keep it damp.

Later in the morning all of the equipment and the nonperishable food may be taken to the beach. If it is a public beach, members of the family or house guests should be assigned to stay and guard the equipment, but this is a pleasant duty on a hot summer day.

About three hours before you intend to put the bake into the pit, the fire must be lighted. It bears repeating that you must use good, big logs and continue to feed the fire regularly, so that the rocks and sand in the pit attain a very high temperature. Once the bake is in and covered, the fire cannot be added to, so the preheating is extremely important.

Just before the guests are due to arrive, a final trip to the house should be made to bring the perishable foods from the refrigerator, carrying them in ice chests or coolers.

**Patio bake** The two large steamers and four additional pots needed for the patio bake will take about two bushels of seaweed. Keep the seaweed in a large covered container (plastic garbage pail, for example) so that the salt water will not evaporate before you are ready to put the seaweed into the pots.

Now you are ready to set your buffet and the tables, and give the grass and patio area a thorough spraying to discourage the mosquitoes.

Check over your cooking equipment, get the charcoal into the grills, and sit back and relax until the guests arrive.

## Party Time

**Beach bake** There is an old saying that "The bake is ready when the bakemaster can no longer stand up!" And there is a seed of wisdom in it, because a clambake is a lengthy party, and there is often a good deal of drinking ahead of time. Part of the fun is seeing the food put into the pit, which means inviting the guests at least two and one-half hours ahead of dinner time. We have two suggestions. First, that you do not serve any hard liquor for the first hour or hour and a half—beer and soft drinks will do nicely for refreshers on the beach. Second, that you plan some games to keep your guests busy. Soft ball, swimming and surfing contests, volleyball—anything that will help to pass the waiting time without a lengthy cocktail hour.

Let us say that you want to open the bake at 7 o'clock. Ask your guests for 4, and at 4:30 start the bake. First, remove all the burning firewood and embers that you possibly can, and pile them to one side. (They will continue to smolder, and can be used for other cooking later on.) Then, line the pit with a thick layer of seaweed, using at least one full bushel and possibly more. The lobsters go in first. If they will not fit in a single layer, put half of them in, add more seaweed, and then the rest. Just be sure to cover each layer of food with seaweed. On top of the lobsters put the bags of potatoes and onions. More seaweed, and then a layer of chicken parts, also in cheesecloth bags. The optional bluefish fillets and sausages come next, and finally the prepared corn on the cob. As you can see, the items that need the most heat are near the bottom of the pit, and those that take less time to cook are on top. When all the food is in the pit, cover it with a final layer of seaweed, and then the tarpaulin, weighting down the edges with substantial rocks. The tarp should be dampened with sea water. As the heat builds up in the pit, the tarpaulin will balloon, and you will know that the bake is cooking as it should.

For the next hour and a half, you can relax and join your friends swimming or playing games. An hour or so before dinner, offer the guests a cocktail, if you wish, and start opening and serving the little-necks and cherrystones. Put the steamer clams in two pots with a small amount of water (about a half inch) in the bottom and set them on a grill laid over the coals you removed from the fire. Or, if those have burned out, light a fresh fire with smaller wood, or use charcoal. Steam the clams until they are all open, and serve with melted butter and cups of the juice they exude as they cook.

When your friends have had their fill, it should be time to open the bake. Remove the tarpaulin carefully so that no one gets burned by the steam. Then the fun really begins. Using a rake or cultivator, pull the seaweed off carefully and remove the food as it comes into view: first, the juicy ears of corn, then the bags of chicken, onions, and potatoes, and finally the pièce de résistance—the lobster.

With one or two helpers, split and clean the lobsters. When they are ready, and all the other food is laid out, call your guests to dinner and enjoy.

## HOW TO CRACK A LOBSTER FOR EATING

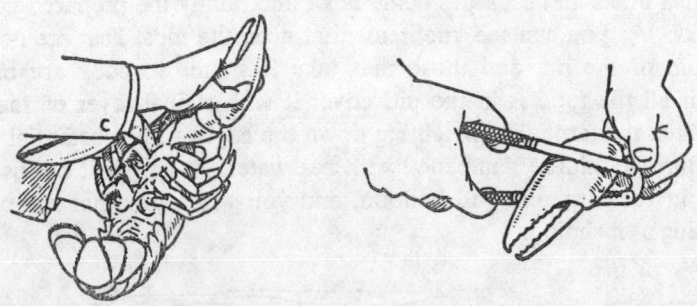

*Twist off the claws. Crack each claw with a nutcracker, pliers, knife, hammer, rock or what have you.*

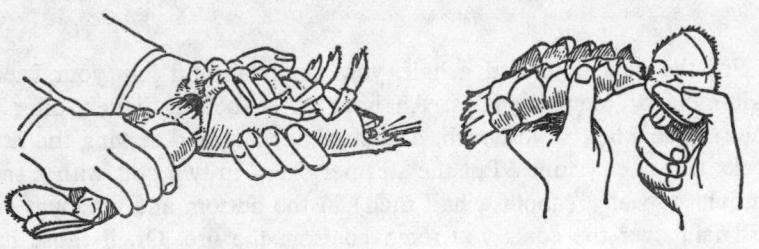

*Separate the tailpiece from the body by arching the back until it cracks. Bend back and break the flippers off the tailpiece.*

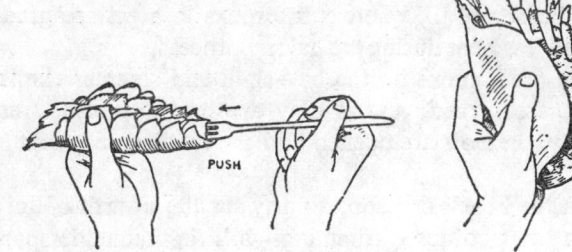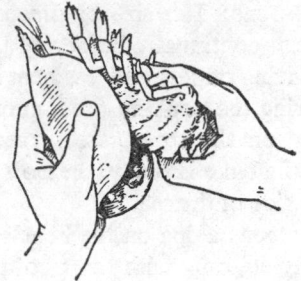

*Insert a fork where the flippers broke off and push. Unhinge the back from the body. Don't forget that this contains the "tomalley," or liver of the lobster which turns green when it is cooked and which many persons consider the best eating of all.*

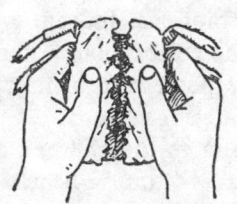

*Open the remaining part of the body by cracking apart sideways. There is some good meat in this section. The small claws are excellent eating and may be placed in the mouth and the meat sucked out like sipping cider with a straw.*

**Patio bake**   The patio bake is not as lengthy a procedure, but it is still a good idea to plan games, a swim in the pool, or whatever is popular with your friends.

Approximately two and a half hours before dinner, or two hours before the guests are to arrive, light the charcoal in the grills. As soon as everyone has arrived, it is time to line the pots with seaweed and assemble the bake. The lobster and corn go into the two large steamers. The potatoes, onions, and chicken go into the other pots with about three inches of water in the bottom. These pots should go on the fire first, as their contents will take longer to cook than the lobster and corn. Their cooking time should be one and a half hours. The lobster and corn should go on about twenty minutes later, and cook for a little over one hour. The time for the patio bake is less than that of the beach bake for two reasons: The size of the containers is smaller, and the source of heat can continually be added to, whereas the rocks in a pit are gradually giving off less and less heat during the baking process.

During the cooking time, clams on the half-shell and steamer clams, cooked on the stove, are served, just as they are on the beach. And when the bake is ready, the pots are opened and the food served, as it is by the side of the sea.

Whether baking on the beach or patio, a party for the Fourth of July is complete only with the traditional trimmings—a little manmade sparkle added to the natural surroundings. On the patio, red, white, and blue floral arrangements strategically placed are appropriate. Accent them with candles and tricolor ribbons to make the outdoor Fourth of July decoration attractive and classic.

Sparklers, firecrackers and Roman candles are traditions dating back to the earliest of Independence Day celebrations. Indeed, a "bang-up" Fourth has become an integral part of the celebration. Although many municipal governments prohibit even the possession of fireworks, they are in wide scale use in many areas. Here are suggestions:

• Sparklers are safe and fun. Give them to the children and/or everyone for an after-dark parade—on the street or on the beach.

• Be certain that Roman candles or rockets are aimed away from houses and rooftops.

• If you want a really memorable display, take a tip from Chinese New Year and set all the firecrackers off at once.

---

## Midsummer Night Party for Forty

---

Clearly, Midsummer Night is an excuse for a party, a lovely way to mark the summer solstice. The antithesis of the haunted spirit of Halloween entertaining, Midsummer Night glistens and shimmers. It is the perfect time of year for an evening pool or patio party. Midsummer parties—and these may include both dancing and swimming if you have a pool—are romantic evenings of candles, soft lights, and mellow music filling the quiet air.

## Menu

*Assorted hors d'oeuvre*
*Cheese platter*
*Avocado halves filled with sour cream and red caviar*
*Rolled, herbed leg of lamb*
*Baby roast potatoes*
*Green peas, braised onions*
*Lemon ice with mandarin orange slices*

### Beverages

*Scotch or bourbon on the rocks*
*Rum and vodka collins*
*Spritzers*
*Soft drinks*
*Wine*

## SHOPPING LIST

*To be ordered*

**5 or 6 legs of lamb, depending on size, boned and left open**

*Other foods*

**Frozen hors d'oeuvre (pastry-wrapped hot dogs, stuffed mushrooms, cheese puffs)**
**1 pound Brie cheese**
**1 pound Havarti cheese**
**½ pound smoked Cheddar**
**2 packages Boursin or Boursault cheese**
**Crackers of your choice**
**20 avocados (if you know ripe ones are hard to find in your area, buy them four or five days ahead so they will have time to ripen)**
**2 pints sour cream**
**2 4-ounce jars red salmon caviar**
**2 pounds butter**
**1 bunch parsley**
**1 garlic bud**

14 pint boxes frozen baby peas
11 dozen small white onions, approximately
 5 pounds small new potatoes
   Thyme
   Tarragon
   Bay leaves
   Chervil
 6 lemons
 1 bottle inexpensive dry white wine
 3 quarts lemon ice or sherbet
10 cans mandarin orange slices
 1 quart unsweetened lemon juice
   Soda water, soft drinks

*Staples*

Salt
Pepper
Cooking oil
Beef bouillon (canned) or bouillon cubes

*Liquor*

½ gallon bourbon
½ gallon Scotch
½ gallon vodka
½ gallon rum
 2 quarts white wine for spritzers
 8 quarts rosé (or white or red if you prefer) wine
   for dinner

## TIMETABLE

*Party Day Minus 3 Weeks*
Figure total available space around pool or in patio
   area
Check and/or order equipment—tables, chairs, clothes
   racks
Send invitations
Plan menu
Plan entertainment and hire orchestra, musician or
   entertainers
Order pool cleaning, if necessary
Order or plan insect protection

Hire caterer and/or temporary help
Begin heavy gardening
Paint or repair yard furniture, if necessary

*Party Day Minus 2 Weeks*
Plan decor
Collect necessities for entertainment
Finish gardening

*Party Day Minus 1 Week*
Prepare pool or patio area
Order legs of lamb

*Party Day Minus 2 Days*
Set up tables and chairs
Order flowers
Shop for food
Buy paper plates, napkins, and plastic utensils

*Party Day Minus 1 Day*
Pick up and arrange flowers

*Party Day Morning*
Pick up meat
Set tables, put out place cards, and finish decorations
Remove cheese from refrigerator
Prepare filling for avocados
Stuff legs of lamb

*Party Day (early afternoon)*
Peel and trim potatoes
Peel onions
Take mandarin oranges out of cans and chill

*Party Day (late afternoon)*
When helpers arrive give complete instructions and
   discuss all details
Rest and relax

*Party Time*
See "schedule" at end of chapter

## Party Day Minus 3 Weeks

**Seating needs**   Seating arrangements for outdoor parties cannot be casual. If you have a pool, it will be the focal point, but it is also a source of potential disaster. To guard against accidentally dunking a guest, plan carefully. To figure the total number of people you can seat comfortably and safely, measure five feet back from the edge of the pool or patio. Plan to place one side of the tables on this five foot mark. Allowing for chair space between table and pool or patio edge and between each table, you will be able to figure the total number of guests that you can seat.

Regular outdoor furniture is designed for basking in the sun, and most chairs and tables are built low to the ground. So don't assume that outdoor chairs can be used with standard 29-inch high tables. Now is the time to check your estimated guest list against your available tables and chairs, and to rent whatever you are lacking.

I want to stress the importance of using *only* plastic glasses around the pool or patio area. Because you cannot see broken glass in the water, "real" glasses are doubly dangerous near a pool. China and silver are still appropriate; they lend a more formal air. However, in the interests of practicality, sturdy paper plates and high-quality strong plastic utensils are perfectly acceptable for *all* outdoor entertaining.

**Guests and invitations**   After figuring the total number of available seating spaces, begin to compile your guest list. Remember that many of your regular partygoers may be away at this time of year. This, then, is a perfect opportunity to invite new friends and neighbors, and distant friends who may be vacationing nearby. Like Midsummer Night itself, your guest list can be new, refreshing, and exciting.

Try a new approach in your invitations, too. For instance, you might write invitations on fabric, and trim them with glitter and foil. For the more elaborate parties, hand-delivered invitations are an unusual means of presentation. Try hiring an actor, put him or her in a costume suggesting Shakespeare's Midsummer Night's Dream and send him or her to your guests' homes with a parchment invitation. This would certainly help to set the tone of the evening from the very start! Of course, this can be done only when the guests live within reasonable distance of each other.

If you have a swimming pool and you choose to make the evening go the full route—from dining to dancing to swimming—then you must alert your guests to what they will need to bring. Your invitation might read:

> *On Saturday, June 24th*
> *When the moon is on the rise*
> *Cricket and Jerry Thompson*
> *are planning a Midsummer Night's Dream*
> *You'll find them at the pool (or patio)*
> *at 2 Milton Road*
> *at 7 P.M.*
> *Many friends will be there and they hope you will be, too.*
> *Please call 259-6078 and say yes.*
> *Dress for dancing and bring your bathing suit (if appropriate).*

**Plan the menu**  Since the party takes place during the summer growing season, tender fresh vegetables will be readily available and should be featured. A delicate meat such as the lamb suggested here, or veal or chicken, is the best choice to go with the baby peas or other fresh produce.

**Plan the entertainment**  The ultimate in entertainment for this kind of party would be Peter Duchin and his orchestra. However, soft piano music, live or recorded, can set a lovely tone, too. Or you might be able to hire a good local group to supply live dance music. Dancing may take place between the main course and dessert as well as after dessert and coffee.

You might also want to consider some live entertainment built around the Midsummer Night theme. Light music—lutes, recorders, bells, and such—suggest the mystery and romance of the occasion. A strolling musician, instead of or in addition to a seated band, is in keeping with the Shakespearian atmosphere.

To make Midsummer Night a very special event, consider a costume party. For simplicity's sake, I'd suggest that your guests' costumes be limited to masks, makeup, and hats. Heavy and elaborate costumes are too much for hot summer months, and many people basically dislike full-costume parties.

The masks and makeup allow your guests to get into the magic while not becoming a victim of it. As the evening progresses, they will probably want to remove their disguises, and you must provide an area to do this, other than the main lavatory. A game room, spare bedroom, a den, or even the dressed-up laundry room are appropriate. Equip the area with some cold cream, and lots of facial tissue and wastepaper baskets lined with plastic bags. Then the lavatories are necessary only for the final wash-up. The same areas may work out well as changing rooms for swimmers.

**The pool or patio area**  If your pool or patio party is to take place entirely on a paved surface, your only concern is drainage and smooth surface finish. This is the time to inspect the fringe areas. If there are cracks or bumps, begin their repair now, or segregate bad areas from traffic in your master plan. For dancing, be certain that your dancing space or floor will be located well out of the range of splashing water. A little water on a dancing surface is very dangerous. Dancing by the pool is lovely, but keep a mop close by, just in case.

**Cleaning and gardening**  All cleaning and major gardening projects should be begun or ordered at this time. That means considering a special pool cleaning, unless you have a regular weekly cleaning service. Gardening problems—high hedges, low-hanging branches, and mosquito hide-outs—should all be cleaned up at this time to leave the last days free for creating the special Midsummer Night effects.

Finally, if you plan to rent a tent or canopy, or a dance floor, this is the time to do so.

**Hire caterer or temporary help**  For a party of this size, it is essential to have catering help. You may hire a caterer who will prepare the food as well as serve it and tend the bar, or you may simply hire a bartender and a cook and waitress for the evening. Whatever you choose to do, be sure to make the arrangements at least three weeks ahead of time.

## Party Day Minus 2 Weeks

**The decor**  A Midsummer Night party is not an easy venture. Its success depends on the little things you do to bring it all together. I discussed various themes for floral arrangements and placements in the chapter on decorating with flowers. On Midsummer Night there really are no rules—anything goes. The best colors are the palest shades of blue, yellow, and pink, spiced with glittering accents of any compatible hue—extra emphasis on silver and gold. The Midsummer Night party should look as if Puck and his fairies have sprinkled "fairy dust" all over it.

To capture the glistening and gleaming of Midsummer Night, use china and silver ornaments and vases. Candles in glass chimneys add a soft glow and, to make them extra special, surround the candles with flowers and shiny silver and pink ribbons. Plan to swag tree limbs and tent corners with glittering angel hair (but be sure it's fire retardant). If you can buy or borrow them, string tiny white lights in bushes and tree limbs—if possible get those that can be made to blink later in the evening when people are in the pool or out on a treasure hunt.

You will find that a number of your Christmas tree decorations will serve perfectly in this new setting. Remember that the next time you pass a 50 percent off Christmas decoration sale—for much less than you would normally spend, you can buy decorations for occasional summer use. Glass bulbs, angel hair, tinsel, certain garlands, tiny string lights, gold or silver wrapping paper, are the ingredients of a good enchanted forest.

**Plan the entertainment** If you have decided to play some group games as part of Midsummer Night, two weeks before the party is ample time to plan this entertainment. If simple charades are the choice, any central location near the tables will suffice, and little, if any, equipment is needed. However, if a treasure hunt is to take place, much more planning is in order.

Nighttime treasure hunting requires several things: a planned and cleared course, lighting for finding and reading clues, and ample instructions. To keep the spirit of Midsummer Night, you might want to try to write your clues in Elizabethan English. Many of the guests may be unfamiliar with your yard in the "forest" at night. Careful forethought will guarantee an exciting and magical treasure hunt.

Midsummer Night is also the night of the *foolish actors*. It's a perfect time to let your hambone friends try some improvisations—equipped with your props, costumes, and script suggestions. Be sure to get their approval and promises to cooperate ahead of time. A few dramatic floodlights and some introductory music and your guests may be set for a fun-filled show.

By the end of this week, major lighting installation should be underway or at least purchased. Indoor Christmas lights cannot go up until the day of the party, but outdoor lights may be strung at any time.

Major gardening and construction jobs should also be finished by this time.

## Party Day Minus 1 Week

If you are planning swimming as part of the evening, during this week you should prepare the changing areas. If the guests are to come dressed for dinner and end up in the pool, they will need some area in which to change and hang their clothes, and later to dry off and change back. You will need only two general changing areas—one for men and one for women. When it is time to start swimming, you may open the doors to the changing areas, or put up arrows pointing toward them, and lay the towels out—alerting the guests to the location of the changing areas and to a new party climate.

This will also be the time to clear away as many tables and chairs as possible. These suggestions are given here so that now, before the actual day of the party, you can make various advance plans: for a location to store all the tables and chairs after they are cleared away, for the number of towels you will need (*at least* one per guest), for shower facilities, etc. And consider providing a warm spot—perhaps lighting a bonfire—for an after-swim brandy and coffee.

Order legs of lamb.

### Party Day Minus 2 Days

This is the time to set up the tables, chairs, and buffet tables. If you have rented this equipment, it should be delivered one or two days before the party, so you can check for omissions and have plenty of time to set it up and arrange and rearrange until it is to your liking. Folding chairs should be left closed, leaning against the tables, to keep seats dry in case of heavy dew or showers.

Flowers for the tables may be ordered at this time for delivery the day of the party. If you are planning to make the arrangements yourself, wait until the day before the party to purchase your flowers.

When poolside preparations are taken care of, it is time to turn to the menu. Today, get all your shopping done, and check your supply of staples. The Midsummer Night menu does not lend itself to advance cooking and freezing, but the purchasing of the food is extremely important, and may require some shopping around. Although the lamb has already been ordered and will be delivered prepared, it is essential to find the freshest young vegetables, the perfect avocados and the cheese that will be exactly right the day of the party. If you have a favorite farm market, ask them today to pick the vegetables fresh for you the morning of the party.

Now is also the time to buy your tableware. Choose sturdy paper plates with a flower pattern, and, if possible, matching plastic glasses. You can also get paper napkins and tablecloths to match the plates if you wish. However, if possible, I would recommend using linen tablecloths in bright colors, coordinated with the flower pattern of the plates. Three or four alternating colors on the tables around the patio or pool make a beautiful sight. A good party supply firm should have colored cloths available for rent.

## Party Day

First thing in the morning, pick up the legs of lamb you have ordered, if they are not being delivered.

Much of the advance preparation of the food can be done in the morning. The final cooking will be done by the people you have hired to help out. As you prepare each dish it is a good idea to write down for them how the final cooking and/or serving is to be done.

### Cheese Platter

The cheeses should not be removed from their wrappings until just before serving, but they should be taken out of the refrigerator and arranged on the serving dish in the morning. Fresh boxes of the crackers of your choice should also be set out, but left unopened until serving time. You and your friends undoubtedly have your own favorite cheeses, but I recommend as a superb combination of textures and flavors: Brie; Boursin or Boursault; a smoky or sharp Cheddar; and a mild Havarti.

### Avocado with Sour Cream and Red Caviar

The avocados should not be cut in half until just before dinner time, as they will turn black. However, the sour cream and caviar filling improves with "sitting," so it should be mixed in the morning. For forty avocado halves, two 4-ounce jars of red salmon caviar are stirred gently into 2 pints of sour cream. Two or three tablespoons of the mixture are spooned into each avocado before serving. This appetizer may also be served by putting 3 tablespoons of plain sour cream into each avocado half and topping it with a teaspoon of caviar. Although I think this is less tasty, it makes a prettier dish. It will require an extra jar of the very expensive caviar, however.

## Rolled Legs of Lamb

Your roasts should be prepared in the morning, so that the flavors of the herbs will penetrate the meat. For *each* leg of lamb, mix:

⅔ stick of butter or margarine
2 cloves pressed garlic
2 tablespoons chopped parsley
1 small onion, minced
1 tablespoon dried tarragon
1 tablespoon dried chervil
 Juice of ½ lemon

Spread opened leg of lamb with one-third of mixture.

Roll and tie carefully. Rub remaining mixture over the outside of the lamb. Sprinkle with salt and pepper, and with juice of other half of lemon. Return lamb to refrigerator until late afternoon, when it should be removed and brought to room temperature.

To cook, heat the oven to 400 degrees and cook the lamb for ½ hour. Reduce heat to 375 degrees and bake for 1 hour.

## Baby Roast Potatoes

Parboil new potatoes, peel, and trim into even ovals, approximately 1½ x 2 inches. If you cannot get new potatoes, peel and cut larger ones in half and trim sharp edges until you have rough ovals. Parboil for 10 minutes. Drain, cover with cold water, and set aside.

When roast is ready to go into oven, roll potatoes thoroughly in cooking oil or melted butter and place around roast. Turn frequently during baking, and add a little oil or butter to pan if potatoes are sticking or charring on outside.

## Green Peas and Braised Onions

Much as we would like to suggest serving fresh garden peas, we realize that few people have the time or help to shell 30 pounds of peas! And that is what it would take to satisfy the appetites of forty people. So, unless you have a corps of assistants lined up, you're better off settling for the tiny or baby frozen peas. You will need 14 pint boxes for your party.

Although the peas will be cooked just before serving, the onions should be peeled in the morning. To facilitate peeling, plunge the onions into rapidly boiling water and boil for 2 minutes. Drain and cool. They may also be browned ahead of time, and set aside until 45 minutes before dinner.

Put 1½ tablespoons butter or margarine and 1½ tablespoons cooking oil in each of 3 large heavy skillets. Cook peeled onions over medium heat until they are delicately brown. Turn them constantly. Do not expect them to brown evenly all over. This will take about 15 minutes. Put all onions into one flameproof casserole. Cover and set aside.

Forty-five minutes before serving, add to the casserole:

2 cups canned beef bouillon
2 cups dry white wine
  Herb bouquet made up of 12 parsley sprigs, 2 bay leaves, ¾ teaspoon thyme

Liquid should just show through top layer of onions.

Simmer, loosely covered, for 40 minutes. Onions should be tender but not falling apart, and liquid should be almost gone. Discard herb bouquet.

Cook peas according to package directions.

To serve, place well-buttered peas on 2 large platters and surround with onions.

### Lemon Ice with Mandarin Orange Slices

Open 10 cans of mandarin orange slices and empty into serving bowl. Chill.

Lemon ice must, of course, be kept frozen until the last moment. When it's time for dessert, the ice should be spooned into large bowls with an ice-cream scoop, and the mandarin oranges arranged around the edges.

When as much of the food preparation as possible is completed, it is time for the final chores—setting the tables, putting out the flower arrangements, and adding the finishing touches to your other decorations.

For as many as forty people, place cards are a necessity, and they should be put in place when you set the tables.

## Party Time

Your caterers or helpers should be asked to arrive one hour and a half before the guests. This will give you time to give them complete instructions about serving, cooking, clearing away dishes, etc. If you have everything possible in writing, it will save time and avoid errors. The bartender must be shown where his supplies are, but he should set up the bar in whatever way works best for him. The cook must be shown where to find all the foods and utensils, and the waiter or waitress, the serving dishes and the general layout. Even though it may be a buffet dinner, it will be necessary to pass the hors d'oeuvre, to clear away used plates and glasses, and to keep the buffet dishes refilled. The final preparation of the hors d'oeuvre—unwrapping the cheeses, filling the avocado halves, and heating the frozen hors d'oeuvre according to package directions—must be discussed and will be taken care of by the help.

These instructions should be completed within a half hour, leaving you an hour to bathe and dress leisurely, and to be ready to receive your guests in the Midsummer Night spirit.

As we have said many times, the single most important thing to guarantee a party's success is planning and preparation. The host and hostess *must* be relaxed, organized, and able to devote their time to their guests. Because you will have help for your elegant party, this should not be difficult. The hard work is already done, and you are free to enjoy the party as much as any of your guests. To be sure that you will enjoy it, have a timetable worked out, and carefully explained to your help.

Here is a suggested timetable:

7–7:30   Guests arrive and are shown to pool or patio area.

7–8:30   Cocktails and hors d'oeuvre are served.
         Strolling musician plays.

8:15     Candles are lighted and filled avocado halves are placed on tables.

8:30     Guests are asked to unmask.

8:40     Guests are invited to be seated (have a master plan in your hand so you can help your friends to find their places quickly).

8:45     The entrées are brought to the buffet table, and the guests are asked to go and help themselves. The waiter (or waitress) removes the avocados when the guests leave their tables.

9:15     Dessert is placed on the buffet table.

9:30     Coffee and liqueurs are served at the tables by the waiter and bartender.

10:00     Entertainment time—dancing, charades, treasure hunt or whatever you have planned.
Bar re-opens.

11:45     Changing areas are opened in preparation for a midnight dip.

?     Party ends.

## Labor Day Luau for Twenty-four

Labor Day—the first Monday in September—marks the unofficial, if not the calendar, end of summer. This long weekend provides the perfect opportunity to say good-by to the friends you have made during the summer, or to celebrate the start of a new season with old friends and neighbors.

The luau is the ideal motif for a Labor Day party because early September, in almost all parts of the country, is the best time to obtain fresh fruits, vegetables, and flowers, so much a part of the luau traditions.

Of necessity, the mainland interpretation of this classic Pacific cuisine has been modified to resemble the more familiar clambake. One might even say that some Americans treat the luau as if it *were* a Hawaiian clambake, but it is not. Unlike the clambake, where all the foods are cooked together in a pit, only the pig is cooked in a pit at a luau. The key to a successful luau is the combination of the classic menu with the right luau atmosphere. Abundant food and lavish decor are the essential ingredients. Because of this, we do not suggest having a luau unless you are committed to doing a great deal of work before and during the party, and have plenty of help—either volunteer or hired.

Luau is a Hawaiian word with two distinct but related meanings. As an adjective it means stuffed or filled. As a noun, it means the supplier of food, or the one a child goes to for food, which would explain the history of the luau in Hawaii.

Traditionally, Hawaiian families have been very large, and very close to each other. The family often was extended to include friends and distant relatives who were alone, or strangers who appeared lost or lonely. The luau was the family form of entertaining, and on some occasions friends were invited, too, and the feast was incredibly lavish. Originally the diners sat in a circle on the ground, with the foods spread out in the center. The traditional hula was danced, and Hawaiian guitar music was played by one or a number of the guests.

Today it is clearly not possible to follow these traditions to the letter, but it's fun to do so insofar as it is practical. People are always seated together at one or more large tables, even at luaus held in hotels or clubs. Unless the luau is small, guests help themselves from a buffet, rather than from dishes in the center of a round table. Tables and chairs are used, because few of us are comfortable seated on the floor for any length of time. Originally all of the food was eaten with the fingers, but today, with the addition of various "foreign" dishes to the menu, knives and forks as well as fingers are used. But the atmosphere, the warmth, the gaiety, and the superb menus have survived, and make the luau one of the truly great forms of entertainment.

Listed below is a complete, authentic Hawaiian luau menu. Many of the ingredients are unavailable on the mainland, and the average home-owner does not have the equipment or the help to provide such a menu, so we have starred the dishes that can be done conveniently or that can be approximated by making substitutions. The pig—the one unchangeable feature of the menu—may be roasted in the oven or in a fireplace if no yard space is available. To make the luau as authentic as possible, prepare as many of the starred items as you can handle.

*Menu*

*Lomi Salmon*
SALTED SALMON WITH TOMATOES AND ONIONS (COLD)
*Maki Sushi*
RICE ROLLED IN SEAWEED CASING (WARM)
* *Poisson Cru*
A TAHITIAN RAW FISH DISH (COLD)
*Poi*
THIN GRUEL PREPARED FROM TARO ROOTS (WARM)
* *Poe*
SAMOAN-STYLE BANANA AND PAPAYA PUDDING (WARM)

*\* Uwala*
BAKED CASSEROLE OF SWEET POTATOES (HOT)
*Chicken Luau*
CHICKEN AND TARO LEAVES WITH COCONUT MILK (HOT)
*Pipi Pulehu*
ROAST BEEF (HOT)
*\* Fresh Mahi Mahi*
DEEP-FRIED PACIFIC DOLPHIN (HOT)
*\* Laiki Loloa Mekamoa*
CHICKEN WITH LONG-GRAIN RICE (HOT)
*\* Kalua Pua's*
PIT-ROASTED PORK (HOT)
*Haupia*
COCONUT PUDDING (COLD)
*\* Fresh pineapple and papaya*
*\*Coconut cake*

*Drinks*

*Mai tai*     *Piña colada*
*Rum punch*
*Pineapple punch*
*Daiquiri*     *Whiskey and soda or water*


## SHOPPING LIST

*To be ordered*

**35- to 40-pound pig (at least 3 weeks in advance)**
 **4 pounds dolphin fillets (or red snapper, sea trout, scrod)**
 **4 pounds flounder fillets (or lemon sole)**
**18 sweet potatoes (not always available, so have your grocer order for you)**
 **6 papayas**
**12 pineapples**

*Nonperishable foods*

 **1 box coarse salt**
 **1 quart chicken broth**
 **1 pound yellow onions**

2 pounds butter or margarine
1 quart vegetable oil
3 packages long-grain wild rice
3 cans artichoke hearts
3 cans shredded coconut
1 can grated coconut
2 boxes white cake mix
2 cans soft icing
1 quart lime juice
1 can green chilies
1 2-pound box dark brown sugar
1 box graham cracker crumbs
1 pint maple syrup
1 9½-ounce box cracker meal

*Perishable foods*

12 firm but ripe bananas
8 whole chicken breasts
1 pint cream (for coffee)
1 head lettuce
3 pounds tomatoes
5 lemons
4 limes
1 dozen eggs
1 carton orange juice

*Staples*

**Salt**
**Pepper**
**Flour**
**Vanilla extract**
**Baking powder**
**Sugar**
**Nutmeg**
**Cinnamon**
**Cayenne pepper**
**Tarragon**
**Paprika**
**Tea**
**Regular and decaffeinated coffee**

*Bar supplies*

2 dozen mai tai mix

2 dozen piña colada mix
2 quarts light rum
1 quart dark rum
1 quart bourbon
1 quart scotch
1 quart vodka
1 quart gin
2 quarts soda water

*For fruit punches*

1 pint unsweetened lemon juice
1 can sliced pineapple
1 quart ginger ale
1 quart soda
  Grenadine
1 jar maraschino cherries
3 oranges

## TIMETABLE

*Luau Day Minus 3 Weeks*
**Order pig and other hard-to-find foods**
**Send invitations**
**Order chairs, tables, tent (if required)**
**Arrange for entertainment and music**

*Luau Day Minus 2 Weeks*
**Hire temporary help**
**Order flowers (and leis, if possible)**
**Buy other decorations**

*Luau Day Minus 1 Week*
**Prepare yard area**
**Dig pit**
**Collect rocks and wood for pit**
**Plan and obtain material to cover hot rocks**
**Buy nonperishable foods and bar supplies**
**Check supply of serving dishes as well as tableware**

*Luau Day Minus 2 Days*
**Buy perishable foods and pick up previously ordered fish, fruit, etc.**
**Pick up pig and start to thaw if necessary**
**Make coconut cake**
**Buy extra ice cubes—5 10-pound bags**

*Luau Day Minus 1 Day*
Set up chairs, tables, place settings, and serving area—
   cold and hot.
Make fruit and flower arrangements
Complete other decorations
Prepare poisson cru
Prepare chicken and rice

*Luau Day Morning*
Prepare pit and light fire
Prepare poe (banana dish)
Prepare dolphin for oven frying
Prepare pineapple and papaya
Prepare sweet potato casserole
Set up bar—make punch

*Luau*
4:30 P.M.—Prepare pig and put into pit
7 P.M. Remove pig from pit—Set out cold foods on
   bed of ice—Serve dinner

## Luau Day Minus 3 Weeks

**Order the pig**  Before sending out your invitations, be sure that your butcher can guarantee delivery of a pig. Without it, a real luau is not possible. Tell the butcher the number of guests you expect, and he will be able to advise you about how large a pig you need. A 35-pound pig will serve 24 people generously. Ask for a written copy of your order, with price and delivery date specified. Find out if the pig will be frozen or not. If so, be sure that it will arrive two days ahead of the party to allow time for defrosting.

**Send invitations**  Although a luau is not a formal party, Labor Day weekend is a busy one and written invitations are in order. Select one with a colorful flower or fruit motif, and you may write "Dress— muumuus and aloha shirts," if you wish, to further set the tone.

Since the pig will be removed from the pit at 7 P.M., guests should be asked to come at 6:30, to be sure that they arrive in time to see the ritual.

Be sure to include "R.s.v.p." or "Regrets only" with your telephone number.

**Order the equipment**  Since your luau should take place outdoors if it is at all possible, you will probably need to rent tables and chairs for the occasion. The best arrangement would be three tables for eight placed in a "U" because guests at an authentic luau sit at the same table. If this does not fit into the available space, two tables of twelve will do nicely.

You will also need a bigger-than-ordinary buffet table, or several tables, a large heating unit, and wide, shallow pans to hold the cold dishes on a bed of ice. You may be able to improvise with your own equipment, but, if not, be sure to rent the necessary items to insure a spacious display of the exotic foods, as this is the focal point of the luau. The hot food may be served on one table, the cold on another, and the pig, in all its glory, on a third. Plan your serving area very carefully, making a sketch of each area before ordering your rental equipment. Reserve extra platters, casseroles, and serving dishes, or contact friends who may lend them to you.

This is also the time to decide if you will need a tent or marquee. If you have an area in which you can set up the tables and the buffet in case of rain (a large garage, a barn, or a big game room area, for example) you can forego the expense of a tent. But if you do not, you may not wish to take a chance on fair weather.

**Entertainment** If you live near a big city where all sorts of entertainment is available, do try to get some Hawaiian or other Polynesian entertainers for the evening. If you cannot, try to hire a musician who will play Hawaiian songs on his guitar. Failing that, you can at least get some Hawaiian records to play during dinner. Although the meal is an entertainment in itself, you may want something for your guests after dinner, so if there are no professionals to be had, plan something like a hula contest. Or, if that doesn't appeal to you, another possibility would be to rent a short movie on surfing or diving in Hawaiian waters.

## Luau Day Minus 2 Weeks

**Temporary help** A luau is *not* a one-man job! Even if you plan to do all of the food preparation yourself, you will need help with digging the pit, collecting rocks, setting up tables, decorating, etc.

Since most colleges are not yet back in session by Labor Day, student agencies or youngsters whom you know personally may provide the best source of help. A professional bartender would be a great asset.

As long as you know your help personally, or have good references, you will do better *not* to hire regular caterers' workers. You do not need the service of professional waiters, but rather a number of "bus boys" and clearers and washers. If you can buy some wild, flowered shirts at the local cut-rate store, you could outfit the boys in shorts and these Hawaiian-style shirts. Girls or women could be given two yards of inexpensive flowered fabric to wrap around themselves Polynesian style.

Your own children, their friends, or neighborhood youngsters might well be delighted to help with the pit, collecting rocks, and splitting wood for the fire—as well as with decorations, flower arranging and so on—for a nominal amount of money.

**Order flowers** Flowers are second only to food at a luau, so special care must be taken in planning what you want and how you will use them. Flamboyant flowers such as birds of paradise, anthurium, and plumeria are perfect, but are often not obtainable, or are too expensive. Less hard-to-get but colorful flowers can be substituted. Poppies, tiger lilies in various colors, black-eyed Susans, and dahlias make eye-catching displays. A variety of ferns and pots of exotic greens—elephant ears, cut-leaf philodendron, etc.—add to the atmosphere. Discuss other details with your florist.

You may also want to inquire about the possibility of ordering fresh leis for all your guests. They are, on occasion, flown in from Hawaii, but this may be too costly for your budget. Instead, you could plan to give each woman a flower to wear behind her ear. Your florist will be able to suggest a variety that will last well throughout the evening.

**Other decorations** Although flowers will provide the main decoration, certain other items will be necessary to augment them. Torch lights add an authentic and beautiful touch, but if you are planning on a tent, and are concerned about open flame near the fabric, big Oriental lanterns are also dramatic and are safer. They may be used alone, suspended over the tables and around the edge of the tent, or in conjunction with the torches.

In the event that fresh flowers are completely unavailable or are too expensive to consider, colorful substitutes can be made with papier maché and crêpe or tissue paper.

### Luau Day Minus 1 Week

During this week, the yard should be cleaned up and the pit dug. For a 30 to 40 pound pig, the pit should be 3 feet deep, 4 feet long, and 3 feet wide. This allows ample room for the sizable rocks that are necessary to line it. These rocks should also be collected early in the week, as well as a substantial enough pile of wood to keep the fire going for four to five hours.

It is essential to have an ample supply of some kind of moisture-retaining leaves to cover the rocks before the pig is laid on them, and to provide the steam that will keep it moist. In Hawaii, ti leaves and banana stalks are used, but the former are unavailable on the mainland, and only a few of us have access to banana trees. If you do, the stalks and leaves will serve very well. The best substitute is seaweed. Again, not everyone lives near the ocean, but seaweed can be ordered from companies that ship lobster and shellfish inland. Ask at your fish market if they can assist you in getting fresh seaweed. If all else fails, it is possible to use live green corn stalks and the leaves and husks. Whatever you do, you *must* have enough greenery to cover the rocks with several layers or your pig will come out charred and dry.

Early in the week, buy the nonperishable foods and bar supplies, to allow yourself more time for preparation of the meal and last-minute chores just before the party.

## Luau Day Minus 2 Days

If your previously ordered food is not to be delivered by the store, this is the time to pick it up. Try to empty your refrigerator of leftovers and nonparty items, so that you will have plenty of room for the fish, fruits, juices, etc.

If your pig is frozen, it should be picked up two days ahead to be sure that it will be defrosted by Luau day. Keep it in a cool place (a basement is usually best) and hang it from the ceiling or cover it with netting or screening to keep insects and mice away from it. If the pig is fresh-killed and not frozen, leave it in your butcher's locker until the last possible moment. If it will not fit in your refrigerator, you must make some arrangement with a friendly restaurant owner, or a friend with an extra refrigerator, to keep it cold for you.

In the afternoon, make your coconut cakes. Simply follow the directions on the packages of white cake mix and icing, adding ¾ cup shredded coconut and 1½ teaspoons grated lemon rind to the batter for each cake. When the cakes are cool and iced, press more shredded coconut gently into icing on top and sides.

If you have a freezer, buy your ice supply now, leaving one less chore for later. You will need at least 50 pounds of ice to fill the trays on which you will set out the cold dishes. And, of course, you will want to have a generous supply for those delicious Polynesian drinks!

## Luau Day Minus 1 Day

By this time, you will be pretty sure of what the weather will be, and you can set up your tables indoors or out. If you have ordered a tent, it should arrive in the morning and you can start to decorate it as soon as it is in place.

A beautiful centerpiece for your buffet can be made of a three-tiered mound of Styrofoam or wood—either round or square—covered with a white cloth. A folded sheet or bridge table cover will do. Make arrangements of fruit on each tier, perhaps a pineapple on each corner surrounded by heaped-up bananas, oranges, apples, etc. Another pineapple makes a perfect top, with more fruit surrounding it. Just before the party, you can add fresh flowers and greens to the piles of fruit, and between them. A smaller, similar arrangement (2-tiered) can serve for the centerpiece on the dining table.

Install the torches, making sure that they are very stable and cannot be easily knocked over. Also be sure you have an adequate supply of kerosene for them. Hang the lanterns, and finish all other flower arrangements and decorating.

You must give special attention to your serving area. It should be near enough to an electric outlet so that hot trays and warming dishes can be plugged in. Or, a heavy-duty extension cord can be run from the nearest outlet, making sure it follows a path where it will not be stepped on or tripped over. The table that will hold the cold food must be strong, because the bed of ice to keep the food cold will be heavy.

With the setting all ready except for last-minute touches, you can turn your attention to preparing some of the dishes. The poisson cru must be prepared a day ahead to allow time for the lime juice to "cook" the fish, and the chicken and rice can be prepared now and reheated at dinner time.

*Poisson Cru*

---

4 pounds flounder or lemon sole fillets
4 cups lime juice
1 cup minced onion
½ cup green chili pepper
2 cups peeled, seeded, and chopped tomatoes

4 **teaspoons salt**
  **Dash of cayenne pepper**

Cut the fish into small pieces and put in a glass bowl. Mix the remaining ingredients and pour over the fish. Be sure the fish is entirely submerged in lime juice. Cover and marinate for 3 to 4 hours, stirring occasionally, then refrigerate until ready to serve.

### *Laiki Loloa Mekamoa (Chicken with rice)*

8 **whole chicken breasts**
3 **onions, chopped**
6 **tablespoons butter or margarine**
3 **packages long-grain wild rice**
  **Salt and pepper**
3 **teaspoons tarragon**
3 **cans artichoke hearts**
6 **tablespoons melted butter**
  **Paprika**
4 **cups chicken broth**

Bone the chicken breasts and cut each into 4 pieces. Sauté the onion in the butter. Divide the onion into two large casseroles and cover each with 1½ packages rice. Sprinkle with salt, pepper, and tarragon. Arrange the artichoke hearts on top of the rice and cover with the chicken, skin side up. Brush the chicken with melted butter and sprinkle with salt, pepper, and paprika. Pour 2 cups chicken broth in each casserole. Cover and bake for 45 minutes in a 400-degree oven. Cool and refrigerate.

### Luau Day Morning

Early in the day the pit must be lined with rocks, filled with wood, and the fire lighted. The fire must burn for a minimum of four hours, and since we have scheduled the pig to go in at 4:30, the fire should be going by 12:30 at the latest. If you have enough wood, it would be better to start it at 11. Someone (not the chef) should be assigned the important task of keeping an eye on the fire and replenishing it regularly throughout the day.

The person in charge of the food has a busy day ahead. In whatever order you prefer, the fried fish, banana dish, fresh fruit, and sweet potatoes must be prepared.

## *Mahi Mahi (Deep-fried dolphin or other fish)*

**4 pounds dolphin, sea trout or scrod fillets**
**1 9½-ounce box cracker meal**
**2 eggs**
**4 tablespoons water**

Dry the fish thoroughly and cut into pieces about 2 inches long, ¾-inch wide, and ¾-inch thick. Pour the cracker meal onto wax paper. Beat the eggs with the water. Roll fish strips in the cracker meal, then dip in egg mixture, and roll again in cracker meal. Cover and set aside to be fried at the last minute.

## *Poe Substitute (Baked bananas)*

**12 firm, ripe bananas**
**1½ cups orange juice**
**1½ cups dark brown sugar**
**1 cup grated coconut**
**1 cup graham cracker crumbs**
**¼ teaspoon nutmeg**
**½ teaspoon cinnamon**

Peel and split the bananas lengthwise. Place them in a baking dish. Mix together the orange juice and brown sugar and pour over the bananas. Mix the coconut, graham cracker crumbs, nutmeg, and cinnamon and sprinkle over the top. Bake 20 minutes in a 325-degree oven.

## *Fresh Pineapple and Papaya (or melon)*

Slice off top end of 4 pineapples. Cut the pineapples in half lengthwise, then quarters, then eighths. Cut core from pointed section of each wedge. Remove outer rind by sliding knife along between pulp and rind. Remove brown "eyes," if any.

Halve and remove seeds from 6 papayas or melons. Cut into wedges. Arrange papaya or melon in center of platter, surrounded by wedges of pineapple, or arrange fruit in any way that appeals to you.

## *Uwala (Baked casserole of sweet potatoes)*

18 sweet potatoes, about 7 pounds
   Salt and pepper
½ cup maple syrup
1½ tablespoons lemon juice
½ teaspoon grated lemon rind
 4 tablespoons butter or margarine

Boil peeled sweet potatoes until nearly tender. When cool, slice them into ½-inch slices and place in shallow greased casseroles or baking dishes. Sprinkle with salt and pepper. Combine the maple syrup and lemon juice and pour over each dish. Sprinkle the tops with lemon rind and dot with butter. Set aside for baking just before the party.

**Set up the bar** While the fire in the pit is doing its work, someone should set up the bar and make the pineapple and rum punches. The recipes for making mai tais and piña coladas are printed on the cans of mix, so check them to be sure you have the necessary ingredients.

## *Rum Punch*

1 tablespoon lime juice
1½ ounces dark rum
   Dash of grenadine
1 ounce light rum
½ slice of orange
   Maraschino cherry
   Pineapple stick

In a highball glass, combine the lime juice, dark rum, and grenadine. Fill the glass with cracked ice and add the light rum. Stir well and garnish with orange, maraschino cherry, or pineapple.

## *Pineapple Punch (nonalcoholic)*

---

1 pint strong tea
½ cup lemon juice
2 cups orange juice
2 tablespoons lime juice
1 cup sugar
1 can sliced pineapple with juice (chilled)
1 quart ginger ale
1 quart soda water

In a large punch bowl, mix together the tea, lemon juice, orange juice, lime juice, and sugar. Chill. When ready to serve, add a block of ice and the sliced pineapple, ginger ale and soda water. Garnish with orange slices.

## Luau Day Afternoon

At 4:30, all burning wood and as many embers as possible must be removed from the pit. It is now time to prepare the pig.

Wipe it thoroughly with a damp cloth and sprinkle the inside generously with coarse salt. Lay the pig on its back, take several of the smaller hot rocks from the pit with tongs or asbestos gloves, and insert them into the body cavity.

Quickly cover the rocks in the pit with one half of the wet seaweed or corn husks you have collected, and lay the pig carefully on its side in the center. (A piece of chicken wire under the pig facilitates putting it in and taking it out of the pit.)

Now cover the pig completely with more seaweed or leaves, and then a *heavy* tarpaulin. This may be held down by additional rocks, or, if sand is available, cover the entire pile with a layer of sand. This will serve to hold the tarpaulin in place and will further insulate the "oven."

And now you can relax and rest for a while before you have to dress for your luau.

## The Luau

Just before 6:30, plug in electric trays or heating devices, and spread ice cubes into the trays for the cold dishes.

As the guests arrive, give each a lei, or, if you do not have leis, a flower for the women to put behind their ears.

When your guests are all assembled and are enjoying their drinks, the ceremony of removing the pig takes place. Have your temporary helpers remove the rocks or dig away the sand, remove the tarpaulin and the top layer of leaves. The pig on its wire bed is carefully lifted and placed on a table. Small pieces of the crisp skin (crackling) can be cut off and served to your guests—the only hors d'oeuvre.

While this ritual is taking place you should cook or heat the dishes that need it, and set the cold dishes out on the trays of ice. So that you will not forget anything:

Sweet potatoes: Bake 30 minutes in 375-degree oven.

Chicken and rice: Heat for 20 minutes in same oven.

Fried fish: Heat oil for frying to 375 degrees. Fish can now be fried a few sticks at a time, drained on paper towels, and kept hot on hot plate.

Baked bananas: Reheat in 350-degree oven for about 15 minutes when other foods are removed.

Carve the pig while food is heating.

All of this heating and finishing will take about 45 minutes. This is just the right time to allow your guests to finish their first drinks, be seated, and enjoy another drink at the table.

When all of the hot dishes are ready, and the cold dishes are in place, summon your guests to the buffet table. There, in all its succulence, is the carved pig, surrounded by fruits, flowers, and the colorful menu selections you have prepared. Glasses are refilled throughout the meal, and the entertainment starts when the last diner is finished. Coffee may be served while the show is on.

A luau may not be the easiest party to produce, but it is indeed a memorable occasion. As your guests leave, you and they can say to each other a heartfelt "Aloha!"

---

## BYO Halloween Party for Twenty

---

Planning a party that requires a number of people to supply the food and/or drink and subsequently the spirit looks deceptively easy. It is not. Before you decide to embark on a BYOF/BYOB party, read this chapter carefully. Select your guests with care. It takes responsible guests to make this kind of entertainment work.

BYOF/BYOB parties are in many ways the exceptions to all the rules. All of my tips about planning your menu and allowing time for food preparation still apply, but they apply to your prospective guests, rather than to you! The role of the hosts in this instance is clearly one of organizer. They supply the framework and the accouterments.

For example, at a BYO party, it is assumed that the hosts will provide bar setups, mixers, and equipment. It is assumed that they will also supply the table service, flatware, linen, and the like. (An exception to this rule might be a BYO cookout/picnic where one guest could be asked to bring all the paper goods. Keep this in mind when using the BYO theme for summertime events.) Our menu calls for the hosts to provide grilled hamburgers, leaving the guests to bring accompanying dishes. One of the following might be suggested to each of the nine couples invited as their contribution. They require no last-minute preparation and are easily carried.

*Menu*

*Any favorite dip and chips    Assorted cheeses and crackers*
*(Grilled hamburgers provençale)*
*Scalloped potatoes    Macaroni and cheese*
*Spinach salad    Green salad with mushrooms*
*Rolls, garlic bread and condiments*
*Dessert    Coffee*

## SHOPPING LIST

½  bushel apples
½  pound spaghetti
 1  bunch carrots or beets
 1  small box dark raisins
 1  bag fresh spinach
 1  bunch celery
 1  crookneck squash
 1  large Hubbard squash
    Pumpkin(s)
½  dozen lemons
 3  quarts club soda
 2  six-packs ginger ale
 2  six-packs cola
 1  six-pack tonic water
 1  gallon cider
 7  pounds good grade hamburger meat
 1  pint tomato juice
 1  pound onions
 1  garlic bud
 1  bunch parsley
 1  bottle natural lemon juice
If providing liquor, buy whatever you and your friends
     like best. Two half-gallons should amply serve
     twenty people.

*Staples*

Salt
Pepper
Ice
Sugar
Regular and decaffeinated coffee

## TIMETABLE

*Party Day Minus 2 Weeks*
Invite your friends
Assign courses and/or dishes
Consider costume party option

*Party Day Minus 1 Week*
**Collect materials for decorations and games**
**Buy paper plates and table accessories**
**Get books of ghost stories from library**

*Party Day Minus 2 Days*
**Check staples**
**Do all necessary marketing**

*Party Day Minus 1 Day*
**Prepare decorations—centerpiece, Guy Fawkes effigy**
**Prepare hamburgers and refrigerate**

*Party Day Morning*
**Set up slide and complete decorations**
**Construct Fun House**
**Get other Halloween games ready**
**Set up buffet table with trivets, serving utensils, plates, and silverware**

*Party Time*
**Guests "slide" into party**
**Everyone passes through Fun House to get to bar**
**Apple games with drinks and hors d'oeuvre**
**Cook hamburgers, set out food**
**After dinner, ghost stories**

## Party Day Minus 2 Weeks

**Invite your friends**   Anyone you know well enough to invite to a BYO party doesn't need a formal invitation. How you get your friends together is more a reflection of personal style than standard form. You may choose to send out an invitation that announces the party and allows the guests to respond with their first and second choice for "course" assignments. Or you may even plan the party casually at a morning coffee or over a bridge game.

The most important thing about your invitation, whether it is by phone or in writing, is that you make it quite clear that it is a BYO party, and to what extent. You as the hostess may provide the meat and nothing else. Or your specialty may be a fabulous dessert, which you would like to prepare for your friends. You may supply beer and wine, and leave it up to them to bring hard liquor, or you need not supply anything other than mixes for their drinks. However you wish to do it, be sure that your friends understand just what is expected. This not only helps to insure a successful party, but it gives them the option of refusing gracefully if they do not wish (or cannot afford) to prepare a dish for a large group.

**Assign the dishes** There are two ways to plan a BYOF party. One is to simply say "Bring a dish that will feed twelve to fifteen people—anything you like." This usually works well for a much larger party, as there always seems to be a broad selection. I would not recommend it for twenty people, however, as you might end up with five salads, four desserts, and one casserole for all twenty people!

Therefore, for a party of this size, it is wise to assign courses, and quite permissible to suggest specific dishes. (See menu above.) Be sure to tell the guests how many people are invited, or you may run very short. If any food is left over, you should insist that the donors take it home, unless they insist that they cannot possibly use it.

To help plan who will bring what, first divide the options into course categories including hors d'oeuvre, condiments, meats, vegetables, salads, and desserts. Dessert is usually the first course for which there are a number of volunteers, so assign two desserts first and you can then tell other guests that the desserts are already spoken for. Knowledge of the culinary expertise of each guest is a big help. Also, plan your serving facilities carefully, taking into consideration such important details as how big the serving dishes are likely to be (and consequently the serving area); how to keep the prepared dishes hot or cold; utensils; wash-up arrangements, etc.

A BYO party is always a buffet. Not only is it less formal and much easier, but everyone enjoys seeing the special casseroles, salads, etc., on display. Much of this pleasure would be lost if dishes were brought in and passed at a seated dinner.

**Costumes or no?** Now is the time to decide whether the guests are invited to come in costume. Here again, an intimate knowledge of your friends is important. If the majority will not feel comfortable in costume, don't force it. It won't work. *You* may dream of a costume party and all of the fun that comes with it, but if most of your friends are not for it, your dream will rapidly turn into a nightmare.

If you do decide on costumes—and I think you *should* for a Halloween party—make sure you plan one for yourself early in the game and get that out of the way. The last thing you need to be doing the night before the party is scurrying around trying to put a costume together!

## Party Day Minus 1 Week

**Collect materials for decorations and games**   Since little time is needed for active involvement in cooking, use some of the surplus time to make the setting right. Halloween tradition is rich in decorative symbols. As everyone knows, they include jack-o'-lanterns, witches on broomsticks, scarecrows, ghosts, and skeletons. And because Halloween falls during harvest time, there are numerous additional materials such as dried corn and exotic gourds, which make splendid tabletop centerpieces and room decorations. Whether your witches are traditionally dressed in grand-mother's old black dress or clad in the modern variety, stretched black Naugahyde, keep the motif related to the time of year by using seasonal flowers, vegetables, and reeds.

Stationery and party stores carry every imaginable accessory for Halloween parties. Unless you have an aversion to them, this is one party where we would recommend taking advantage of plasticized paper plates, napkins, serving dishes, etc. Not only will they save you a great deal of work, but their colors and motifs will add tremendously to the spirit of the party. Buy them now while there is still a good selection available, and buy some cardboard skeletons, ghosts, etc., for wall decorations. This is also the time to buy the prizes for the best costumes.

If you live in the suburbs or country, go to the nearest farm stand and select the most interesting gourds, the most beautiful pumpkins, and the finest ears of decorative corn to make into table, door, and window sill decorations. Look for a very large Hubbard squash, with which you will make your Halloween centerpiece.

You will need a large washtub if you plan to bob for apples.

During this week, you should also locate and borrow a children's slide, if you do not have one. If possible, get a bale of hay to put at the foot of the slide.

**Ghost stories**   The ideal after-dinner entertainment is a series of blood-chilling ghost stories. If one of your guests is a skilled raconteur, you might ask him to tell them, but otherwise, go to the library and get several books of stories. Select the most exciting ones and practice reading them so that you can really scare your friends on Halloween night.

## Party Day Minus 2 Days

Now that the party is drawing near, it is time to check your staples and do the marketing. Refer to the shopping list and be sure that you haven't left anything out.

It is also time to buy the mixes if it is a BYOB party, or the liquor, wine, and beer if you are providing the liquid refreshments yourself.

There may be some guests who do not drink. For them you will want to supply soft drinks and apple cider; don't assume that mixes will do. If it is a true BYOB party, you won't have to worry about whether you have enough vodka, rum, scotch, etc., because those who drink scotch will bring it themselves. Guests who like wine may wish to deposit it with you in advance for chilling. Guests who favor drinks that require several liquors or unusual ingredients are expected to bring all the materials needed. Of course, having a little dry vermouth on hand is a thoughtful touch if you have martini drinkers among your friends.

## Party Day Minus 1 Day

Today, the fun begins. First of all, you are ready to make the centerpiece for your buffet table. One suggestion might be a turkey, made entirely of fruits and vegetables surrounded by fall flowers.

Take the Hubbard squash, lay it on its side on a platter and cut off the stem end. Hollow out the top part of the end so that the small end of the crookneck squash will fit into it. Set the small squash in so that the fat base curves forward like a turkey's head. This can be secured by two long skewers forced through the crookneck squash into the Hubbard squash. With a sharp knife, fashion a beak and a comb from slices of carrots or beets. Affix them, and two raisin eyes, with toothpicks. Make a tail by affixing several stalks of celery, with leaves, to the other end of the big squash. Finally, make wings by laying overlapping spinach leaves against the sides, and holding them in place with toothpicks or hairpins. Just before the party, you can surround your turkey with autumn leaves, chrysanthemums, or both.

Another decoration that is fun to make is a Guy Fawkes man to greet your guests. To make him, first cut a grinning face out of a pumpkin. Then find an old shirt and a pair of trousers and stuff them with hay or straw. Tie the ankles and wrists to keep the sleeves and legs firm. Jam a stick or pole into the bottom of the pumpkin, and stuff the other end down through the neck of the shirt. Tie a colorful bandanna around the "neck," to hide the pole. Put an old straw hat or a ski hat on the "head" and add any other touches your imagination can devise. Set "Guy" on a chair beside your front door with one arm propped out for a handshake—a fine greeting for your guests!

**Prepare hamburgers** Later in the day, you can prepare your hamburgers:

## Grilled Hamburgers Provençale

7 pounds hamburger
2 cups tomato juice
4 medium onions, chopped
4 cloves garlic, minced or crushed
1 tablespoon salt
1 teaspoon pepper
½ cup chopped parsley
4 tablespoons lemon juice

Combine the hamburger and tomato juice. Thoroughly mix in the remaining ingredients. Form into patties, wrap in foil and refrigerate.

### Party Day Morning

**The slide** Set up the children's slide just far enough inside the front door so that the door will open fully. Make a wall of cornstalks leading to the slide so that no one can walk around it. Put a large canvas or piece of plastic at the foot and break up a bale of hay for the guests to land on. If you cannot get hay, put an old mattress down to soften the landing.

**The fun house** It may be impossible for you to do this in a small apartment but if you can arrange it in any way, it is a very successful Halloween stunt. The idea is to make your guests pass through a fun house to get to the bar. Therefore, a hallway leading to the kitchen is ideal. However, a room such as a den that can be darkened by curtains and shades may provide the appropriate passageway.

First construct an alleyway by setting up clothesline or rope handrails on either side. They may be laid along the backs of chairs or other furniture to keep the guests on the path. The fun house need be only 10 or 12 feet long, but everyone must negotiate several obstacles. First put down a piece of thick foam rubber. This is difficult to walk on in the dark, but provides a cushion if someone falls. As they step off that they will run into strands of wet spaghetti hanging from strings stretched above their heads—a cobweb in the dark. Next, the room will seem to tilt as they step on a platform raised at one side and a second tilting the opposite direction. At the end, they emerge through a door or curtain to their reward—the bar. Use your ingenuity to provide other obstacles, and hang skeletons, witches, bats, etc., along the way, lighted by little penlights so as not to brighten the whole passageway.

**Other games** Set your washtub up on a large piece of plastic, newspapers, or whatever will keep the floors driest. It is wise to do the bobbing for apples in the kitchen, or on a tile or linoleum floor. Have a large basket of apples beside it ready for the bobbers, and towels for drying dripping faces.

You may wish to play "pin the heart on the skeleton" or other foolish games. If so, get them ready before the guests arrive.

**Finishing touches** Arrangements of cornstalks, gourds, and apples should be completed in the morning, to allow you time for a rest in the afternoon. And be sure that there is space in your refrigerator for the cold dishes your friends bring. Have oven and hot tray space to keep other things warm, or to complete heating of casseroles, rolls, etc. Prepare the table on which the food will be laid out with trivets, serving utensils, plates, silver, napkins, and, of course, your centerpiece.

## Party Time

As your guests arrive—in full costume, if you've agreed on a costume party—and literally slide into the party, the stage is set for an unusual evening. The host or hostess must remain by the door to relieve the guests of their food and drink contributions or the slide could end in a disaster! Put hot dishes into a warm oven or on the hot plate at once, cold dishes (salads, etc.) into the refrigerator, and hors d'oeuvre right onto the buffet table.

When the guests have removed their coats, they follow "to the bar" signs through the fun house. When everyone has arrived and has a drink, games can be started. Four or five people bob for apples at a time. Others may form a circle. One person holds an apple by squeezing it between chin and neck. The idea is to pass it around the circle without touching it with your hands. "Pin the heart on the skeleton" is simply a Halloween version of "pin the tail on the donkey." These games may sound childish, but you will be surprised how much your friends will enjoy them.

Just before dinner is served, pass out pencils and paper and conduct a secret vote for the best costumes. You may have several categories, and you should award small prizes for each.

An hour or so after the guests arrive, start to grill the hamburgers. (If you are planning to grill them over charcoal, remember to light the coals about a half hour beforehand.) While they are cooking—about five minutes on each side—put the rest of the dishes on the buffet. When everything is ready, call the guests in to help themselves.

After dinner, coffee, and a period of conversation and relaxation, turn out the lights in the living room and light the fire if you have a fireplace. Get everyone to sit in a circle and, by the light of a flashlight (or candle, if you prefer) read your ghost stories.

---

## Election Night Buffet for Sixteen

---

Election night is one night when the emphasis is definitely on the occasion rather than the food. And since the entertainment is provided by the television set, it is a very easy and rewarding night on which to entertain. Because the returns will not become very exciting until later in the evening, you will want to give your guests a delicious but simple dinner fairly early, and then have a supply of snacks and late-night sandwiches for those who stay on until the victory statements are made.

### *Menu*

*Liver pâté-consommé mold with melba toast*
*Alaskan king crab claws with lemon-mayonnaise*
*Polynesian beef and vegetables*
*Rice pilaf*
*Apple crisp*
*Irish (or Spanish) coffee*
*Sandwiches and snacks*

### *SHOPPING LIST*

1  **can Sell's liver pâté**
1  **can consommé**
1  **envelope unflavored gelatin**
2  **8-ounce packages cream cheese (1 for sandwiches)**
2  **packages frozen Alaskan king crab claws**
1  **jar mayonnaise**
3  **lemons**

1 bag yellow onions
1 jar horseradish
3 pounds butter or margarine
5 green peppers (1 for tuna sandwiches)
1 pound mushrooms
2 cans water chestnuts
4 large tomatoes
4 pounds beef tenderloin or top sirloin
1 bottle red wine
Cornstarch
1 bottle soy sauce
2 pounds long-grain rice
5 13½-ounce cans chicken broth
3 pounds tart apples
1 bottle cinnamon sugar
1 orange
1 bottle Grand Marnier
1 bottle amaretto
1 pound brown sugar
1 quart vanilla ice cream
1 loaf pumpernickel bread
1 loaf thin-sliced rye bread
2 loaves thin-sliced white bread
1 loaf firm white bread
2 cans tuna fish
2 pounds thin-sliced corned beef or pastrami
1 jar Dijon mustard
1 bottle dried dill weed
1 stalk celery
1 cucumber
Chopped chives
½ pound lox (or smoked salmon)
Nuts, fritos, pretzels, etc.
Coffee
Whipping cream

*Staples*

Flour
Eggs
Sugar
Prepared mustard
Salt, pepper
Monosodium glutamate (MSG)
Worcestershire sauce

*Bar supplies*

- **2 quarts vodka**
- **1 quart bourbon**
- **1 quart blended whiskey**
- **1 bottle dry vermouth**
- **1 bottle kahlua**
  **Soda water and soft drinks**
- **32 beers**

## TIMETABLE

*Party Day Minus 3 Weeks*
**Send invitations**

*Party Day Minus 1 Week*
**Buy necessary materials for election charts and decorations**
**All foods except beef can be bought at any time this week, as the beef is the only perishable item on the menu**
**Check staples, clean and check serving dishes, china, silver, and glasses**
**Stock bar**
**Plan seating, buy place cards**

*Party Day Minus 2 Days*
**Prepare the hors d'oeuvre and the dessert**

*Party Day Minus 1 Day*
**Set tables**
**Arrange television area**
**Buy beef**
**Remove king crab claws from freezer**

*Party Day Morning*
**Make sandwiches**
**Prepare Polynesian beef and vegetables**
**Whip cream and refrigerate**

*Party Day Afternoon*
**Set out snacks**
**Prepare rice pilaf**
**Crack crab claws**
**Prepare coffee cups**

*Party Time*
**6:30-8 Last-minute preparations and cocktails**
**8-8:30 Dinner**
**8:30 Guests move to television area for Irish coffee**
**10:30 Serve sandwiches and snacks**

## Party Day Minus 3 Weeks

Because election night is a popular night to entertain, you should issue your invitations at least three weeks in advance. Since it is an informal party, you may telephone your friends if you wish, but a printed, fill-in invitation is more festive and serves as a reference as to the hour, the location, etc. Be sure to include R.s.v.p. or "regrets only" with your telephone number. If you do telephone your invitations, send a reminder card a week before election day—just in case.

## Party Day Minus 1 Week

**Buy materials for election charts and decorations** If you have an enormous wall space on which to hang cardboard charts with boxes for all of the states and hourly returns, then sheets of white cardboard and black Magic Markers will be all that you will need. The average home does not generally have so much space, however, and a blackboard and chalk are more practical. If your children do not have a blackboard, try to borrow one from a friend or from the nearest school. If you must buy a board (or two boards), you can plan to use it afterward for your children or grandchildren, or as a gift. In any case, you will need enough blackboard area to list the states in one direction and the candidates in the other. Plenty of chalk and two good erasers complete the list.

If you have, or can get hold of, easels to support the blackboards, that is ideal. If you cannot, then they can be rested on straight chairs or bridge tables.

Of course, all the information will be flashing constantly on your television screen, but it is fun to keep your own tally going, and the opportunities for all sorts of betting are endless.

Few decorations are necessary, but a centerpiece of toy elephants and donkeys is appropriate, and you will find papier-maché and cardboard political symbols at your local party or stationery store.

**Do the marketing** The beef is the only perishable item on the shopping list, so do the rest of the marketing early in the week. Keep the ingredients for each dish together when you put them away, which will save you considerable time when you go to prepare the dishes.

Be sure your silver is polished, and your good china and glassware sparkling. Make sure that tablecloths and napkins are clean and ironed. **Stock the bar**   Make a list of bar supplies and purchase everything. Since it will be a long evening, you should plan to serve beer during the evening unless anyone specifically requests hard liquor. So have plenty of beer on hand—both regular and light.

You will know what cocktails and liquors your friends prefer, so stock the bar accordingly, and have plenty of soft drinks, too. Many people who do enjoy a cocktail do not like to drink liquor after dinner. Do not forget to get a bottle of Irish whiskey for your Irish coffee, or Kahlua if you plan to serve Spanish coffee.

**Seating and place cards**   Plan your seating carefully. If possible, do not have a table or tables in the television area. The best service for sixteen is semi-buffet, so plan on a sideboard or a large table for the serving and set your dining table plus two card tables for the diners. If you do not have a dining room, or space enough for four small tables, your meal may be served as a real buffet, but be sure you have enough small folding tables and side tables to provide each guest with a space to set his plate down.

If the guests *are* to be seated at tables, place cards add a nice touch. If you do not care to use them, tell each guest where he is to sit as he leaves the buffet. This avoids confusion, and you do not end up with all the husbands and wives or the same people that see each other every day at the same table.

## Party Day Minus 2 Days

The hors d'oeuvre and the dessert can be done well ahead, and today is none to soon.

### Liver Pâté-Consommé Mold

1 can consommé
1 envelope unflavored gelatin
1 8-ounce package softened cream cheese
1 can Sell's liver pâté

Heat the consommé slightly. Soften the gelatin in a little water and add to the consommé. Pour a small amount into a small fluted mold, or a mold with a design. Chill. Refrigerate the remainder until thick but not stiff. Beat together the cream cheese, liver pâté, and remaining consommé mixture. Press into mold and chill until ready to serve.

Cut 16 very thin bread slices into quarters (remove crusts first) and toast in a 250-degree oven until golden and very crisp. Store in airtight container.

### *Lemon-Mayonnaise Dip for Alaskan King Crab Claws*

1½ cups mayonnaise
3 teaspoons Worcestershire sauce
1 medium onion, grated
1½ teaspoons horseradish
2½ teaspoons lemon juice

Thoroughly mix all ingredients, cover tightly, and refrigerate.

### *Apple Crisp*

3 pounds tart apples
2 teaspoons grated orange peel
2 teaspoons grated lemon peel
1 teaspoon cinnamon sugar
1 jigger Grand Marnier
1 jigger Amaretto
½ cup white sugar
½ cup brown sugar
1½ cups flour
½ teaspoon salt
2 sticks butter or margarine

Peel, core, and slice the apples. There should be about 10 cups. Arrange the slices in two well-buttered baking dishes. Sprinkle the orange peel, lemon peel, cinnamon sugar and both liqueurs over the apple slices. Mix the white sugar, brown sugar, flour, and salt and cut in the butter with two knives, pastry blender or food processor. When crumbly, spread the mixture evenly over the apples. Bake in a 350-degree oven for 1 hour, or until the topping is golden. When cool, cover with foil and refrigerate.

## Party Day Minus 1 Day

**Set the tables**   Now is the time to set your tables and see how everything looks, and what you may be missing. Make out the place cards and be sure you like your seating plan.

Comfort in the television area is most important. If you have two sets, or can borrow a second one, so much the better. You must have comfortable seats for everyone and plenty of small tables for drinks, snacks, etc. If there are some smokers in the group, put tables with ashtrays at one side, nearest a window, which should be opened slightly at the top.

If you have just one television set you would do well to have it elevated. A couple of wooden crates, covered with a tablecloth, set on top of a sturdy table will raise it so that everyone will have a better view.

**Buy the beef**   When your tables are set, make your last trip to market for the beef, and for any other items you may have overlooked. Do you have fresh candles, hangers for coats, fresh soap for the powder room? This is the time to check those easily forgotten items.

**Defrost crab claws**   Finally, late in the day, remove the king crab claws from the freezer and put them in the refrigerator.

## Party Day Morning

**Make the sandwiches**   Butter pumpernickel slices liberally and heap generously with sliced corned beef or pastrami. Spread with a good herbed or Dijon mustard.

Mix together 2 cans of tuna fish, ½ cup finely chopped green pepper, ½ cup chopped celery, 1 tablespoon chopped chives, 2 tablespoons lemon juice, and mayonnaise to bind. Taste for salt and pepper and spread on white bread.

Spread one slice of rye bread with butter, another with soft cream cheese. Lay slices of lox (or smoked salmon if you can afford it) on the cheese. Sprinkle with freshly ground pepper, and a little dried dill (optional).

Peel and slice cucumber very thin. Cut crusts from thin white bread, spread with mayonnaise and arrange cucumber on bread slices. Sprinkle with salt and pepper and dried dill weed.

Cut all sandwiches in half, place in airtight bags or wrap in foil and refrigerate.

Prepare the Polynesian beef and vegetables.

### *Polynesian Beef and Vegetables*

---

1½ sticks butter or margarine
4 green peppers, chopped
4 large onions, chopped
1 pound mushrooms, sliced
2 cans water chestnuts, sliced
    Salt and pepper
    Monosodium glutamate (optional)
4 large tomatoes, peeled and chopped
4 pounds beef tenderloin or top sirloin
8 tablespoons red wine
4 tablespoons soy sauce
2 tablespoons cornstarch

The vegetables will cook more rapidly and better if you sauté them in two skillets rather than trying to do it in one large pan. Divide the butter and the vegetables between the two skillets and sauté the peppers, onions, mushrooms, and water chestnuts just until tender. Sprinkle with salt, pepper, and monosodium glutamate. Put half the tomatoes in each skillet and cook for 5 minutes. Cut the beef into thin strips. In a separate skillet, sauté the beef in butter, in three or four batches, until brown outside, pink inside. Do not overcook.

Combine all the vegetables with the beef and add the wine, soy sauce, and cornstarch mixed with 3 tablespoons water. Heat for a few moments, cover, and set aside. You do not need to refrigerate this dish.

Whip the cream for Irish coffee and refrigerate.

### Party Day Afternoon

After lunch, open up the cans or bags of snacks and set them out in your hors d'oeuvre dishes.

Crack the defrosted king crab claws, drain away juice, arrange in a circle on a round platter, and refrigerate.

Prepare the rice.

## Rice Pilaf

---

1  stick butter or margarine
2  medium onions, finely chopped
4  cups long-grain rice
8  cups chicken broth
2  teaspoons salt
1  teaspoon pepper

Melt the butter in a large, flameproof casserole. Cook the onion in the butter until golden. Add the rice, stirring, and cook until rice starts to brown. Do not let it burn. Add the chicken broth, salt, and pepper. Cover tightly and bring to a boil. Reduce heat to simmer (as low as possible, or set casserole over a Flame Tamer) and cook until rice absorbs all liquid and grains are soft but separate—about 45 minutes. Leave cover on and set aside.

Put 1 jigger of Irish whiskey and 1 teaspoon of sugar, *or* 1 tablespoon of Kahlua, in each of 16 coffee cups.

### Party Time

Since the raison d'être of this party is to watch the election returns, you should stick fairly close to a schedule. Let us say that you plan dinner for 8 so that you can be settled down to watching the returns by 9.

Just before 7, unmold your liver pâté and surround with the melba toast. Take the crab claw platter out of the refrigerator and put a bowl of the lemon-mayonnaise in the center of the plate. Pass the hors d'oeuvre as soon as all the guests have arrived and have their cocktails.

While they are enjoying their drinks, slip out to the kitchen and put the casserole of rice back over the Flame Tamer, or between warm and low on an electric stove.

At 7:30, preheat your oven to 350 degrees. At 7:40, put the Polynesian beef into the oven. Set the food on the buffet table at 8 and call your guests to dinner. As soon as you remove the beef from the oven, put the apple crisp (uncovered) into the oven at the same temperature.

When you finish eating, excuse yourself and prepare the dessert plates in the kitchen. Slice the apple crisp into 16 portions and top each portion with a scoop of vanilla ice cream. While you are in the kitchen, turn on the coffee maker.

When your guests have finished their dessert, shepherd them in to the television area, and get them settled for the evening's entertainment. Pour the coffee into the prepared cups, top with a heaping spoonful of whipped cream and serve.

About 10:30 or 11, arrange the sandwiches on platters and pass them around. Leave them on the buffet, where people can go and get more as they wish. Set out a stack of small plates or paper plates and plenty of napkins for those who wish to use them. Set out dishes of snacks.

Offer regular and decaffeinated coffee to go with the sandwiches, as well as beer and soft drinks.

---

### Pre-Christmas Open House for Thirty-six to Forty

---

There are certain holidays whose celebration is very much a family tradition—perhaps none more so than Christmas. Various ethnic and religious customs are the basis for much family entertaining. Because Christmas is such a festive season, many hostesses choose this special time of year to share their holiday spirit with their friends. Since an open house is such a flexible party and people can come and go as they wish during this busy season, it is one of the most popular forms of holiday entertaining.

*Menu*

*Chicken livers wrapped in bacon*
*Sour cream and red caviar dip with corn chips*
*Oyster stew      Ham-filled cheese puffs*
*Spinach quiche*
*Cauliflower, broccoli, zucchini and dip*
*Mocha balls      White fruit cake*
*Eggnog, fruit punch, wassail bowl*

*SHOPPING LIST*

*To order*

**9 pints oysters**

*Ingredients for fruit cake, ham-filled cheese puffs, and
   mocha balls*

    5  pounds flour
    3  pounds butter or margarine
    4  dozen eggs
 1½  pounds Swiss cheese
    1  pound ham slice
    1  jar Dijon mustard
    2  12-ounce packages semisweet chocolate bits
    2  pounds confectioners' sugar
    1  jar instant coffee
    1  bottle brandy
    1  bottle vanilla extract
    1  bag chopped pecans
    1  can baking powder
    4  pounds assorted candied fruits
    4  cans candied whole cherries
    4  boxes white seedless raisins
    1  bottle dark rum
    2  pounds granulated sugar

*Other ingredients*

    3  2-ounce jars red caviar
    3  ½-pint cartons sour cream
    3  packages chips for dip
    3  pints chicken livers
    2  pounds bacon
    3  pints heavy cream
    5  quarts medium cream (for eggnog and oyster stew)
    2  quarts milk
    3  dozen eggs
    6  packages frozen chopped spinach
    6  frozen pie crusts
    1  bunch parsley
    1  quart plain yogurt
 1½  pounds feta cheese
    1  dozen apples
    3  bunches broccoli
    3  heads cauliflower
    4  medium zucchini
    1  bunch asparagus (if available)
    3  boxes cherry tomatoes
    6  aluminum pie plates

1 can crushed pineapple
1 pint cranberry juice
1 small can frozen orange juice
1 bottle lemon juice
1 bottle maraschino cherries
1 quart soda water

*Staples*

Mayonnaise
Lemon juice
Curry powder
Tabasco sauce
Nutmeg
Tarragon
Salt
Pepper
Ground ginger
Whole cloves
Allspice
Stick cinnamon
Cayenne pepper
Paprika
Toothpicks
Tea
Sugar

*Liquor for eggnog and wassail bowl*

1 quart light rum, brandy or bourbon
1 pint brandy
4 bottles sherry

## TIMETABLE

*Party Day Minus 3 Weeks*
Plan party
Send invitations

*Party Day Minus 2 Weeks*
Order necessary equipment
Order oysters
Buy ingredients for cheese puffs and mocha balls and
    prepare and freeze these dishes
Make fruit cake

*Party Day Minus 1 Week*
**Wash and polish china, crystal, silver**
**Start Christmas decorations other than greens**

*Party Day Minus 3 Days*
**Buy, set up and decorate tree (if not to be trimmed at party)**
**Buy or cut holly, evergreens, finish decorations**

*Party Day Minus 2 Days*
**Buy all remaining food**
**Check recipes; be sure you have seasonings, staples**

*Party Day Minus 1 Day*
**Obtain oysters and rented equipment**
**Arrange flowers, if necessary**
**Prepare raw vegetables and dip and refrigerate**
**Make spinach quiches and refrigerate**
**Prepare chicken livers in bacon and refrigerate**
**Clear space and set buffet table**

*Party Day Morning*
**Remove cheese puffs and mocha balls from freezer**
**Remove fruit cake and quiches from refrigerator**
**Arrange vegetables on platters**
**Mix sour cream and caviar**
**Prepare eggnog, wassail bowl, and fruit punch**
**Set out serving dishes**

*Party Time*
**Food service—three separate servings**
**Entertainment—tree trimming (if not done beforehand)**
**Carols**

## Party Day Minus 3 Weeks

**Plan the time for your party**  To begin with, schedule your open house at the most convenient time possible. If most of your guests commute to work and your party is planned for a weekday evening, allow time for them to get home. Remember, too, that your open house will be competing with the extraordinary number of events and activities that go hand in hand with Christmas—shopping, caroling, sleigh rides, gift-wrapping, etc.

If you decide on a weekday for your party, *early* evening, perhaps 8 to 10:30 is the best time. If the weekend before Christmas is your choice, a late afternoon party—say, 4 to 8—allowing people to go on to a later party or a family gathering is better.

Christmas Eve is a lovely time to have an open house, but you may get a lot of refusals from people who are just too busy to socialize. To insure that most of your friends will accept, plan a Christmas Eve party for *early* suppertime, say from 5 until 9. For the sake of those who will be up at the crack of dawn with children or grandchildren, I suggest that you end the party early enough to allow them a good night's sleep. In the true spirit of Christmas, include your friends' children and visiting relatives in the invitation. Remember that some of your friends will have to get home in time to make last minute preparations. There are always toys to be assembled, stockings to be filled, and many other chores to be done before Mom and Dad can fall in for their "long winter's nap."

Four hours is about the maximum time that you can be expected to juggle people coming and going, to keep the food fresh, hot and appetizing, and to keep the beverages flowing. So whichever day, and part of the day, you select for your open house, keep it to no more than four hours.

Although much of your Christmas festivity will involve family and close friends, remember that it is an ideal opportunity to entertain other friends who spend Christmas alone. "Being home for the holidays" is more than just a custom in America. It is a way of life. When you know someone is alone, Christmas is the time to bring them into your family.

**Send invitations** Invitations for holiday parties should be mailed *at least* three weeks ahead of time. A written invitation to serve as a reminder and to provide the information about time, address, etc., is essential during the busy Christmas/Hanukkah season.

The most popular and practical invitation (unless you wish to be very formal and have engraved invitations made) is the attractive, decorated, fill-in invitation found in every stationery store. Simply choose the one that suits you—and the occasion—the best.

Open house invitations do not always include an R.s.v.p. Since the hours are so flexible, it is assumed that *most* of the invitees will be able to attend, at least for a short time. However, if you feel that you must have an approximate estimate of guests, I suggest that you write "regrets only" followed by your telephone number at the bottom of the invitation. This should elicit enough replies so that you will have quite a good idea of how many to expect.

I'd like to make a suggestion about selecting your invitations: The *reason* for the celebration of Christmas is often overlooked at this time.

Perhaps the best, or should I say the worst, example of this offense is the use of the word "Xmas," commonly understood to mean Christmas. "Xmas" literally takes Christ out of Christmas by substituting the letter "x." It is inexcusable that we allow the presence of Christ to be removed from this holiday with a vulgar abbreviation. One way we can help put Christ back into Christmas is to refuse to buy invitations—or Christmas cards—that use the abbreviation.

**Plan the menu**   There are countless Christmas delicacies that may be added to standard entertainment fare. However, at an open house your choice of menu is confined to those foods that will survive prolonged service. Since your invitation allows considerable leeway for your guests' arrival, the menu must be tailored accordingly. Foods that must be kept hot should be prepared and served in such a way that there will be a constant supply throughout the party. If you are brave enough to serve a soufflé or even a hot quiche, your best bet is to prepare three or four identical dishes. A two-quart soufflé will serve approximately eight people. If you expect to serve forty guests over an extended period of time, five separate two-quart soufflés brought out at regular intervals, instead of two five-quart soufflés, would make much more sense. It is easier to bake five soufflés at different times, and have all of them turn out well, than it is to keep one or two large soufflés fluffy and hot throughout the party.

Of course this prolonged service will require some careful preparation and it would not be wise to try it without some part-time help, just to keep the food flowing and the supply constant.

I strongly suggest avoiding intricate and delicate foods for an open house—dishes that can be prepared and frozen in advance are best for this kind of party. At Christmas time, some of your guests may have had some food at another party before coming to your open house, or they may be going on to a later party. Light hors d'ouevre, dips, and salads, along with one or two more substantial dishes will provide something for everyone. Perhaps you may have some family recipes for Christmas treats. This is the time to bring them out and share them with your friends!

**Line up the necessary equipment**   Very few of us have enough china, crystal, and silver to serve forty people. So we must make plans to *acquire* enough for our Christmas open house.

## Party Day Minus Two Weeks

For smaller holiday parties, I would recommend using your very finest china, your gold-rimmed glasses, and your damask napkins—those treasures that are likely to be hidden away the rest of the year. But for a large party there are two courses open to you. First, you may go to a party supply service and rent the necessary equipment. The best companies can offer you a selection of china and glassware, ranging from thick white "coffee shop" mugs to very good quality china. They can also provide you with platters, serving dishes, tables, chairs, decorations, and almost everything you will need. But this will, of course, cost a considerable amount, depending on the equipment you rent.

The second possibility is to turn to paper and plastic. If you do this, it must be of the best quality you can find. Full-size, heavy dinner plates, 15 × 17-inch napkins, and rigid plastic glasses will insure your guests' comfort and pleasure. Most holiday plate patterns have matching tablecloths, serving dishes, and even centerpieces to go with them. And paper plates undeniably have the advantage of making the clean-up easy.

Outside of large bowls for the punch, eggnog, and wassail, the only other special equipment you will need is a table large enough for your buffet. If you have a dining table and sideboard that will hold all your dishes and the punch bowls, that is fine. But if not, you must plan to rent a folding table at this time. Or, if you have wooden sawhorses in your basement, three or four smooth planks can be laid across them and, covered with a plastic under-mat and a pretty cloth, they will make a very serviceable buffet table.

**Order oysters**   Oysters are in great demand at Christmas time, so you should ask your fish market to reserve 9 pints of oysters for the day before your party.

Purchase ingredients and prepare fruit cake and dishes to be frozen.

### White Fruit Cake

(This recipe is for one cake that serves ten to twelve. It would be best to make four separate recipes—four cakes—to serve forty people.)

¼  **pound butter**
 1  **cup sugar**
 5  **eggs**
 2  **cups plus 4 tablespoons sifted flour**
⅛  **teaspoon salt**
 2  **teaspoons baking powder**
 1  **pound assorted candied fruits**

1 can candied whole cherries
1 box white seedless raisins
8 tablespoons dark rum

Cream the butter with the sugar. Beat in the eggs one at a time. Add the 2 cups flour, salt, and baking powder. Mix together the candied fruits, raisins, and 4 tablespoons flour and add to batter. Pour into a greased 10-inch tube pan. Bake for 1½ hours at 350 degrees. After 15 minutes, add 2 tablespoons dark rum. After next ½ hour, add 2 tablespoons rum. After ½ hour more, add 2 tablespoons rum. When cake is done, sprinkle on 2 more tablespoons rum. When cool, wrap in foil and keep in cool place. Fruit cake improves when it is kept for some time before using.

### Ham-filled Cheese Puffs

(This recipe makes 48 puffs. Double recipe, if desired.)

¼ pound butter
3 cups flour
1 dozen eggs
1½ pounds Swiss cheese, grated, about 2⅔ cups
⅔ pound ham, trimmed of fat and finely diced
4 tablespoons Dijon mustard

In a saucepan, combine the butter with 3 cups water. Bring to a boil and add the flour. Stir until mixture pulls away from sides of pan. Put into electric mixer and add the eggs, one at a time. Beat 5 minutes at high speed. Stir in 2 cups grated cheese.

With a tablespoon, shape 48 rounds of the dough and put on cooky sheets. Dampen a finger and make a large depression in each round. Mix the ham and mustard and spoon onto rounds of dough. Dot with butter. Sprinkle with remaining ⅔ cup grated cheese. Bake at 375 degrees for 30 to 40 minutes. When cool, wrap in foil and freeze.

### Mocha Balls

2 12-ounce packages semisweet chocolate bits
8 egg yolks

3 cups confectioners' sugar
1 pound soft butter or margarine
4 teaspoons instant coffee
8 tablespoons brandy
4 teaspoons vanilla extract
   Chopped pecans

Melt the chocolate bits. Beat the egg yolks and gradually add the confectioners' sugar, beating until smooth. Beat in the butter.

Dissolve the instant coffee in the brandy and add the vanilla. Combine with egg yolks and sugar. Add the melted chocolate, mix thoroughly, and chill. Shape into little balls and roll in chopped pecans. Wrap in foil and freeze.

## Party Day Minus 1 Week

**Wash and polish china, crystal, and silver**   Even though you may decide to use plasticized plates and paper napkins, you will surely want to use some of the treasures that go so well with Christmas: silver platters and serving dishes, silver candlesticks or candelabra, a lovely china compote to hold a Christmas fruit pyramid, your best crystal wine or champagne glasses for one holiday toast, etc. A week before the party, take all these things out, wash them thoroughly, polish the silver until it gleams and cover with plastic.

**Start Christmas decorations other than greens**   Decide which old and beloved Christmas decorations you want to use, and put up those that do not need fresh greens to complete them. You can tie colorful bows on your wall sconces, fasten tiny colored balls and a bright red bow onto some of your house plants, and replace the picture over your fireplace with a simple felt cutout picture of the three kings, or of children hanging their stockings at a felt fireplace. Now is the time to order flowers and greens from your florist.

During this week you can make a new decoration for your sideboard or buffet, or to hang from a chandelier. Here are instructions for two that we think are especially festive-looking.

## Choirboy and Choirgirl Wreath

Make a tiny hole in the narrow end of an egg and a larger hole three-quarters of the way down toward the rounded end. Blow out the contents. Rinse and drain. Do this with eight eggs.

Glue scraps of knitting or embroidery yarn on the pointed ends, fashioning various hair styles—braids, bangs, etc.

With Magic Markers, draw faces on the eggs using the larger hole as the mouth. Make red lips around the hole, use blue or brown for eyes, black for lashes and eyebrows, pink for the cheeks, etc.

Fashion peaked caps for some, using two triangles of felt stitched together at the sides. Others might have bows on their heads, a scarf, or a little felt bonnet. Trim the hats or tie back the hair with narrow Christmas braid. Make bows of red ribbon and glue below the mouths, like choirboys' bows. Run strong thread through the hair or hat and suspend from a round Styrofoam wreath, wrapped in ribbons or covered with green roping or rope tinsel. Hang the wreath from a chandelier, a beam, or a doorway.

### Cookie Tree for Buffet

Using ¼-inch plywood, cut fine 1-inch-wide strips in the following lengths: 3 feet, 2 feet, 20 inches, 16 inches, 12 inches.

Sand and paint the strips green or red. Shape the ends of the four shorter strips into a point. (You may also use pine strips, and varnish instead of paint.)

Spacing them evenly, lay the four shorter strips across the longest strip, with the 12-inch strip at the top and the 2-foot strip at the bottom, forming a "tree." Glue or screw into position.

Make at least twenty-four gingerbread cookies in different Christmas shapes—stars, trees, Santa Claus, Mrs. Santa Claus, bells, etc. Before baking, make a hole in the top of each cooky with a plastic straw. When the cookies are baked and cooled insert a 6-inch piece of narrow red ribbon in each hole and decorate the figures with white fosting.

Paint a large flowerpot red and fill it with pebbles or sand. Bury the "trunk" of the tree well into the fill. Hang the cookies from the cross pieces—eight on the bottom "branches," six on the next two, and four on the short top "branch."

Shine eight very red apples, cut a wedge out of the stem end, and jam the apples onto the pointed ends of the branches. With a red ribbon, tie on a sprig of greens to hide the top of the "trunk," lay some greens around the base to hide the pebbles, and lo and behold, your cookie tree is completed!

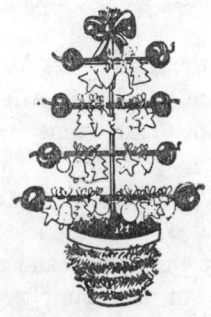

## Party Day Minus 3 Days

If you have not already done so, now is the time to buy (or cut) and set up your Christmas tree. You can decorate it now yourself, or put on the lights and the top decoration and leave the rest to your guests as part of the entertainment.

Every family has its own favorite decorating scheme, but perhaps this is the first year you have had a home of your own, or the first time you have entertained during the holidays, so that you want to make a special effort. Open fires, candlelit rooms, carols and Christmas music as a background, and a certain formality are the basic elements that create a Christmas atmosphere. Red, green, and white mean Christmas to everyone and are the perfect colors, but vary them with accents of silver, gold, pink, or blue. Evergreens, holly, and wreaths of nuts or flowers are in keeping with the current emphasis on natural things and they all help to capture the Christmas spirit. Poinsettias, carnations, and red roses are the choice flowers for the season. Candles, strategically placed, add a tremendous amount of atmosphere and symbolize the glow of Christmas. Of course, you must be *very* careful not to have lighted candles near greens or other flammable materials.

## Party Day Minus 2 Days

This is the time to check all your remaining recipes carefully and make sure that your supply of staples is adequate and that you have all the seasonings you will need. Then, using the shopping list on pp. 207–209, spend the morning making your purchases. For this particular menu, all food may be bought now except the oysters that you ordered for the day before the party.

Insofar as possible, store the ingredients for each recipe close to each other, and nearest the area in which you will prepare the dish. A little forethought now will save considerable time the next day.

## Party Day Minus 1 Day

Early in the morning pick up the oysters and any rented equipment that is not to be delivered. Call your party supplier and/or caterer to be sure that these things *will* be delivered in time. If you are planning on fresh flowers for your table, buy them now and arrange them as soon as you get home.

In the afternoon, you can prepare, or partly prepare, most of the dishes on your menu.

*Raw Vegetables and Dip*

3 bunches broccoli
3 heads cauliflower
4 medium zucchini
1 bunch asparagus (if available)
3 boxes cherry tomatoes
1 cup mayonnaise
1 tablespoon Dijon mustard
1 tablespoon lemon juice
2 teaspoons curry powder
  Tabasco sauce

Break the broccoli and cauliflower into flowerets. Cut the zucchini into 3-inch lengths and then into ½-inch strips. Cut off and discard all but about 2 top inches of asparagus stalks. Stem the cherry tomatoes. Put all the vegetables except tomatoes into bowls of cold water and store in the refrigerator.

Mix the remaining ingredients for the dip. Stir well and refrigerate.

### Chicken Livers in Bacon

3 pints chicken livers
¼ pound butter
2 pounds bacon

Trim fat from chicken livers and sauté gently in two frying pans, using ½ stick of butter in each. Cook only until they are firm and still red in the center. Wrap each liver in ½ strip bacon and secure with a toothpick. Cover and refrigerate.

### Spinach Quiche (*Six 9-inch quiches*)

6 packages frozen chopped spinach
6 frozen pie crusts
2 egg yolks
1 teaspoon nutmeg
6 teaspoons dried tarragon
6 tablespoons lemon juice
Salt and pepper to taste
½ cup chopped parsley
1½ pounds feta cheese
1 dozen eggs
6 cups heavy cream
3 cups plain yogurt

Thaw and drain the spinach.

Thaw and bake the pie crusts for 15 minutes in a 450-degree oven, pricking the crusts in several places. Brush each with beaten egg yolk and return to oven for two minutes, to seal and crisp shells.

Combine nutmeg, tarragon, lemon juice, salt, pepper, and parsley and mix into the spinach. Spoon the spinach into pie shells and sprinkle each with ½ cup feta cheese.

Beat the 12 eggs lightly and add the cream and yogurt, mixing well.

Pour the mixture evenly over each quiche. Bake in a 300-degree oven for 30 minutes. Cool, cover lightly, and refrigerate.

**The buffet table** If you are not too tired, it is a good idea to prepare your buffet table the evening before the party. By doing this you can check to see what may be missing, whether you need more flowers, how the lines will form so that you can rearrange the furniture if necessary, etc. Unlike most buffet situations where each course is served, consumed, and removed to be followed by the next course and so on, an open house requires that all courses, from hors d'oeuvre to coffee and dessert be made available to your guests simultaneously.

People will be coming in while others who may still be present will have already eaten. A little extra planning, therefore, is essential in keeping an aging party looking young and fresh.

### Party Day Morning

The first thing to do the morning of the party is to remove the cheese puffs and the mocha balls from the freezer. Remove fruit cake and quiches from refrigerator.

Then arrange one-third of the vegetables on a platter, and place a small bowl of dip in the center. If you have room in the refrigerator, keep the platter there, but it may be set on the buffet and covered with foil or plastic wrap.

Mix ½ pint sour cream with a 2-ounce jar of red caviar. Keep in refrigerator.

Lay out all the platters, bowls and serving utensils you will need for the party.

The eggnog should be prepared in the morning, as it must stand for several hours to "ripen." The wassail bowl spices may also be mixed early in the day, and the apples may be cored and baked in a moderate oven until tender but still firm, but the remaining ingredients must be combined and heated when the party is starting.

The fruit punch may be prepared, too, except for adding soda water.

### Eggnog

12 eggs, separated
 1 pound confectioners' sugar
 4 cups light rum, brandy, or bourbon
 2 quarts medium cream
   Nutmeg

Beat the egg yolks until lemon-colored. Beat in the sugar and slowly add 2 cups liquor. Let stand for at least 1 hour. Then add 2 more cups liquor and the cream. Cover and refrigerate for at least 3 hours.

Just before serving, beat the egg whites until stiff and fold into the liquid. Sprinkle with nutmeg.

### Wassail Bowl

 4 cups sugar
 1 tablespoon nutmeg
 2 teaspoons ground ginger
 6 whole cloves
¼ teaspoon allspice
 1 stick cinnamon
 1 dozen eggs, separated
 4 bottles sherry
 2 cups brandy
12 baked apples

Combine the sugar and spices with 1 cup water and boil for 5 minutes. Just before the party, beat the egg yolks until lemon-colored and beat the whites until stiff. Fold the whites into the yolks. Add sugar and spice mixture and bring to a boil. In separate pots, bring the sherry and brandy to a boil. Stir sherry slowly into egg mixture. Then add brandy. Just before serving, add the baked apples.

## Non-alcoholic Fruit Punch

1½  cups sugar
1½  cups water
 2  cups strong tea
 1  can crushed pineapple
 3  cups cranberry juice
 6  tablespoons lemon juice
 1  can frozen orange juice (6 oz. size)
 1  quart soda water
 1   bottle maraschino cherries

Boil sugar and water together for 10 minutes and add tea. When cool, add crushed pineapple, cranberry juice, and lemon juice. Mix frozen orange juice according to directions on can and add. Chill.

Just before serving, add 1 quart soda water and maraschino cherries. Pour over cake of ice in punch bowl.

### Party Time

You should plan to offer three complete servings during the party hours so that every guest, no matter what time he comes or goes, will have an opportunity to enjoy each of your dishes.

Just before the guests are due, the first serving of each dish should be set out on the buffet. The caviar and sour cream dip should be placed in the center of a platter and surrounded with chips.

The chicken livers should be broiled about 4 inches from the flame and turned several times until the bacon is crisp. This will take 5 or 6 minutes.

The quiches and cheese puffs should be warmed for 15 minutes in a 350-degree oven.

The hot dishes should be served in chafing dishes or set out on an electric hot plate.

Oyster stew takes only a few minutes to prepare, and should not be served until a number of people are there to enjoy it. Each batch should be prepared separately, and will provide approximately 16 small servings.

## *Oyster Stew*

1 **stick butter or margarine**
3 **cups oysters**
2 **cups milk**
4 **cups medium cream**
 **Salt and pepper to taste**
 **Cayenne pepper**
 **Paprika**

Melt the butter and sauté the oysters until edges curl, about 3 minutes. Add the milk and cream and bring the mixture to a boil. Season with salt, pepper, and cayenne and sprinkle with paprika.

During the party, you must keep an eye constantly on the buffet table to be sure that there are no empty platters and that a new supply of food keeps coming from the kitchen. The same attention must be paid to the eggnog, punch and wassail bowls, which should be refilled before they are completely empty.

**Entertainment** Although it is not necessary to plan any special entertainment at an open house, where people are coming and going, there is one form of entertainment that is traditional at a Christmas party—tree trimming.

Many people feel that they should take their hostess a gift, especially at Christmas time. Calling your open house a "Tree Trimming Party" will solve their problem. Most will bring an ornament for your tree. But whether they do or not, trimming your tree can be fun for everyone. Put out baskets of ornaments, boxes of tinsel, and bowls of cranberries and popcorn with a supply of waxed thread and needles. The youngsters present will be kept busy and happy making chains of either or both. There is always room for one more ornament, another handful of tinsel or an extra strand of roping, so the trimming will last throughout the party.

The other traditional entertainment is carol singing. If you are fortunate enough to have a family member or friend who plays a guitar or the piano, ask him, in advance, if he would be willing to lead the singing. Get three or four strong voices to lead, and you will find that your guests will join in heartily and enthusiastically. Nothing sends people away happier and more filled with Christmas spirit than a chance to sing the beloved, familiar carols.

# 11

# *Children's Parties*

When preparing to give a party for your youngster, there are two essential things to remember: Careful planning is crucial, and your child *must* be involved from the outset. Too often, parents make all the decisions, leaving the child to be merely a guest at his or her own party.

Even with a very young child, it's a good idea to discuss the theme and event around which the party will be planned. It helps to bring a little background to the occasion. Tell the child something about the history of St. Valentine, Hanukkah, St. Patrick, Independence Day, or whatever, and how and why the day has traditionally been celebrated. Youngsters are truly creative; once they have accepted an idea, they will come back with incredible suggestions and innovations.

Getting the child involved also establishes his or her responsibility, and making the occasion a success provides a valuable social lesson: planning, cooperating, working and interacting with his peers as well as his parents. Parties for young children also provide one of the earliest occasions at which they can be taught "party manners"—the arts of greeting, saying good-by, and thank you.

Children's parties are much like any others in that they require careful planning and advance preparation if they are to be a success. In addition, there are certain limitations—the frequently short attention span of youngsters, and the fact that small children tire easily, among others. Far more than at adult parties, every moment of a small child's party should be filled with an organized activity, except possibly for the first few minutes when the excitement of arriving at the party is itself enough to keep the interest and provide the action that is so necessary. As children get older, they are of course more able to make their own entertainment and the structure may become much looser, but even for the teenagers, plenty of *action,* whether it's provided by their own activity (dancing, for example) or by other entertainment (movies, spectator sports, etc.) is the key to success.

## TIMETABLE

*Party Day Minus 3 Weeks*
Select a theme
Get the family involved
Choose a location
Make up the guest list
Establish a budget
Hire entertainers

*Party Day Minus 2 Weeks*
Send out the invitations
Arrange for rental of equipment if necessary

*Party Day Minus 1 Week*
Prepare the location
Order food
Purchase foods that can be frozen and nonperishable
    foods
Buy decorations and favors

*Party Day Minus 2 Days*
Buy ingredients for foods to be prepared at home

*Party Day Minus 1 Day*
Decorate the party rooms
Check with caterers and suppliers
Prepare all foods that can be done ahead

*Party Day Morning*
Pick up last-minute items and catered food
Make sandwiches
Remove previously prepared food from freezer
Set the table
Blow up balloons
Prepare coat room and bathroom

*Party Time*
The first stage—greetings and gifts
The second stage—games and contests
The third stage—entertainment and/or outings
The fourth stage—refreshments

## Party Day Minus 3 Weeks

**Select a theme**   Almost any excuse will do for a party. There are the standards: Christmas, Hanukkah, birthday, Halloween, pajama and Sweet Sixteen. If it's seasonal—or in celebration of a definite event—a motif may be immediately apparent. Halloween, for example, is almost always a costume party, and the decorations are black and orange. There are other parties, however, that do not spark distinct or immediate theme solutions, such as a birthday.

I have listed below a number of events and possible themes around which you might wish to build a party.

### *Occasions to Celebrate*

| | |
|---|---|
| Birthday | Saint Patrick's day |
| Bar mitzvah/confirmation | Easter |
| Sweet sixteen | July fourth |
| End of school | Halloween |
| Going away (to camp, school, etc.) | Thanksgiving |
| | Christmas |
| Valentine's day | Hanukkah |

### *Themes/Motifs*

| | |
|---|---|
| Around the world | Monsters |
| Biblical | Nautical |
| Circus | Pirate |
| Comic book characters | Railroad |
| Dance—ethnic & square | Space—Star Wars & Star Trek |
| Fairy tales | Sports |
| Historical | Safari |
| Kings & Queens | TV characters—muppets |
| Magic | Zoo/animals |

**Get the family involved**   After deciding on the event and theme with your child, it is time to call a meeting of all of the family members who will be involved to get some definite input and help. With small families —particularly an only child—you might include the child's closest friend(s).

This is also the time to mention the problem of slighting your other children. If, for example, you are planning a birthday party for twelve-year-old Stephen, do not overlook the sensitivity of a small sister or brother. Try not to make *too* much of the exclusiveness of celebrating just Stephen's birthday. Wherever possible, include Sally and Johnny in all the planning—it helps keep a potentially tense situation much calmer.

There are many things that children can do to help. An artistic child might be put in charge of decorations. A sports lover might plan and collect equipment for outdoor games. A big cleaning task might be given to a team of your children and their friends. Whatever the talents and responsibilities are, division of labor—taking as much as possible off your shoulders—is desirable. And, once again, it allows the youngsters to feel they are an important part of the event.

**Choose a location** Deciding on a realistic locale is the first consideration. A cookout for thirty would obviously be impossible if yard facilities are limited. Also avoid an area where you will spend the entire day of the party policing the children with, "Don't sit there," "Don't touch that." If the party is to be indoors, the best choice is some area in your home that is easily stripped of furniture. Living rooms are a rather risky venture—especially if they are decorated with your finest possessions. Kitchens are dangerous for obvious reasons and often create traffic jams, as well as creating interference with food preparation. The best alternatives are playrooms, garages, cellars, and enclosed porches.

You'll need enough space for eating, game playing, gift opening, and entertainment. Try to choose an area with natural boundaries and points of segregation from the rest of the house. From this point of view, the garage or basement is ideal.

If there is not sufficient space in your own home, try to "borrow" the yard or the basement of a relative or close friend for the occasion. For a very large party, you may choose to rent space—the local Grange, a church or synagogue's social rooms, the Y, or a school hall are logical choices. A country club, if you belong to one, is a good possibility because of the facilities provided.

**Make up the guest list** From the beginning, set a number that is manageable and affordable, and, within reason, stick to it. Whatever the magic number (and it should be agreed to by your youngsters), be prepared to cut the invitations off at your figure. Be wary of the famous last words "Oh, Mom, just a few friends," or "just the team," or "just my class."

After establishing how many you can handle and afford, give the child several days to make up the list. Some advice and direction from you will help to get it completed quickly.

If another one of your children is helping out substantially, allow him or her to invite *a* friend. If the hostess is twelve for example, and her nine-year-old brother is doing a lot of the work, this will provide him with an extra incentive. As a basic rule, however, keep the majority of the guests within the same age group.

When inviting just one or two children from a family, but not others, remember to make that clear by the plainly written address. Age, or membership in the same class or club, is an important criterion for which ones will be invited. In most cases, all the brothers and sisters within a year or two of the host or hostess should be included.

Usually it is impossible to invite your child's entire class to a party. But it's a nice gesture to send enough cupcakes or brownies to school with your child the day before or after the party so that all of his classmates can share a little celebration with him during recess or at a time agreed upon with his teacher.

**Establish a budget**   Once the invitation list is completed and the theme selected, a budget should be established. First of all, estimate how much you really want to spend and what you can afford to spend. This means budgeting everything: refreshments for chaperoning parents and helpers, cleanup equipment, decorations, food, beverages, entertainment, invitations, stamps, prizes, favors, and a host of smaller items.

Armed with the figures, sit down with your child and the family and figure out how much it will cost per head. If the expenditures go higher than planned, you must reduce the costs by cutting the list, and by reconsidering the menu and the kinds of invitations and decorations you have chosen. For example, telephoned invitations may be issued if printed ones are too expensive.

When you see how much you can allow for food, the menu is ready to be planned. There are suggestions throughout the chapter, particularly on pp. 231–232, 235, and 244–245.

I suggest figuring an additional 10 percent into the budget for the cost of those additional things that always seem to come up, no matter how meticulous the planning.

Someone, presumably one of the parents, should keep track of all money spent. If he is old enough, the host should be involved with this process. It is a good and practical lesson. Your child will know what the picture is—dime for dime. If the budget becomes strained, he will be aware of the need to cut back. When certain items do have to be sacrificed, he will be a part of the decision as to what and where. Only an informed child can understand what the situation is.

**Hire entertainers**   If you are hiring a professional entertainer such as a magician, be certain that you book him well in advance. Confirm the date with a deposit check and a letter discussing what you expect: show time, setup needs, how long you expect the show to go on, distribution of prizes, children's names, dressing facilities, etc.

## Party Day Minus 2 Weeks

**Send out the invitations** Invitations for children's parties need not be expensive or elaborate. Your party or stationery store sells them in varying styles, colors, and themes for every conceivable occasion.

A written invitation does more than just invite. It serves as a reminder as to who is giving the party, why, when, where, at what time, etc. The invitation may even establish the theme from the very beginning—a circus costume party, for example. A written R.s.v.p. is usually not requested. The best way to get responses quickly is by giving a telephone number to call and perhaps a suggested time to make the call.

---

OCCASION: *Lora Jean's 9th birthday*
TIME: *1-4, Saturday, November 11, 1981*
PLACE: *666 Verne Street*

*It's a circus, so come as a clown or a fat
lady, or a muscle man, or whatever you like.
R.s.v.p. (or please answer): 666-6666, between
7:30 and 9:30 P.M.*

---

If transportation to or from the party is arranged, add appropriate instructions. If special equipment such as sneakers, bathing suits, towels, or sports equipment is necessary, make that clear, too.

The time section of the invitation supplies very important information. It tells parents not only what time their child has to be at the party, but what time to expect him home. The young guest knows when the party will break up, and he and his parents can decide whether they will pick him up or whether he will get a ride home with a friend.

Parties for young children should never be too long—two to three hours at most. Long parties are expensive, exhausting, and tend to end with a whimper—or a fracas. Send the children home begging for more; they'll have nothing but happy memories and you'll have rave reviews.

When you're buying invitations, purchase a few extra. It's nice to send them to aunts, uncles, grandparents, and godparents who cannot possibly attend. Or you might send an invitation *after* the party with a few memorable snapshots enclosed—it's a truly considerate way of including shut-ins and distant relatives. In any event, a few extra invitations are always fun for scrapbook mementos as well as for last-minute guests.

If it's a birthday party, I suggest that you purchase some thank-you-note stationery or cards at the time you buy your invitations. You'll want your child to get thank-yous out promptly for gifts received by mail, and having the notes available will encourage him to do so. He need *not,* however, write notes to those he has thanked in person.

**Homemade invitations**    Making the invitations by hand is a good rainy day project and it builds enthusiasm and anticipation. You are bound in design only by the limits of your children's imagination and creativity. For example, a cardboard tube from inside a wax-paper roll can be cut into shorter lengths, decorated and used to hold a scrolled invitation made from construction paper. A clothespin soldier can be enclosed to hold an invitation card, or an origami (folded paper) animal may have the written invitation inside—ideas to start the party off with imagination. *Making it fun is part of the fun.* For other ideas, try your local library craft section. There are also some suggestions in the bibliography.

You are the best judge of your child's handwriting. If he does address —or helps to address—the invitations, screen them before they go out. It may well avoid confusion and embarrassment.

If it's basically a neighborhood affair, naturally you don't have to mail the invitations. They can be delivered by hand or they can be telephoned.

**Arrange for rental of equipment if necessary**    For seated meals, it may be necessary to rent chairs and tables. Rentable children's tables are designed with expandable legs so that they can be fixed for any age and size.

Movie projectors and record players or tape decks should be reserved well in advance—especially if the party is to be held on a Saturday.

If the budget allows, you can purchase or rent up to four hours of uninterrupted taped music, in any style. More economically, however, the host or hostess can borrow some of the latest from friends. Make certain that all borrowed tapes and records are labeled in advance. This is the only way to insure their proper return.

Someone who has had previous experience with a projector should be assigned to showing movies. A similarly qualified person should supervise all of the record entertainment. To insure the safety of the sound system, this same person (or persons) should manage it throughout the party. Good candidates for this duty: an older brother or sister, a close neighbor who is familiar with the type of equipment, or an adult relative.

If you are planning on games or sports for which you do not have the proper equipment, now is the time to locate it. Use the yellow pages, and go to your local sports stores to see if they have equipment available for rental. You may also go to friends and relatives to borrow baseball mitts, croquet sets, etc., but be sure to do it now, while there is still time to change your plans if you cannot rent or borrow what you need.

## Party Day Minus 1 Week

**Prepare the location** Everyone wants to decorate rooms and blow up balloons, but hardly anyone wants to rake the yard or clean the basement. Deciding on the location establishes the immediate cleanup goals: painting, raking, and the like. If a major effort has to be made to get the rooms cleaned, start on it at least a week in advance. Too often, as the hour of the party draws near, the atmosphere gets frantic with simultaneous food preparations, decorating, errands and cleanup. Avoid too much last-minute work—it's something I've stressed in this book, and for a children's party it certainly bears repeating.

**Order food** If you don't have the time or facilities to cook for fifteen children yourself, I suggest you consider take-out food. A call on Tuesday or Wednesday will bring buckets of chicken or mountains of Big Macs to your Saturday party. If hamburgers are your choice, split the order evenly between hamburgers and cheeseburgers. Pizzas and tacos are the two other take-out alternatives.

Since the turnover in help is so frequent at take-out places, the person who takes your order might not be on duty when the order is to be delivered. Therefore, I suggest that you speak with the manager or person in charge, and be sure to make a written note of his name. A quick confirmation call the morning of the party will put your mind at ease and give you a chance to order anything that might have been forgotten.

Some of these outlets will deliver (make sure that they do when you call them), and you may order all your extras, too—French fries, mashed potatoes and gravy, macaroni or bean salad. Some delicatessens also offer special buffet platters for children. Others will include paper plates, cups, napkins, etc. If these extra supplies are not necessary, a price reduction might be negotiated, or extra condiments included instead. It won't be much, but it is a small way to save.

When working with the local take-out spot, ask for the children's plan and do not hesitate to request changes in the plan to fit your needs. That's why these places are listed in the yellow pages under caterers.

**Purchase foods that can be frozen and nonperishable foods**   Cake and ice cream are of course *the* standard party dessert. There is a way to eliminate about one-half of the starchiness of this combination and about 30 percent of the cost: ice cream cake. Ice cream cake servings are sold by the pound and they usually serve four to five people per pound. If proper freezer space is available, an ice cream cake may be purchased up to six weeks in advance.

Ice cream cakes can be molded to just about any shape, from Snoopy to turkeys. They may also be ordered in different flavor combinations. Many bakeries and ice cream shops will make them up to your order, if given several days notice.

If, however, you prefer to serve plain ice cream and a birthday cake, buy the ice cream and order the cake now. The cake may also be baked and frozen, but I prefer cake that is baked the day before the party.

The more chores that you can do one week ahead, the less harried you will be one day ahead! The following foods and beverages can also be purchased, and stored together in a cupboard or where they will not be in the way, and will not tempt snackers:

Bottled or canned soft drinks and fruit juices
Cookies, pretzels, snacks
Candy
Popcorn
Condiments for hamburgers and hot dogs
Peanut butter, jelly, mayonnaise
Bread for sandwiches may be bought and frozen

**Buy decorations and favors**   The theme you choose for the party will most assuredly spark dozens of decorating possibilities. Decorations should, of course, be bright, colorful, truly festive and, above all, safe.

As a rule, paper decorations are the cheapest and simplest to use. Crêpe paper has become a standard decorating tool and the variations it offers are numerous. It can be twisted, used to wrap gifts and prizes, or pipes and poles. It can be layered in different colors, scalloped, crushed, shredded, folded, pleated, slit, etc. Streamers come in rolls 2 inches wide by 15 yards long and are fire retardant but not colorfast—avoid getting them wet, they will run. They can be purchased with Happy Birthday or Merry Christmas written on them, or in color combinations—red, white and blue, or black and orange, for example. Crêpe paper also comes in wider and shorter rolls in various finishes: puckered, smooth, and crêped. It is truly a versatile and practical tool.

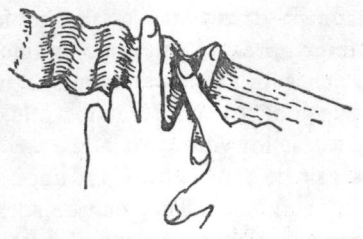

**Scalloping Crêpe Paper.** *Spread the index and middle finger of your left hand along the outer edge of the crêpe paper. With your right index finger alternately push and pull the crêpe paper to create a scalloped effect. Use to trim tables, walls and food dishes.*

Whenever possible, decorations should also be useful. Add color and zest to a party with the necessities: tablecloths, napkins, cups, plates, etc. Party and paper goods stores stock numerous theme combinations for children's parties. If you don't see what you want, ask the dealer if there is a catalogue available, and if it's possible to order what you want.

Favors and prizes are intrinsic parts of every child's party. Here are some suggestions for them, keeping in mind price, practicality, and safety: caps, whistles, coloring books and crayons, children's books (Golden Books are very good for this), jacks, yoyos, pocket puzzles, pails and shovels, water colors, flutes, horns or harmonicas, comic books, jump ropes, rubber balls, bubble-blowing sets, inexpensive costume jewelry.

## Party Day Minus 2 Days

**Buy ingredients for foods to be prepared at home** In order to save time the following day, when you will be busy with the actual food preparation, do all the marketing two days before the party. Make a careful list, going through recipes and checking off ingredients so that you will not discover, in the middle of mixing your cake batter, that you do not have any vanilla.

At the same time, check to be sure that you have an ample supply of toilet paper, Kleenex, paper towels, Band-Aids—those things that we take for granted, but are so often missing when we need them most.

## Party Day Minus 1 Day

**Decorate the party rooms**   Prizes and favors should be wrapped ahead as part of the decorating chores. If you are planning a grab bag, cover a large plastic garbage pail with crêpe paper and then stick pompons of a contrasting colored paper all over it. Or glue felt cutouts or yarn pictures onto an old pillowcase for your grab bag.

Colorful streamers can be attached to just about anything, including walls, the ceiling, or a chandelier. They can be surrounded by balloons or mixed with balloons, and are suspended best with masking tape, which should not remove paint or finishes. Avoid thumbtacks as they leave holes and are a potential source of danger should they fall out.

Unless you have absolutely no other place to sit, you should get the party room or rooms ready the day beforehand.

If you are using a den or living room, remove all bric-a-brac. If the youngsters are going to dance, you will have to make space for a dance floor. If possible, remove the rug. Be certain that all vases and fragile lamps are stored away. Dancing makes floors vibrate—and things *will* fall over.

I suggest protecting upholstered furniture with temporary cloth or plastic slipcovers. This protection also applies for antiques. Don't try roping off a couch—it doesn't work. If the couch or other piece of furniture must remain in a room, and there is no way to protect it, cover it with a colorful sheet and use it for a gift depository, opening area, favor, or costume nucleus. If you can't cover all the upholstered furniture, at least apply a good protective spray.

Placing serving or card tables over smaller pieces of furniture provides them with some protection. If you aren't renting tables and chairs, and your budget is limited, try using mock furniture. For tables, use a piece of plywood on wooden crates or sawhorses; for chairs, use brightly painted or glittered crates, nail kegs, or milk containers, if you can find them. Add a special touch by painting each guest's name on the side. It's fun and it's inexpensive.

Be sure to nail the plywood top to the table base, whether crates or shortened sawhorses. It is worth the extra trouble; an unsecured table could easily tip over.

Finally, if any of your adult helpers are bringing their toddlers or infants to the party, you will be well-advised to make arrangements for facilities to handle these younger guests: disposable diapers, highchairs, possibly a crib, playpens, etc. The party will be lively enough without trying to cope with uncomfortable infants. If their presence will present a problem, ask parents in advance if they could possibly get a sitter, or ask them to bring appropriate equipment.

**Check with caterers and suppliers** Have you ever stopped by to pick up something you had ordered only to have the clerk say, "Oh, I'm sorry, but we have no record of your order"?

Don't let it happen on the occasion of your child's party. The day before, call everyone from whom you have ordered food, furniture, or whatever. Ask for the person with whom you spoke before and make sure that it will be delivered either that day or the next, or that it will be ready for you to pick up at a specified time.

**Prepare all foods that can be done ahead, including cake if you do not purchase it** Here is a list of foods that can be prepared the day before a party.

Raw vegetable strips—carrots, celery, zucchini, etc.

Punch

Cookies

Macaroni and cheese, scalloped potatoes, tuna and noodles—or any casserole that need only be reheated the following day

Salads (do not put dressing on until just before serving)

Bread may be sliced, buttered, and wrapped in foil

The birthday cake (Avoid inordinately rich cakes such as those with layer upon layer of fillings. Let your child decide whether he would prefer a white cake, a chocolate cake, an orange cake, etc.)

Unless you are an expert baker, and have your own favorite recipe, I would suggest that you buy commercial cake mixes and prepare them according to the directions on the package. When the instructions are followed carefully, they make as good (or better) a cake as the average person can bake.

## Party Day Morning

Early in the morning, pick up all last-minute items and/or catered food that is not to be delivered. This will insure that you have time for an alternative menu in case anything has delayed your order.

Remove all previously prepared foods from the freezer. Lay out all the dishes and serving utensils you will need to serve the meal. Sandwiches can be made in the morning if they do not have gooey fillings; otherwise they must be prepared just before the guests arrive.

**Set the table** Now it is time to set the table, which is usually the focal point of your whole decorating scheme. It is always fun to open up and lay out the tablecloth, napkins, paper plates, cups, etc., that you bought the week before. After setting the table with these, you can go on to the trimmings.

Fold-out centerpieces, made of honeycombed paper and cardboard, are very effective. These are usually available to match the other table products you have chosen.

Hats and snappers are old standbys and they do put the guests in a party mood and add to the favors they will take home.

Horns and blowers are noisy additions—think twice about having them if you live in an apartment. Otherwise, they add to the fun if your nerves can stand it!

**Blow up balloons**   Balloons, too, are standard decorating items, but, if you wish to have them plump and gorgeous, they must be blown up at the last possible moment. Regular balloons will stay on the walls and ceilings if you rub them on your clothing to create a little static electricity. If you prefer rising balloons, some party suppliers keep helium tanks available and they may allow you to fill the balloons free if they have been purchased at their store. Otherwise, consult the yellow pages under Bottled Gas for helium sources.

**Coat room and bathroom**   Shortly before the guests arrive, prepare an area where they may leave their coats. A library or den, or a guest bedroom are good choices as they have a bed or couch on which coats may be piled.

The bathroom that the children will use must be clean, of course, and I suggest that you get a supply of paper towels, rather than using your good guest towels. Otherwise, simply be sure there is soap, Kleenex, and an extra roll of toilet paper on hand.

With these last-minute chores taken care of, you and the guest of honor are ready to greet his friends.

## The Party

**The first stage—greetings and gifts**   The young host (or hostess), whether he be 4 or 14, should say hello to every guest, and should say thank you for every present. This is an elementary lesson in common courtesy, but it is often forgotten. The very young child, who has had no previous experience, should have some practice sessions with his parents—learning to shake hands, and to say "Hi, Tommy," "Hello Mrs. Smith," etc. A familiarity with the phrases works wonders—often children clam up because they are faced with something they simply don't know how to do.

At adult parties, gifts are usually collected and opened when everyone has arrived, but it is better for youngsters to open gifts as they are received. The guests would soon get bored watching their host sit and open ten or fifteen presents, and his own attention span might not last throughout a big pile. So he should open each gift at the door, and thank the donor then and there. When all the guests are present, there may be a period of fifteen or twenty minutes for them, and their host, to play with the new games and toys. This, too, is a good lesson in sharing.

**The second stage—games and contests** Various games and contest possibilities are listed below. They are divided into three age groups, but in many cases a particular game, with modifications, would be enjoyed by two, or even all three of the groups. I hope the list will give you and your child some new ideas. A brief description of the more unusual games, marked with an asterisk, follows the list.

### Games and Contests

#### 4 to 7 years

Pin the tail on . . .
Musical chairs
Egg rolls
Three-legged race
Potato race
* Statues
* Peanut hunt
* Spider web
* Art projects

#### 8 to 10 years

* Races
Twist-'em and other commer-
  cial games
Gymnastics contests
Sardines
Treasure hunt
Darts (rubber tipped)
Bobbing for apples
* Balloon sculpture
* Origami
* Piñata

*Pre- and early teens*

Records and dancing
* Board games
* Word and parlor games
Outdoor activities
   swimming
   volleyball
   softball
* Scavenger and treasure hunts

**4 to 7 years**  Two old-fashioned favorites that have been neglected recently but are lots of fun are statues and spider web.

In statues, a record is played for a few seconds while the children run around. When the music ends, each child stops and holds perfectly still in the position he was in at the moment the record stopped. The children are eliminated by a jury of older people who tell them to step out as they see the slightest move. The last one to remain still is the winner.

To play spider web, someone on the family "committee" cuts a long (50 feet or so) length of light string for each child coming to the party. These strings are then run all over the downstairs of the house or apartment, around, behind, under or over furniture. The children are each given one end and they wind up their string, following its course until they come to a small favor or prize at the end.

A peanut hunt is a good way to end the party. Peanuts are hidden all around the downstairs rooms, or outside. About ten minutes before the mothers are due to pick up the guests, each child is given a plastic bag and, at a signal, the hunt starts. The peanuts found by the time the guests leave go home as favors, and the children are kept busy while waiting for their parents.

Youngsters of 4 to 7 love to make things, and they are very creative. Provide them with felt remnants on which you have drawn all manner of simple designs—trees, houses, people, animals, cars, etc. Have a supply of blunt scissors, paste, and squares of cardboard ready, and offer a prize for the prettiest "picture" made with these materials. Or give the children wire hangers and string and let them make mobiles by hanging their felt cutouts from them.

Coloring contests with enough categories to provide a prize for everyone will keep the guests busy and happy for quite a while. The categories might be neatness, good color combinations, originality, brightest, darkest, etc.

**8 to 10 years** Active games are a must for this very energetic age group. All kinds of races—relay, three-legged, hop, skip, and jump—that involve physical activity and are contests will be a success. A hilarious outdoor race is a water relay in which each team passes buckets of water along to fill a tub or spoons of water to fill a glass. Be sure to have plenty of towels on hand! Another amusing form of relay race is to pass an apple from under the chin of one team member to the next without using hands.

Other outdoor games for this age group are volleyball, croquet, cops and robbers (if you have a large enough yard) swimming—being sure there are enough adult lifeguards on hand—softball, hopscotch or jump rope contests.

Indoor games such as carpet bowls, rubber darts, Twist-'em, knock-hockey and Ping-Pong are ideal for this age group, as well as for older children.

Remember, these games provide competition. Competition implies winning and losing. In order to avoid creating a party of winners and losers, you might want to try a grab bag. The winner is the first to grab, the second-place contestant is the second to grab, and so forth. The grab bag or box should be stocked with equal but different gifts or favors. The prize—grabbing first—becomes a psychological form of winning. Since everyone gets to grab, the prizes also become the favors. Separate favors and prizes would be unnecessary.

At first glance, balloon sculpture might seem a bit intimidating but with a little practice and perseverance, everyone can become a pro. The balloon masterpieces may also be used as favors, gifts, and decorations, and you may offer prizes for the best ones.

Consult the Source Manual for more information regarding balloon sculpture.

Origami, like balloon sculpture, is wonderful entertainment for a party that must be held indoors, and when there is not enough space for more physical activities. Origami is the ancient Japanese art of paper folding. The bibliography suggests books on the subject.

Piñatas come to us from Mexico, where they are a popular part of the Christmas traditions. They were originally large clay pots suspended from balconies and poked at by blindfolded participants until the pot broke and released a shower of gifts. In their present form, they are made of papier maché and brilliantly colored paper—Mexican in design and folklore. Piñatas now can be purchased or made in numerous shapes: clowns, birthday cakes, donkeys, drums, jack-o'-lanterns, witches, etc.

Whether you make your own or buy an imported one, stuff it with inexpensive gifts: whistles, tops, caps, jacks, wrapped candies, etc., and hang it from a ceiling, in a stairwell, or wherever possible. One child at a time swings a pole (a broomstick will do) at the piñata until the papier maché finally ruptures, resulting in a shower of gifts. Everyone scrambles for the gifts each time the piñata bursts wider open.

**Pre- and early teens**   Board games are not practical for large parties, but for small groups, such as at a pajama party, they can be great fun. Borrow enough games—checkers, Monopoly, Chinese checkers, or whatever is popular in your neighborhood—so that all of the children can play at once. Set a time limit of twenty to thirty minutes for each game. Those who have not finished lose points to those who have. Make a contest of it, and move the players to a different game after each set.

Parlor games should be played in between more active games to give everyone a rest and provide a change of pace. Girls tend to like them more than boys and you may have to push a little to start them in a mixed group, but if you and your youngster can get the game going, you will find they love it.

Many children are hidden Sarah Bernhardts, and others are natural hams. They may blanch at the idea of standing up and acting out words for charades, but when they see someone else doing it, they will want to try, too. So start the ball rolling by giving an example yourself, or have the hostess volunteer to be the first actor.

Identifying slogans is fun and full of surprises. Cut out familiar slogans from magazines and have the youngsters write down what they think the slogan advertises. The one who gets the most right wins the prize.

A taste test can be hilarious. Put out small dishes of familiar foods and let the blindfolded guests take turns in tasting them. You—and they —will be surprised at how many they will miss. Some sample foods: macaroni, parsley sprigs, Cheerios or Rice Krispies, diced cucumber or eggplant, pieces of chunk tuna, etc.

To play Who am I? pin the name of a famous person on each guest's back. They each stand up in turn and show the others who they are. They are allowed twenty yes or no questions to identify themselves— "Am I a man?" "Am I under twenty?" "Am I American?" "Am I a sports figure?" etc.

A treasure hunt may be held indoors or out, but a scavenger hunt can take place only in an area where the children can go from one house in the neighborhood to another.

The treasure hunt involves a series of clues, written and hidden by you in advance. The children are given the first clue, which leads them to the second, which in turn suggests where to hunt for the third, and so on. The final clue leads to the treasure. Since several of the children will probably get through the course at the same time, it is wise to have several treasures, or one that can be divided a number of ways, at the end of the trail. Making up funny, tricky or clever clues—in poetry if you can—is a wonderful family project that can be worked on for weeks ahead of the party.

In a scavenger hunt, the children are given a list of eight or ten objects they must find in the neighborhood and bring back to home base. Neighbors should be alerted that they may have several visits from youngsters hoping to find a piece of red thread or a stick of spaghetti, and in turn the children should be told exactly how far they may go, and which houses are off-limits.

**The third stage—entertainment and/or outings**  These suggested entertainments are divided in the same way as above, but even more of them are interchangeable among the age groups.

### Entertainment

*4 to 7 years*

Puppets
Magician
Clowns
Storyteller
Santa Claus, Easter bunny, Halloween witch, etc.

*8 to 10 years*

Magician
Clown or acrobat
Movie cartoons

*Pre- and early teens*

Movies
Magician
Musician

**4 to 7 years**  For children of this age it is not necessary to get professional entertainers. Instead, I encourage getting people you know to provide the entertainment. Make certain that at least one rehearsal is scheduled if a friend volunteers. The young host or some of his brothers or sisters might want to do the magic tricks, but if a youngster is going to do the entertaining, have a backup in case of last-minute panic.

If you know of someone who is a clever storyteller, or even a dramatic reader, ask them to help you out with an hour's entertainment. These youngsters, who are not old enough to read for their own pleasure, love nothing more than listening to stories. They are also just the right age for puppet shows, either put on for them by an adult, or put on by themselves. Cardboard cutout puppet stages, door frames with a suspended stage, plywood theaters, or simply a draped table from behind which you can work, are all satisfactory options for stages. The construction of a puppet stage and the making of the puppets is a wonderful pre-party project.

For plots and characters, use various children's stories, cartoon series, television programs, or make it part of the general theme of the party. You may use the puppets as favors and/or gifts. Fill hand puppets with goodies after the show is over and put one at each place at the dining table.

*Outings*

The zoo
Animal farm
Fire engine ride
Children's theater
Rodeo or circus
Sports event
Hay or sleigh ride
Nature center hike
Miniature golf
Picnics
Amusement park
Museum or planetarium
Cruise or sightseeing boat
Bowling
Roller or ice skating
Disco

An outing, which means that you have decided to take the party from your home to another location, becomes a major undertaking if you take too many children. The first move is to make certain the chosen location is available or will be open the day of the party, that it will accommodate the estimated number of guests, and that it is equipped to handle children's groups. When you are sure of this, send out the invitations, making certain that parents know what your plans are.

Outings may be anything from going to a park or a basketball game, to a farm, a skating rink, an amusement park, or even to an educational demonstration such as the U.S. Mint, a newspaper plant, etc. Whatever the choice, *you* are responsible for the safety of your guests, so you must think carefully about the ramifications and logistics. Make certain that you and/or someone you know has visited the spot, and has checked on any potential trouble spots or hazards, as well as the facilities.

Museums, planetariums, and some other educational institutions make good outings for older children. Many science and natural history museums are partially designed for a children's audience, and are entertaining as well as educational.

**4 to 7 years** Younger children love a trip to the zoo. Picnic lunches can be taken, or hamburgers can be purchased at the refreshment stands. However, limit the number—it is very difficult to keep track of eight or ten energetic six-year-olds or to keep sixteen pairs of hands out of the lion's cage.

One of the most successful outings I have seen was one where the parents called the local fire department and found that, for a small contribution, they would be delighted to take the children for a short ride on the hook and ladder. Several volunteers went along to see that the children were safely ensconced in the truck. It wasn't necessary to tell the driver to go slowly, but he made up for lack of speed by blowing the siren—the children were ecstatic.

**8 to 10 years** Rodeos and circuses are perhaps the most popular outings for this age group. However, picnics in a park or at the beach are just as much fun, and less expensive. Be sure that the location is safe—not too close to the highway, no deep water nearby, etc.—and that there are some recreational facilities. Nature centers often provide attractive settings and a little ecological education can be an added plus.

Another delightful form of outing, if you live outside the city, is a hayride or a sleigh ride. The latter depends, of course, on snow conditions, but a hayride is fun at any time. If your yellow pages do not list anyone providing such equipment, and if your local police, Grange, or men's organization cannot help you, try advertising in your local paper.

**Pre- and early teens** Children in their pre- and early teens like nothing better than a professional sporting event—if you can afford it. Your fourteen-year-old son might well prefer to take two friends to a hockey game than have twelve classmates to a party at home. It is something to consider—and the cost would be far less.

If your town does not have a professional sports event at the time of the party, perhaps a high school or university game will do just as well.

Amusement parks make fine outings, but strict supervision is necessary and arrangements must be made for paying for rides, food, etc. You can suggest in the invitation that each guest bring three dollars for rides, and you provide box lunches, or, if the group is small and you can afford it, you can give each youngster a certain sum for so many rides and a hamburger, and he can pay for extra snacks himself. You will have to use your own discretion in deciding which rides are safe enough for your young charges, and this may entail trying them out yourself!

Before I leave the subject of entertainment, I would like to leave you with one last recommendation: Have every minute planned. The unsuccessful party is the one where the children sit around and say, "What'll we do now?" Not only are they bored, but the boredom will soon lead to trouble. The successful party has every minute filled in one way or another. For example, half an hour is allotted for one game, another half for a different type of activity, an hour for the movie or the magician, and another half hour for eating and a final game. The time flies so fast that before the young guests know it, their mothers have come for them, and they go home tired but happy.

**The fourth stage—refreshments**   First of all, let's talk about beverages. Don't serve only soda pop—in fact, avoid it entirely at parties for the very young. Fruit juices, cider, punch, cocoa, milk, and orange- or lemonade are nutritious, appropriate, and popular drinks for any occasion. To add variety and color you may add a piece of fruit, a scoop of sherbet, or a marshmallow to each glass.

Candy, chips, pretzels, etc., are often offered as snacks or favors, but they are not particularly good for small children, and there are alternatives. Letting the youngsters pop their own corn, for example, is lots of fun, and it's far more nutritious than seasoned storebought popcorn. Candy apples are year-round inexpensive favorites. Other fruits, decorated with marshmallow, raisin or nut faces, make fine treats and are much healthier than candy. Most children like raw carrots and celery—serve them instead of corn chips, salted nuts, potato chips, etc.

Sandwiches are always popular, and don't shy away from peanut butter and jelly, or a fluffer-nutter (peanut butter and marshmallow fluff). They are universal favorites and very nutritious. They are best choices for the very small partygoers, but for the older ones who have slightly more sophisticated tastes, chicken, tunafish, ham or bologna and cheese, grilled cheese, or egg salad offer reliable alternatives. Make two or three varieties and let the guests select their own. Also, try cutting sandwiches into different shapes. Little children, especially, love to look for a star, a heart, a diamond, etc.

If you would like your guests to have something to take away with them, bake a special batch of brownies or cookies to be wrapped in foil and taken home as an additional treat.

If you are serving cake and ice cream, rather than ice cream cake, small portions of both will satisfy small stomachs, already on edge with the excitement.

Standard cookout fare is, of course, hamburgers, hot dogs, corn or salad, baked potatoes or chips, watermelon or ice cream, soft drinks, etc. But the variations are numerous. You may prefer chicken legs or spareribs in lieu of hot dogs and hamburgers, or, if you want to be fancier, shish kebabs and steak are sure-fire hits. Pizza is always popular, too. Your child will know what his friends prefer—don't force lamb if they would rather have hot dogs.

With a little imagination and taking some tips from the above, you should have no trouble in creating a children's banquet with a minimum of tooth decay and stomach aches.

## Parties for Toddlers Up to Four

For the two and under group a birthday is really just an excuse for mother and dad to acquire some material for the photograph album or Memory Book. It means nothing to a child, except possibly that he gets a new toy and ice cream and cake. These "parties" you can plan yourself but I suggest that you invite *only* relatives and neighbors and perhaps one or two friends with children of similar ages, who regularly play with your child. Too many guests, or ones who are strangers to him, will only confuse your child and can ruin the day for him.

You and your spouse may prefer to celebrate alone with your youngster with just a birthday cake, ice cream, and a gift. He will enjoy it, and you will have some nice memories.

Above all, don't invite all the nine-year-olds in the neighborhood. The two-year-old won't enjoy it, and nine-year-olds have nothing whatsoever in common with someone seven years their junior.

Three- and four-year-olds, however, are old enough to enjoy parties— as long as they are not overwhelming. Two hours is the maximum time because children of this age have short attention spans and they tire quickly. Five or six guests are about right—not enough to cause confusion, and yet enough to make it a special occasion.

Refreshments should be very simple. As I mentioned earlier, a peanut butter and jelly sandwich is sure to be popular, and ice cream and cake and milk or hot chocolate complete the menu.

A good timetable for a successful party follows:

| | |
|---|---|
| 4–4:30 | Guests arrive, gifts are opened, guests are allowed to run around and get adjusted. If possible, outdoor play on swings or Junglegyms is ideal for this free period. |
| 4:30–5:30 | Organized games and/or entertainment. Simple races, musical chairs, pin-the-tail-on-the-donkey, treasure or peanut hunts, hide and seek, are all possible for 3- to 4-year-olds. Entertainment might be a clown, a magician or cartoon movies. |
| 5:30 | Refreshments are served. |
| 6:00 | Children are picked up, or taken home. |

## Supervisors and Other Guests

For a party of ten or more guests, there is a need for at least one extra supervisor. This might be a neighbor, a parent of one of the guests, a relative, or the host's older brother or sister, etc.

Don't forget to have a pot of coffee in the winter, or iced tea or coffee in the summer, for your adult helpers. There should also be enough birthday cake and ice cream for them to enjoy.

An assistant who drives a car can be a great help at the end of the party by taking some of the children home. Be sure to check with the parents of the guests to see if this would be a help to them.

## Safety Tips

I certainly don't intend to frighten you away from giving this party. However, there are certain precautions you should consider:

Have a first-aid kit available.

In apartments, keep all windows locked, except ground-floor windows that are low to the ground.

Buy fire retardant articles whenever possible—costumes, paper goods, hats, horns, etc.

In blowing out the birthday candles, hold the cake some distance from guests at the table to avoid igniting anyone or anything.

Avoid open flames: lighted fireplaces or candles in pumpkins. Use small flashlights instead.

Avoid sharp corners and breakable objects—things that might cause puncture wounds or cuts.

Choose safe games—use only rubber-tipped arrows or darts, blunt scissors, etc.

In garages and cellars, be certain that paints, flammables, poisons, etc., are stored out of the way.

Remove or securely lock up all firearms, weapons, etc.

Remove any toxic medicines from the medicine chest in the bathroom the children will use. If possible, make bathroom doors unlockable.

At outings, stay away from areas with steep rocky cliffs or potential water hazards.

Don't give swimming parties for children unless they are very well supervised by adults at *all* times. This applies to beaches, lakes, ponds, and streams, as well as to pools.

*For Halloween outings remember the following:*

Parents or older teenagers should accompany small children.

Advise your children to approach homes only if there is a porch or yard light on.

Children should always walk on sidewalks and should cross streets only at intersections, not between parked cars.

Costumes should be lightweight, easily visible, and flame retardant. Reflective tape can be used creatively on the front, back, and sides of costumes.

Use flashlights to help light the way up stairs, across streets, and such. Candles and torches invite trouble.

Whiskers, beards, wigs, hats, and the like need to be fastened securely so they don't block vision or become a fire hazard.

# 12

# *Other Get-Togethers*

In addition to seasonal celebrations, there are a host of day-to-day entertainments, as well as some very special occasions, that require their own approach. This chapter describes many of these get-togethers and provides the information necessary to plan them.

### Coffees

Coffees, or coffee parties, used to be better known in the South than in the North. However, they are becoming more popular all over the country because they offer an opportunity for young women to get together during the hours their youngsters are in school, or are often so informal that preschool toddlers can accompany their mothers.

Coffees may be extremely simple—just a group of neighbors getting together for a cup of coffee and Danish pastry or a doughnut—or they may be an elaborate party held in a club or hotel. Many busy women use this type of get-together to plan promotional parties, charity balls, etc. More elaborate menus may include sandwiches, chafing dishes of scrambled eggs, fresh fruits, and pastries, as well as exotic coffee flavors such as mocha and capuccino.

Dress is usually whatever is standard for morning wear in your neighborhood, generally slacks or skirts. But be certain you do not look as if you have just come in from weeding the garden. For very special coffee parties, dress is an "afternoon" dress, a suit or a dressy pants suit.

Invitations are issued by telephone except to the more formal coffees, which are generally held in honor of someone or something. In the South, coffees are frequently given for brides-to-be and may or may not be showers.

## Teas

Afternoon teas are given in honor of visiting celebrities, new neighbors, or a house guest, as a housewarming, or for no reason other than that the hostess wants to entertain her friends.

**Invitations** Invitations to an informal tea are almost always telephoned. However, if the occasion is more formal, an invitation is sent on the face of fold-over note-paper, or inside if the paper has a monogram on the front.

---

> *January 10*
> *Tea at 4 o'clock*
> *105 Springvale Avenue*
> *Boston, Mass.*

---

When the tea is given in honor of someone, you write "In honor of" or "To meet Barbara Withers" at the top.

**The tea table** The dining table is the simplest and most comfortable place from which to serve. However, the tea table may be set up in any room that has adequate space and easy access and exit. The guests should be able to circulate freely without becoming trapped in a corner after they have been served.

A cloth must always be used except on a glass-topped table. It may barely cover the table, or it may hang half a yard over the edge. A tea cloth may be colored, but the conventional one is of lace or white linen with needlework, lace, or appliquéd designs.

Large trays are set at either end of the table, one for the tea, one for the coffee.

The tea tray holds a pot of boiling water—with a flame under it, if possible—a full pot of tea, cream pitcher, sugar bowl, and thin slices of lemon on a dish.

The coffee tray is simpler. The coffee is in a large urn or pot with a flame under it. A pitcher of cream and a bowl of sugar (preferably lumps) complete the tray. If chocolate is served instead of coffee, there is nothing needed other than the pot of steaming chocolate.

If the trays are carried by a maid, the flames under the pots are not lighted until the trays are set down in order to avoid the danger of fire.

The cups and saucers are placed within easy reach of the women who are pouring, usually at the left of the tray, because the cups are held in the left hand while the tea (or coffee) is poured with the right. On either side of the table are stacks of little tea plates, with small napkins matching the tea cloth. Arranged behind these, or in any way that is pretty and uncluttered, are the plates of food and whatever silver is necessary. Forks should be on the table if cake with soft icing is served. If the table is not large enough to hold all the plates, some may be placed on a sideboard or a small table in a convenient location.

Food for a tea party is quite different from that served at a cocktail party. For one thing, much of the food is sweet—cookies, cupcakes, fruit cake, or slices of iced cake. In addition, for those who do not have such a sweet tooth, tea sandwiches are served. They are small and made on very thin bread—watercress rolled in thin bread, a cherry tomato sliced on a round of bread, cream cheese on datenut bread, or crabmeat on toast rounds are typical choices for tea-party menus. In the winter, there is sometimes a tray of hot cheese puffs, pastry filled with mushrooms, etc.

Because nothing needs to be passed to the guests, it is perfectly possible for a hostess to give a formal tea without help. If she has no maid, she sets out the tray with everything except the boiling water before her guests arrive, leaving the kettle on the stove in the kitchen. She greets the guests at the door, telling them where to leave their coats. When she is ready to serve the tea, she fills the teapot from the kitchen kettle and carries it in to the tea table.

**Making good tea**    The most important part of the tea service is boiling water and plenty of it. To make good tea, half-fill the teapot with boiling water, let it stand a moment or two to heat the pot, and then pour it out. Put in a rounded teaspoonful of tea leaves or one tea bag for each person. Half this amount may be used if the tea is of superb quality.

Then pour enough rapidly boiling water into the pot to cover the tea leaves about half an inch. It should steep at least five minutes (for those who like it very strong, ten) before additional boiling water is poured on. When serving, pour half tea, half boiling water for those who like it weak. Increase the amount of tea for those who like it strong. The cup of good tea should be too strong without the addition of a little lively boiling water, which gives it freshness.

When tea has to stand a long time for many guests, the ideal way is to make a strong infusion in a big kettle on the kitchen stove. Let the tea actually boil three to four minutes, then pour it through a sieve or filter into your hot teapot. The tea will not become bitter, and it does not matter if it gets quite cold. You need only a small amount of such tea, and the boiling water poured over it will make the drink hot enough.

**Those who pour**   The pouring is usually done by close friends of the hostess. These women are asked beforehand if they will "do the honors" and, unless they have a valid excuse, they should accept. After an hour, the first two may be relieved by two other friends.

Each guest simply walks up to the table and says, "May I have a cup of tea?" The one pouring should smile and answer, "Certainly! How do you like it? Strong or weak? Would you like cream or lemon?" If the guest prefers coffee, she asks for it at the other end of the table. Try to keep the traffic flow even.

**Tea-party guests**   When there is a guest of honor, the hostess introduces her to each woman as she arrives. But rather than forming a receiving line, they stand together near the door and talk for a little while with the arriving guests. The hostess should see that guests who are strangers to the others are introduced to two or three people when they arrive.

## Tea Dances

An afternoon tea dance occasionally takes the place of a debutante party. It may also be given to honor a birthday or anniversary or to celebrate a holiday.

Invitations are usually written on the hostess's visiting card, on a fold-over informal, or on a fill-in invitation.

Since houses with rooms large enough for dancing are comparatively few, a tea dance is usually given at a club or in a small ballroom of a hotel. Remember, however, that it is a mistake to choose too large a room, because too much space for too few people gives an effect of emptiness that throws a pall on the party. Also remember that an undecorated public room needs more people than a room in a private house to make it look filled. Although a crush may be unpleasant, it does give the effect of success. Nothing is more dismal than a half-empty room with scattered guests.

The arrangements for a tea with dancing are much the same as for an evening dance. A screen of greens behind the musicians and flowers on the tables are all the decorations that are required.

Tea, coffee, tea sandwiches, and cakes are served. In addition, there is usually a table nearby with pitchers or bowls of fruit juice or punch, and a bar for those who wish stronger drinks.

## Formal Luncheons

The formal luncheon, although less formidable than the formal dinner, differs from it only in details. Therefore, this chapter will be confined to the variations.

The most significant difference is that luncheons are generally given by and for women. However, an equal number of men may be included on a weekend or a holiday, and their presence affects certain considerations such as the heartiness of the menu.

**The invitations** The word "lunch" is used much more often than "luncheon." Luncheon is rarely spoken, but it is written in books like this one and sometimes in third-person invitations.

Although invitations may be telephoned, occasionally an engraved card is used for an elaborate luncheon, especially for one given in honor of a noted person. If written, a formal invitation is nearly always in the form of a personal note, which is rarely mailed more than a week in advance. For instance:

---

*Dear Mrs. Adams (or Linda),*
    *Will you come to lunch on Friday, the tenth at*
*half past twelve at the Hillsboro Country Club?*
*I look forward to seeing you then.*
                    *Sincerely,*
                    *Carol (or Carol Binen)*

---

If Mrs. Binen's luncheon were given in honor of someone, the phrase "to meet Mrs. Lawrence" would be added immediately after the location. If it is a very large luncheon, for which the engraved card is used, "To meet Mrs. Lawrence" is written across the top.

**Cocktails**  Cocktails may or may not be served before lunch. If they are, they differ from those offered before dinner. Although a martini can be offered, sherry, Dubonnet, Bloody Marys, or daiquiris are more usual. As always, there must be tomato juice, soft drinks, or plain fruit juice available for those who wish it.

**The table**  Candles are not needed on a lunch table, but are sometimes used as ornaments, but they should never be lighted in the daytime. The plain white tablecloth that is correct for dinner is not used for luncheon, although colored damask is acceptable. Traditionally, the lunch table is set with place mats made in any variety of linen, needlework, or lace. A runner, matching the mats but two or three times as long, may be used in the center of the table.

The decorations are practically the same as for dinner: flowers or an ornament in the center, and two or four dishes of fruit or candy where they look best. If the table is very large, four small vases with flowers matching those in the centerpiece—or any other glass or silver ornaments—may be added.

The places are set as for dinner, with a service plate, a butter plate and knife, and a fork, knife, and spoon for each course. The lunch napkin is much smaller than the dinner napkin and is not folded in the same manner. Generally it is folded like a handkerchief, in a square of four thicknesses. The square is laid on the plate diagonally, with the monogrammed (or embroidered) corner pointing down toward the near edge of the table. The upper corner is then turned sharply under in a flat crease for about a quarter of its diagonal length; then the two sides are rolled loosely under, with a straight top edge and a pointed lower edge and the monogram displayed in the center. Or it can be folded in any simple way one prefers.

If it is a large luncheon, place cards are used just as they are at dinner.

A goblet for water is at each place, and a wine glass if wine is to be served. If the hostess chooses to serve iced tea or a similar beverage in the summer, a highball glass on a coaster replaces the wine glass.

**The service**  If the luncheon is to be formal, the hostess must have help, whether her own servants or temporary ones.

The formal service is identical with that of dinner. Carving is done in the kitchen and, except for the ornamental dishes of fruit, candy, and nuts, no food is set on the table. The plate service is also the same as dinner. The places are never left without plates, except after the salad course, when the table is cleared and crumbed for dessert. The dessert plates and finger bowls are arranged as for dinner.

**The menu**   Five courses could be served, but more usually four are sufficient for the longest and the most elaborate luncheons. The possible courses include:

1. Fruit, or soup in cups
2. Eggs or shellfish
3. Fowl or meat (not a roast)
4. Salad
5. Dessert

The menu for lunch eaten in a private house never consists of more than four courses. Any one of the courses above may be omitted except for the fowl or meat.

Melon, grapefruit, or fruit cup, with or without a liqueur poured over it, is a popular first course. Fruit cup may be served in special glass bowls that fit into long-stemmed and much larger glasses with a space for crushed ice between, or it can just as well be served in champagne glasses, after being kept as cold as possible in the refrigerator.

Soup at a luncheon is never served in soup plates, but in two-handled cups. It is eaten with a teaspoon or a bouillon spoon, or, after it has cooled sufficiently, the cup may be picked up and lifted to the mouth with one or both hands. In the winter it is almost always a clear soup: a bouillon, turtle soup, or consommé. In the summer, a chilled soup like jellied consommé, madrilène, or vichyssoise is appropriate.

Hot breads are an important feature of the luncheon—hot croissants, baking powder biscuits, muffins, rolls, or corn bread—and they are passed as often as necessary.

There are innumerable egg and fish dishes suitable for a luncheon. A first or second course that is substantial and rich, such as eggs Benedict or crab meat au gratin, should be balanced by a simple meat, such as broiled chicken served with a salad, combining meat and salad courses in one. On the other hand, if you serve eggs in aspic, or shrimp cocktail first, you could have meat and vegetables, as well as salad and dessert.

**Beverages**   In the winter a wine is usually served with lunch. Sherry may also be served with soup, or a liqueur after dessert, but one wine is sufficient, and it should be a light one such as a dry Rhine wine or a claret.

### Bridge Luncheons

The size of your bridge luncheon depends on the number that you can seat and the help that you will have with the serving. If you have no dining room but you have several available rooms or a large enough living room, you may set up three or four card tables to accommodate the number of guests you wish to invite. For those who can manage to seat their guests in this way, a luncheon for twelve or sixteen people, followed by bridge, is one of the nicest parties imaginable.

Each card table should be covered with a white or colored cloth. The cloths may be of any style, but they should be exactly alike or complement each other and be well coordinated. A small flower arrangement makes the prettiest centerpiece.

**Serving the luncheon** If you are serving without the help of a maid, you will be wise to make your party a buffet. The food is set out as for a buffet dinner on the dining-room table or on any table with sufficient space, and the guests eat at the card tables.

As soon as you announce that luncheon is served, your guests serve themselves. If you are having a course before the entrée it should be on the tables when your guests sit down. While they are helping themselves to the main course, you remove the soiled dishes to the kitchen.

The same procedure is followed when everyone is ready for the salad or dessert. When they have finished the last course, you ask them to go to another room to have their coffee. This gives you a chance to clear away the glasses, silver and cloths from the tables, and to set out the cards. There should always be two decks of clean cards and at least two score pads and two pencils on each table.

A maid can serve twelve or sixteen guests quite easily if the first course is already on the table. The main course should be limited to a single dish and salad, as otherwise it will take a rather long time to serve. The salad may be in small bowls or plates, which are brought in two at a time and placed on the guests' left. If there is no first course, the salad may be on the table when the guests sit down. Rolls, butter, ice water, and any other beverage should also be put on the table beforehand.

When dessert is finished, the maid carries the coffee tray to another room and, if it is a bridge party, readies the tables while the hostess pours the coffee.

**On food and drink** If you wish to serve cocktails before lunch, you should limit the time, especially when everyone is looking forward to playing cards. And the drinks should be of a milder type than those served before dinner: sherry, Dubonnet, or Bloody Marys.

Two or three courses are sufficient at any informal luncheon. If you serve many more than that and then move to the bridge table, you will find some of your players falling asleep over their hands! Furthermore, among a group of eight or twelve women, there are always some who are watching their calories, so a delicious but light meal is far more appreciated than one dressed with rich sauces and ending with sweets.

Iced tea and iced coffee are delicious with luncheon, especially in the summer. It is nice to give your guests a choice by passing a tray with a pitcher of each or by having both available close to the buffet table. A bowl of fruit punch may take the place of iced tea or coffee and appears cool and refreshing if it is prepared with floating slices of orange and lemon and is surrounded by glasses or cups adorned with fresh sprigs of mint.

In the winter, many hostesses like to have hot coffee or tea in a convenient spot where the guests may help themselves.

A light wine may be served, although it is not necessary, especially if you have offered cocktails.

A pitcher of ice water, from which the guests may help themselves, should always be in evidence, or glasses of water should already be on the table if the luncheon is not buffet.

On a hot summer day when people have been playing cards for an hour or more, a tray should be brought in with a large pitcher of ice water and perhaps another pitcher of iced tea, and put down on a convenient table. Hostesses tend to forget that five out of six long for a cold drink in the afternoon more than anything else. Sandwiches and cookies may also be served, but these are not necessary when bridge follows a luncheon. If you invite people to come at 2 o'clock and play for the afternoon, light refreshments may be served between 4:30 and 5.

## Progressive Dinners

An imaginative and inexpensive alternative to standard entertaining is the progressive dinner. It requires careful planning, coordination between a number of hostesses, and locations that are easily accessible to all guests.

Progressive dinners are usually divided into three courses—the first for appetizers and cocktails, the second for soup and the main course, and the third for salad and dessert. Sometimes a fourth course of fruit, cheese, and liqueurs is included.

It is permissible to mix the fare; if the main course is to be Italian food, for example, appetizers need not be of Italian origin. Be careful though that the chosen menu is complementary.

It is important, too, that a menu be planned that allows for some delay. Don't choose dishes that must be timed perfectly—allow for the unexpected.

If the setting is a rural one, chances are all the guests will have their own automobiles or access to one. Pairing couples to limit the number of cars not only avoids traffic jams at each setting, but also helps to conserve gas. In urban centers, where settings are too far apart for walking, cabs, subways, or buses must be used to get from one course to another.

Timing counts. As the guests leave one setting, the hostess there should phone ahead to alert the next hostess that the guests are just leaving.

Since the hostesses should be at home to greet the guests as they arrive, they may not be able to join the group for the course immediately preceding their own. They should use that time to make last-minute preparations and to ready everything at their own houses.

The hostess of the first session joins her guests at the second session, so that at the last course, all hostesses are present. The final stop will also be the time for entertainment, games, or dancing.

Before guests are invited to a progressive dinner, the hostesses must meet to plan a complementary menu and a workable time schedule. They should also plan a route between the locations so that the guests easily progress from one house to another. There should be no backtracking, or a gap of more than fifteen to twenty minutes between the stops.

If necessary, a map should be made for each guest, including time and location of each course and the telephone numbers of the hostesses. This information is sent either with the invitations or after the guests accept. Guest lists are usually made up by allowing each hostess to invite a certain number of couples.

## Informal Dinners

Although most of this book is devoted to rather elaborate entertaining for the simple reason that that is the time when hostesses most need help with the planning, it is undeniable that far more of our entertaining is simply the "Come on over for dinner tomorrow night" variety. Then maybe another friend or two are included, and you have on your hands a real—but very informal—party. You do not need much help with this sort of entertaining, you simply do what comes naturally. However, there are certain established guidelines—ways of preparing and presenting the meal for example—that make a super hostess out of a run-of-the-mill one.

**The table**    Although you certainly *may,* there is no reason to stick to a white tablecloth when you entertain informally. Use your creativity to combine a bright modern print with solid color napkins, or use interesting place mats if you have room. Candelabra are too formal for such an occasion, so use candlesticks—as many as you wish. They can be grouped in different ways and can be of varying heights, or use a candlestick with a ring of flowers around it to make a lovely table decoration. Centerpieces can vary from traditional flower arrangements to fresh fruit, a wooden carving or a china or glass ornament. Dried flowers or grasses on a brown cloth, with beige or orange napkins, make lovely winter centerpieces.

The place settings are simple—only the silver or stainless you will actually use is set out. If the main course is a casserole that requires no knife, don't put one out. If you are serving wine, a water goblet is not necessary, but it is a nice touch. Butter plates, however, I do recommend. Bread that has slipped from the edge of the plate and gotten soggy in the gravy is less than appetizing, and butter melting on the hot plate doesn't last for long! For somewhat the same reason, I recommend using salad plates when serving salad with the main course. If your entrée has a sauce or gravy and the salad must be placed on the same plate, the resulting mixture of dressing and gravy is scarcely a gourmet's delight.

Service plates are not used at informal dinners, but a small glass or plain china plate should be placed under fruit cups, seafood shells, or soup bowls.

Dinner plates should be heated (if the meal is hot) so they must be brought in at the last moment.

You may mix wood and pewter, two or more kinds of china, stainless steel and pottery in any way you wish, as long as the result is harmonious and each item is in keeping with the others. In other words, you would not use plastic glasses with fine bone china, or trenchers with delicate wine glasses.

To minimize your running around after your guests are seated, the butter should be on the butter plates, the candles lighted, the water glasses filled, and the wine opened and in a holder on the table when the guests sit down. The salad may also be on the table, either dressed, or with a tray of the ingredients necessary for each guest to make his own dressing.

Condiments and accompaniments should be served in appropriate containers—not in their jars or cartons.

If there is to be a first course, it, too, should be on the table before the guests sit down.

All of these things, if planned and prepared in advance, will make your party run smoothly, and will allow you to be relaxed and to enjoy the evening yourself.

**Serving the meal** The simplest and most efficient way to serve an informal dinner when you have no help is what we call semi-buffet. The food is placed on a side table or sideboard, the guests serve themselves and are directed to their places by the hostess, who stands close to the buffet. The table is set as described above.

A first course may be on the table when the guests come in or it may be served in the living room with the last cocktail. If it is eaten at the table, the hostess gets up and removes the empty plates and then asks the guests to go to the buffet table to get their main course. A close friend, or the host, may help her, to speed up the process. However, *all* of the women should not try to help as that invariably causes more confusion than assistance.

Dishes should be removed two at a time, without stacking. Butter plates, however, may be placed on the dinner plates for removal. Salts, peppers, and condiment dishes should be cleared away also.

If you have a dining room, there is no need to clear the dessert dishes. If, however, your dining tables have been set up in the living room, they should be cleared completely and removed, unless you are planning to use the tables for card games later.

Don't let your guests do your dishes. You have invited them over to give them a good time, and to relieve them from everyday mealtime chores. If they offer (as they undoubtedly will), say firmly, "No thanks, the dishes will be here in the morning and you won't, so I'd rather enjoy your company *now*."

After-dinner coffee should be served in the living room, unless everyone is enjoying a lively conversation and doesn't want to leave the table. Many hostesses serve nothing but decaffeinated coffee today, and it should certainly be available, but it is also nice to offer "real" coffee or espresso, or, as a special treat, Irish coffee or Spanish coffee—whatever you think your guests would enjoy.

These casual dinners are certainly the kind of entertaining that most of us enjoy best of all. But no matter how well you know your guests or how often you see them, the evening will be more fun and more special if you make that little ounce of extra effort.

## Late-Night Suppers

Hostesses don't give late-night suppers the way they used to. The elaborate, multicourse supper has given way to the less formal after-the-show or après ski intimate supper.

Suppers are almost always buffets. They are perfect ways to extend the evening's entertainment just a little bit longer. A supper provides a splendid opportunity for friends to discuss the movie or concert they have just seen, or to warm up together after a night of ice-skating or skiing.

The most important thing to consider is the time you will have to get the food ready when you and your guests return home. If you have help, or are able to get someone to prepare the meal while you're away, coming home to a supper that's all ready, and a roaring fire, is a real treat. A quick call to your helper, alerting her that your guests are on the way, insures the supper will not sit out too long waiting for the party to begin.

If, on the other hand, you are executing this supper alone, you will need to allow extra time and planning before you depart. The buffet and tables can be set, candles placed, casseroles readied for immediate heating, and all the equipment set in place.

The key to a successful late-night supper is to do everything you can before you leave so that when you return the party is instantaneous. At a late-night supper, you can "lose" your guests if the preparation takes too long. Be certain to provide little snacks or hors d'oeuvre for your guests while the main course is being prepared.

The meal served at a late-night supper should be light and easy to prepare, serve, and eat. A hearty soup or chowder served with French bread and green salad, eggs Benedict (everything except the eggs and muffins can be prepared before you go out), Reuben or club sandwiches accompanied by assorted pickles and potato chips, or, on a hot night, a chef's salad all make simple but filling late-night menus. It's always a good idea to allow for a few extra guests whom you may invite on the spur of the moment—other chilled skiers, or associates or friends you may chance to meet at a concert or play.

The night's entertainment will be subdued and relaxed conversation among good friends savoring your late-night meal.

## Anniversaries

It takes a very remarkable person to remember all the anniversaries and birthdays that he should—especially if he has a large family. Here are three suggestions to help you:

Make a chart of twelve squares—one for each month of the year. Label them January, February, etc., but do not put in the days of the week. In each square, note the appropriate dates, occasions, and names. In the square marked January, you might list:

12th—Anne's birthday

17th—Fred and Sue's anniversary

This chart is good forever and should be hung by your desk, your bulletin board, or wherever it will be noticed.

At the beginning of the year, take a regular calendar and fill in all the anniversaries and birthdays you want to remember on the appropriate days. Each January, spend a few minutes transferring the notations to your new calendar.

At the beginning of each month, address cards to the people you will want to send them to that month. Have them stamped and ready to go, and keep a list of the dates when they are to be mailed on top of the pile. Again, keep the pile in a place where you will be sure to notice it.

**Planning an anniversary party**   The party may be held in the home of the couple, in the home of the person planning the party, in a church parish house, or in a room of a hotel, restaurant, or club.

If the party is a dinner or a small reception, the guests are primarily family, members of the original wedding party, and closest friends. If it is to be a large reception or an open house, the list may include business acquaintances, church and club members, and, in very small communities, everyone in town.

**Invitations**   The form of the invitations depends entirely on the degree of formality of the party. They may range from an informal telephone call to an engraved invitation. In between lie the most common forms—handwritten notes, or the necessary information written on a visiting card, an informal, or a fill-in card. Formal invitations for a twenty-fifth anniversary are often bordered and printed in silver; those for a fiftieth, in gold.

For the large open house, the invitation may simply be an announcement in the local paper or the church or club bulletin. The danger with this form of invitation is that more people than the hosts expect may appear, or that some who are really wanted may fail to read the announcement or hear of the party. If the only invitation is the announcement in the paper, anyone who reads it may attend, but if invitations are extended personally, only those who receive them may go.

The following are some sample invitations.

When the couple are giving the party themselves:

---

*1960–1985*
*Mr. and Mrs. Harvey Langdon*
*request the pleasure of your company*
*at a reception in honor of*
*their silver wedding anniversary*
*on Saturday, the eighth of December*
*at eight o'clock*
*Barrymore Country Club*
*R.s.v.p.*
*12 Corning Road*

---

On an informal or visiting card (name engraved):

---

*1960–1985*
*Mr. and Mrs. Harvey Langdon*
*Cocktail Buffet*
*March 1 at 6 P.M.*
*12 Corning Road*
*R.s.v.p.*

---

When the children of the couple give the party:

---

*Dear Anne (or Mrs. Franklin),*
*Will you and Joe (or Mr. Franklin) join us for dinner*
*at the Rosemont Club on Saturday, May 4, at 7 P.M.*
*to help us celebrate Mom and Dad's twenty-fifth*
*anniversary? Hoping to see you then.*

> *Helen and Bill*
> *(or Helen and Bill Porter)*

---

Or if they have a card printed:

---

*In honor of the*
*fiftieth wedding anniversary of*
*Mr. and Mrs. Harvey Langdon*

*Mr. and Mrs. William Porter*
*(or "their sons and daughters")*
*request the pleasure of your company*
*on Tuesday, the fourth of July*
*at seven thirty o'clock*
*10 Glenwood Road*

*R.s.v.p.*

---

The newspaper or church-bulletin announcement reads:

---

*Open House*
*to celebrate the fiftieth anniversary*
*of Mr. and Mrs. Harvey Langdon, Sunday,*
*March 4, 4 to 6 P.M., 12 Osborn Road*

---

**Refreshments** The refreshments depend on the type of party being given. If it is a luncheon or a dinner, the hostess simply chooses whatever menu she thinks will please the couple and the guests most. Since the later anniversaries attempt to re-create the wedding day to some extent, the food might be the same as that served at the original wedding reception.

If the party is a cocktail party, hors d'oeuvre are served, but a wedding cake should be cut and passed with a round of champagne for toasting the couple before the guests leave.

At an afternoon reception or an open house, the menu varies according to the formality of the party and the pocketbook of the hosts. The refreshments may consist of sandwiches, snacks, and punch, or a complete buffet—cold ham, turkey, sliced fillet of beef, and chafing dishes filled with hot snacks or hors d'oeuvre. Whatever the other food, as close a replica of the couple's wedding cake as can be made is often a feature of the menu.

Drinks may range from tea and coffee at an afternoon reception to wine, champagne, or highballs at an evening affair. Soft drinks should always be available for those who prefer them. Punch made with or without liquor is often served at open houses and other daytime parties. When the family does not object to alcoholic beverages, a glass of champagne is the traditional drink for toasts—at any hour of the afternoon or evening. Otherwise, the toasts may be made with punch or whatever drinks are available.

**Decorations** Decorations need not be elaborate, but the twenty-fifth anniversary party should feature white and silver ornaments and flowers, and the fiftieth, gold (or yellow) and white. Flowers make the loveliest decoration of all, and the "bride" should always be presented with a corsage.

**With or without music** There need not be any entertainment, but a strolling accordion player adds a touch of romance, and he can be asked to play the couple's favorite tunes, wedding music, etc. If the hosts wish to hire an orchestra or provide records, dancing will be all the entertainment necessary.

**The receiving line** One of the distinguishing features of an anniversary party is the receiving line. Except for a somewhat elderly couple celebrating their fiftieth, the couple stand near the door and greet the guests. Their children may join them in the line, and, if the party is given by someone else, that person always heads the line as host or hostess.

**Receiving Line.** *A receiving line is always headed by the hosts. In this instance, the event is an anniversary celebration. Immediately following the hosts are the honored couple, followed by their children. If the original maid of honor and best man are in attendance, they would end the line. Guests are often treated to champagne or a mixed drink as they finish paying their respects.*

**Gifts** When gifts are brought to the anniversary couple (as they should be, unless "no gifts, please" was written on the invitations), the opening of the packages is a feature of the party. After everyone has arrived, or perhaps after dinner while the guests are enjoying their coffee, everyone gathers around and the couple open the gifts and thank the donors. One of their children, or anyone they choose to designate, helps by taking care of the wrappings, making a list, collecting the ribbons, etc. The couple do not need to write notes later to those they have already thanked in person, unless they wish to do so.

### *Traditional Anniversary Gifts*

1. Paper or plastics
2. Calico or cotton
3. Leather or simulated leather
4. Silk or synthetic material
5. Wood
6. Iron
7. Copper or wool
8. Electrical appliances or bronze
9. Pottery
10. Tin or aluminum
11. Steel
12. Linens

| 13. Lace             | 30. Pearl           |
|----------------------|---------------------|
| 14. Ivory            | 35. Coral and jade  |
| 15. Crystal or glass | 40. Ruby            |
| 20. China            | 45. Sapphire        |
| 25. Silver           | 50. Gold            |

**Marking gifts**   Gifts of silver are still often given on twenty-fifth anniversaries. A couple's children, for example, may get together and give their parents a beautiful silver tray, a bowl, a coffeepot, etc. These gifts should be marked to commemorate the occasion.

*1960–1985*

*to*

*Mom and Dad*

*on their twenty-fifth anniversary*

*from*

*Sally, Bill, and Ted*

Once in a while, the children giving a party for their parents present mementos of the occasion to all the guests. These gifts, too, are monogrammed. There are several choices, depending on relationships and costs. If it is not too expensive, it is nice to have silver, leather, or glass marked with the anniversary couple's name and the date. The articles for their parents might be engraved:

*Mom and Dad*

*October 10*

*1960–1985*

and those for friends:

*Jean and Harry*

*October 10*

*1960–1985*

If this is impractical or too expensive, simple mementos such as paper matchboxes or coasters could be marked and distributed.

*Jean and Harry Porter*
*October 10*
*1960–1985*

**The main table** The table should be as much like the bridal table at the couple's wedding reception as possible. The "bride and groom" sit together at the center of a long table or in the places facing the guests if the table is a round one. The original bridesmaids and ushers, if any are present, are seated next to them; their husbands or wives are also included at the table. The couple's children are seated with them, in whatever way they will enjoy most.

When the party is given by a married son or daughter of the anniversary couple, the host and hostess sit at either end of the table, or, at a round table, opposite the "bride and groom," who always sit together.

The table is decorated with white flowers, or, for a fiftieth anniversary, gold or yellow flowers. If there is room, the wedding cake may be in the center of the table, but if it is large it is more convenient to place it on a side table.

**Elderly couples** Some couples who are celebrating their fiftieth anniversaries are so elderly or infirm that they must be given special consideration. They should not be asked to stand to greet their guests, but should be seated in a central spot where people can pass by comfortably to offer congratulations. It is best to plan to have the party in their home, or perhaps in the home of one of their children, rather than in a restaurant or hall.

If the couple are not up to any party at all, a lovely thing to do is to arrange a card shower. A daughter or son sends out cards saying that the parents' anniversary will be celebrated by a card shower, and would the "guest attend" by sending a card. No other gift is expected, but the couple will be delighted with the messages of love and congratulations carried in the cards.

Some couples who marry late in life feel that they will never reach their Golden Anniversary and ask whether they may have a big celebration on their thirty-fifth or fortieth. Of course they may! There is nothing magical about the fiftieth, and a couple may celebrate any anniversary they choose to.

**Widows and widowers** Even though you want someone who has lost his or her mate to know that you haven't forgotten their anniversary, you should not send a congratulatory card. The nicest thing you can do for people who are recently bereaved, if you live close enough, is to take them out to dinner, or have them to your home that day. This will give them something to look forward to and keep them from being lonely and sad.

For those farther away, to whom you have always sent a card, write a letter instead. You need not mention the bereavement or the anniversary other than to say, "We want you to know we are thinking of you today."

When one member of a couple is ill, or perhaps in a nursing home, the other will not feel like celebrating alone. But family and friends can make it a special occasion in the same way mentioned above—by taking him or her out to dinner, or inviting him or her and a few close friends for dinner in their home.

**A conference call** A lovely gift to a couple whose children are scattered and far away is a conference call. The person giving the party can arrange with the telephone company to connect the lines so that all members of the family can talk together at an appointed hour. This could, in many cases, be the most wonderful gift the couple could receive.

**Reaffirmation of marriage vows** Some couples want to reaffirm their marriage vows on the twenty-fifth or fiftieth anniversaries. They should not try to duplicate their entire original wedding ceremony, but rather have a simple repetition of the vows. As many members as possible of the original wedding party gather for the service. If there are any children, they sometimes stand with the couple, or, if the best man and maid of honor are present, they may stand and the children sit nearby.

The "bride" should not wear her wedding dress, nor should the couple and attendants walk up the aisle or otherwise try to reenact the wedding. Women wear dresses appropriate to the hour of the day, and men wear business suits in the daytime and suits or tuxedos, whichever is indicated, in the evening.

After the service, everyone may be invited to the couple's home for a reception, and a replica of the wedding cake may be served as dessert, or with coffee or champagne. Toasts are in order.

## Bon Voyage Parties

Saying good-by with a party is a thoughtful and gracious way to entertain.

Most bon voyage parties take place at the departure location, whether at an airport, or aboard ship. In all cases, it helps to know in advance what facilities are available. At an airport, the best approach is to reserve the particular airline's lounge or a portion of it for one or two hours before the trip is to begin. For shipboard departures, you may use the stateroom or a lounge aboard the ship.

The shipboard bon voyage party may be given by friends or relatives or by the couple about to embark. Guests should bring small useful gifts such as a magnetic backgammon board, a traveling sewing kit, or food and liquor that can be used at the party and during the voyage. Heavy gifts are inconvenient for travelers. Streamers, confetti, and balloons are the standard decorations.

Usually a tab for all drinks and hors d'oeuvre is kept by the waiter or steward and presented at the end to the host, or it may be added to the traveler's bill.

If you plan to leave by bus or auto, or if the departure point is simply too inconvenient for friends to reach, a friend of the couple may hold a bon voyage celebration at his home. Usually the bon voyage party is held just before the actual departure, so using the couple's own home presents logistical and cleaning problems that are best avoided this way. Someone should keep an eye on the clock to be sure that the travelers will make their plane, train, ship, or whatever.

### Farewell Parties

Farewell or going-away parties are like any others in most ways, but there are one or two things to be remembered.

If you are planning a party for someone who is leaving town for good, coordinate your efforts with other friends. I know a popular couple who moved away from my hometown recently, and there were thirteen parties held for them! By the time the departure date arrived, their exhausted friends could hardly wait for them to go! So if you find that your friends are being overly fêted, plan something different—take them to the theater, or a hockey game, or whatever they will miss most in their new locale.

While friends are expected to take farewell gifts to one party, they should not be obligated to take gifts to several. This should be made very clear on the invitations. In choosing a gift try to think of something that will serve as a memento to the ones going away. A picture of their home, of their friends, or candids of the going-away party will be treasured. A subscription to the local newspaper will help them to keep up with news of their old friends. And a gift certificate for a store in their new locality will relieve them from having to pack some additional items.

The guests of honor obviously cannot reciprocate by giving a party for those who have entertained them. But they should show their appreciation by sending flowers or a small gift to their hosts.

## Housewarmings

When you have put a great deal of time and effort into making a lovely home, you are naturally as eager to show it off as your friends are to see it. The nicest way to do so is to call your friends and ask them to a housewarming. Invitations on notepaper or commercial fill-in cards are quite suitable, too. Because the object of the party is to show your guests the house, it is far better to have two or three small parties at which you will have to make the tour only a few times. If you have too many people at once, you may spend the entire time leading groups from one room to another.

A housewarming is generally a cocktail party or a cocktail buffet. It may be as simple or as elaborate as you wish, but you should keep the style of your house in mind when you plan your decorations. For instance, if it is an Early American type, a brown tablecloth set with copper or pewter may be more appealing than lace with crystal and silver.

The guest generally takes a small gift to a housewarming and the hostess should be prepared to open these gifts and display them as her guests arrive.

## Wine and Cheese Parties

An appetite for wine has swept the country in recent years and with it a new form of party has become popular—a wine tasting, or wine and cheese party. It is a wonderful way of entertaining your friends. The informal atmosphere and the simplicity of the requirements are ideal for those who have little time to devote to elaborate preparations.

The wine and cheese party may be held at the cocktail hour, or later in the evening. Other liquors are not served. A variety of wines—red, white, rosé, and sparkling (if you wish)—are set out on your dining table, or any convenient table or counter area. Select wines of different types—some sweet, some dry—and include both inexpensive selections and moderate to higher-priced varieties. To accompany the wine buy several cheeses ranging from very mild to go with a medium dry white wine to stronger varieties, such as Roquefort, to go with a hearty red wine. For specific suggestions about what cheeses to use with which types of wine, consult the wine and cheese table in the Appendix (page 298).

Set the cheeses out on a large tray or on individual plates, with a separate spreader for each. As an accompaniment, set out very bland unsalted crackers, or best of all, thinly sliced fresh French bread.

Wine tasting parties should be restricted to 12–16 guests, or the area around the table is sure to become very congested—and messy. Since each guest should have a new glass for every wine he tastes, you will undoubtedly have to buy clear plastic glasses.

Open the wine and allow the cheeses to warm to room temperature before the guests arrive. The red wine is served at room temperature, so it may be stood on a coaster or wine holder on the table, but the white wine must be kept in a cooler of ice to retain its chill. Allow at least a half bottle of wine per person, so 4 bottles would probably serve a party of 8. However, it would do no harm to have one extra bottle of red wine and one of white. Whatever is left will keep for another meal.

You may place the cheeses next to the wines they are supposed to accompany, or you can simply let everyone experiment. It is, however, a good idea to label the cheeses, since many are impossible to identify by sight alone.

The guests help themselves to a small amount of wine and a little piece of bread and cheese, and leave the table to allow others to move up. A very small group can be seated around the table, then, the host serves each with one wine and then the next, and so on, and the cheese is passed around each time. This is often done when the host is a connoisseur (or perhaps a wine dealer) and he gives a brief description and comment on each wine.

Since the idea of the party is to learn about wines as well as to enjoy them, it is an ideal time to experiment. Don't buy your usual favorites but ask your dealer's help in selecting an interesting variety. Even a very inexperienced wine drinker (including the host) can learn to discriminate and to develop his or her own tastes at this very pleasant kind of gathering.

## Picnics

Although picnics can be utterly delightful when well managed, they can be perfectly awful when bungled! Therefore, here are a few general directions for the benefit of those who want to have a really outstanding picnic.

**What kind of picnic**   There are several ways to organize a picnic. The first is to give the picnic yourself, inviting the guests by telephone. If they accept, tell them the hour, where to meet, and possibly ask them to bring a blanket or backrest if the party is large and you do not have enough for everyone.

Or you may call and say, "Mike and I are trying to get a group together for a picnic Saturday night. We'll bring the steaks, and we're asking each couple to contribute one dish. Would you rather bring dessert or salad?" Others might be asked to bring the condiments, chowder, corn, or the drinks.

Lastly, a group of friends may simply arrange to picnic together, each family bringing its own food and cooking it over a community fire. It is fun to see what the others have prepared, and often there is considerable trading and sharing. "I'll trade you a chicken leg for a lobster claw," or "Do try some of this special steak sauce that Susie taught me to make." This sort of picnic is especially good if children are included, as each mother knows best what her young ones will eat most happily.

**Choose your guests**   If you wish to entertain friends by taking them on a picnic, your first task is to consider your guest list very carefully. Nothing is so dampening to the enjoyment of a picnic as the presence of one or more faultfinders who never lift a finger but sit and complain of the heat, of the wind, of a possible shower, of the discomfort of sitting on the ground, or of their personal sufferings caused by mosquitoes or flies. On the other hand, if you select your company from friends who really enjoy picnics, you'll all have a good time and most likely they will work like beavers.

**Choose the location**   If you live near the mountains, you will probably decide to climb or drive to a site that has a beautiful view, but if there are children in the party, be sure there is a field nearby for games or races, or a stream in which they may swim. It should scarcely be necessary to remind you to select a site that you know something about— because you or your friends have picnicked there before. Be sure that the ground is not swampy, that it is not more mosquito-ridden or ant-infested than any place else, and that it is not covered with poison ivy.

If you choose a beach, remember to make some preparation to shield both your guests and the food they are to eat from blowing sand. For this nothing is better than some five-foot garden stakes and a few yards of burlap with a wide hem at each end through which stakes are inserted. Thrust the stakes into the sand to form a windbreak. If you are going to be on the beach all day, an umbrella is a must for those who are not tanned or accustomed to the sun.

If you are giving a large picnic and including a number of people who are not necessarily picnic addicts, it is important to select a site that is easy to get to. Don't expect your average guest to tramp through miles of soft sand carrying blankets, beach towels, and backrests.

**Plan the menu** The very simplest type of picnic is a Continental one. It consists of a loaf of bread, a piece of cheese, and a bottle of wine. If the cheese and wine are good and the bread fresh, this menu has all the advantages of being delicious and nourishing, requiring no preparation, and not costing a great deal. However, in spite of the ease of getting together and carrying the ingredients of a Continental picnic, most Americans prefer to expand the menu in varying degrees. Using the three items above as a base, you may add whatever you wish—fruit for dessert, little tomatoes as a vegetable, tins of sardines or meats, and so on.

If there are children at the picnic, sandwiches are the most popular food of all. Peanut butter and jelly still outstrips any other variety in popularity contests among the very young. Adults and children alike enjoy meat sandwiches, well-seasoned and with plenty of mayonnaise to moisten the bread. Don't, however, make the mistake of using too much mayonnaise or too many tomatoes as the sandwiches will turn to mush on the way to the picnic grounds. Don't attempt to take bread and fillings separately and let people make their own. The messiest picnic imaginable is one at which knives and plates and bread and butter and a half-dozen jars of jams and meat pastes are all spread around and flavored with sand or ants.

It is a good idea to offer a choice of two or three kinds of sandwiches, and by all means label each variety, especially if they are wrapped in foil. Wrapping and unwrapping and pulling apart to view the insides can make a hash of the most beautifully prepared sandwich.

To accompany the sandwich menu, offer a selection of potato chips, pickles, tomatoes, carrot and celery sticks, or disposable containers of potato or macaroni salad. Cake or cookies or any other dessert that may be eaten with the fingers (seedless grapes or watermelon are among the most popular with all ages) make a perfect ending. Thermos jugs of milk or soft drinks for the children, and beer, iced tea, or coffee for the adults complete the meal.

Cold menus may be much more elaborate than sandwiches. In fact, if you have the necessary equipment, you may have an entire buffet spread on a folding table. But most people prefer a simpler picnic, and the main requirement is that the food be the best of its kind. Cold fried chicken, or cold boiled lobster, accompanied by coleslaw or lettuce brought in a damp cloth and mixed with dressing when the group is ready to eat, bread and butter, and fresh fruit for dessert make a meal that is truly fit for a king.

When the nights are cool, or simply because you prefer it, you may wish to serve a hot dish on your picnic. Again you have a choice to make. Do you wish to bring a main dish already made in an insulated container, or do you wish to build a fire and heat your meal at the picnic site? Stews with potatoes and other vegetables, creamed chicken with noodles, roast beef hash made with potatoes, or filling chowders are all excellent choices. All keep indefinitely in big Thermos jugs or any other well-insulated container.

If you enjoy cooking over an open fire, there is nothing more delicious than steak, lamb chops, chicken, swordfish, or lobster cooked over coals. Even hot dogs and hamburgers change from an uninspired meal to a delectable treat. Whole potatoes or corn, wrapped in foil and roasted in the coals, and a mixed green salad make the best accompaniments, along with as many condiments such as mustard and ketchup as you can fit into your baskets. Cold watermelon, or perhaps fresh strawberries, already sugared, might finish the meal.

Your plates for hot picnic food must be more substantial than uncoated paper. Hard plastic or stoneware ones are really the most satisfactory, even though they must be taken home to be washed. Plastic bowls or cups for chowder are far more leakproof and easier to hold than paper cups. As long as you are bringing the utensils for this type of meal, there is no reason not to accompany your main dish with a salad already mixed in a big bowl and breads kept warm by several layers of foil wrapping.

Good strong coffee in a Thermos and plenty of beer and soft drinks kept cold in a tub of ice should be on hand for the singing around a roaring fire that should be a part of every evening picnic.

If you plan to serve wine, you might consider a red wine because it does not need to be chilled. Also, if you forget to bring a corkscrew, here's a handy way to get the cork out of the bottle. First, remove the labels and seals from the cork top. Next, wrap the bottom of the bottle in some heavy cloth—a sweater, shirt, towel, whatever is handy. Holding the wrapped bottle at right angles, gently tap the neck against a tree or rock—the cork will inevitably work itself out, and there is no broken bottle or cork pieces left inside.

**Equipment** Several items of equipment available at hardware stores, chain stores, or specialty shops are a delight to any picnic enthusiast. Styrofoam containers, which will keep food hot or cold and weigh almost nothing, are a must. Another excellent item is an insulated wide-mouthed jug or Thermos to carry anything from cold vichyssoise to hot lamb stew.

Portable grills with folding legs are a great help if you are planning to cook, although on the beach you may simply scoop a hole in the sand, put in the charcoal, and lay a grill from your oven across it, resting it on sturdy boards pressed into the sand on either side of the hole.

Charcoal briquettes packaged in a cardboard container save the trouble of taking newspaper or lighter fluid, and they are easier to carry than a large bag of charcoal. All one has to do is touch a match to the cardboard and the fire is started. One warning: don't try to cook before the flame has died down and the coals have turned white, with a faint red glow here and there.

A two-sided grill, hinged on one end and with a long handle, is wonderful for holding and turning hamburgers, hot dogs, and steaks. It eliminates the danger of the hot dogs rolling between the rungs of a larger grill into the fire, or the hamburgers sticking and crumbling when they are turned.

A pair of long tongs is useful for arranging coals and for moving anything that is hot. They are ideal for turning corn or potatoes as they cook in the coals and better for turning a steak than a fork, which pierces the meat and allows the juices to escape.

There are many other items that add greatly to the ease of preparing a picnic, and each picnic fan must decide which pleases him most. In general, choose those articles that are the most compact and lightweight and those that serve several purposes—useful for transporting or preparing either a hot or cold picnic.

Like the perfect traveler, the perfect picnic manager has reduced the process to an exact science. She knows very well that the one thing to do is to take the fewest things possible and to consider the utility of those few.

Fitted hampers, tents, umbrellas, folding chairs and tables are all very well in a shop, and all right if you have a trailer or a station wagon for hauling them. But the usual flaw in picnics is that there are too many things to carry and look after and too much to clean and pack up and take home again.

Therefore, people who go on picnics frequently should make up a list of all items that may be needed and check it each time before leaving. All the equipment may not be necessary for every picnic, but a list will prevent the salt or the bottle opener from being omitted! If you are a picnic fan, post the following list in a convenient place, and use it whenever you plan a picnic.

## *Picnic Check List*

Can and bottle opener, corkscrew
Forks, knives, spoons
Plates, cups, plastic glasses
Containers with covers (various sizes)
Stoppers and corks
Condiments: salt, pepper, sugar, ketchup, mustard and
    seasonings
Cooking forks, knives, spoons and long tongs
Pots and pans appropriate for outdoor cooking
Napkins and paper towels
Tablecloth(s)
Thermos containers
Aluminum foil or plastic wrap
Canvas carrying bags or picnic baskets
Blankets, backrests
Wind screens
Umbrellas
Large plastic trash bags
Insect repellent and suntan lotion
Small first-aid kit
Matches (in waterproof wrapping)
Grill, charcoal, and lighter fluid
Hinged grill for hot dogs, hamburgers, fish fillets, etc.
Styrofoam ice chest
Ice
Newspaper
Flashlight
Candles with glass chimneys
Equipment for sports or fishing
Extra socks and sweaters
Rain gear
Swimwear, towels, and bags for wet clothes
Packaged moist towels
Clean up equipment

**Leaving the picnic site**   No matter where your picnic has taken place, be sure to tidy up before you leave so that no trace will be left, and be careful, while you are eating and opening papers, not to throw them carelessly aside where they will blow out onto the road. Many of our highways have pleasant wayside parks for picnickers, equipped with rustic tables, safe drinking water, and incinerators. On the property of a private owner, the least payment you can make is to be sure that you do nothing that might despoil any of his property.

Most important of all, never leave a fire without being absolutely certain that it is out. In the woods, water may be poured on the logs until there is no sign of steam, or, if you have a shovel or other means of lifting them, the embers may be carried to a nearby pond or stream and thrown in. On the beach, a fire should also be put out with water. *Never* cover the coals with sand, as they will retain the heat for hours, and someone walking by with bare feet, unable to see the remains of the fire, may step on the hot sand and receive a terrible burn.

# Appendixes

## Sentimental Meaning of Flowers

*Acacia*—platonic love

*Acacia rose*—elegance

*Agrimony*—thankfulness

*Ambrosia*—love returned

*Bachelor's buttons*—hope in love

*Begonia*—fame

*Cactus*—burning love

*Carnation*—pride and beauty

*Pink carnation*—women's love

*Chrysanthemum*—cheerfulness under adversity

*Spring crocus*—youthful gladness

*Daisy*—cheerfulness and innocence

*Fern*—sincerity

*Geranium*—bridal love

*Honeysuckle*—bonds of love

*Iris*—message

*Jasmine*—amiability

*Lemon blossoms*—fidelity in love

*Purple lilac*—first emotion of love

*Magnolia*—love of innocence

*Mistletoe*—surmounting all difficulties

*Tuft of moss*—maternal love

*Myrtle*—love, fertility

*Orange blossoms*—purity and loveliness

*Periwinkle*—sweet remembrance

*Blue periwinkle*—early friendship

*Rose*—love, happy love

*Garland of roses*—reward of virtue

*Shamrock*—lightheartedness

*Red tulip*—declaration of love

*Pink verbena*—family union

*Blue violet*—faithfulness

*Wisteria*—welcome to strangers

*Zinnia*—thoughts of absent friends

*Reprinted by permission from* Green Magic *by Leslie Gordon, Viking Press, 1977*
© *Webb & Bower, Ltd.*

## Chinese Floral Calendar

*January* Plum blossom
*February* Peach blossom
*March* Tree peony
*April* Cherry blossom
*May* Magnolia
*June* Pomegranate
*July* Lotus
*August* Pear blossom
*September* Mallow
*October* Chrysanthemum
*November* Gardenia
*December* Poppy

*Reprinted by permission from* Green Magic *by Leslie Gordon, Viking Press, 1977*
© *Webb & Bower, Ltd.*

## The Months with Their Birthstones and Flowers

| Month | Birthstone | Flower |
|---|---|---|
| January | Garnet | Carnation |
| February | Amethyst | Violet |
| March | Bloodstone or Aquamarine | Jonquil |
| April | Diamond | Sweet pea |
| May | Emerald | Lily-of-the-valley |
| June | Pearl, moonstone, Alexandrite | Rose |
| July | Ruby | Larkspur |
| August | Sardonyx or peridot | Gladiolus |
| September | Sapphire | Aster |
| October | Opal or tourmaline | Calendula |
| November | Topaz | Chrysanthemum |
| December | Turquoise or zircon | Narcissus |

## The Signs of the Zodiac and Their Colors

| | | |
|---|---|---|
| **Aries:** Ram | March 21–April 19 | Red, green |
| **Taurus:** Bull | April 20–May 20 | Blue |
| **Gemini:** Twins | May 21–June 20 | Green |
| **Cancer:** Crab | June 21–July 22 | Blends |
| **Leo:** Lion | July 23–August 22 | Blue, red |
| **Virgo:** Virgin | August 23–September 22 | Red, brown, green, yellow |
| **Libra:** Scales | September 23–October 22 | Green-blue |
| **Scorpio:** Scorpion | October 23–November 21 | Blends |
| **Sagittarius:** Archer | November 22–December 21 | Gold |
| **Capricorn:** Goat | December 22–January 19 | Red, blue, green |
| **Aquarius:** Water boy | January 20–February 18 | Dark red |
| **Pisces:** Fish | February 19–March 20 | Purple |

## Permanent Holiday Calendar

Jan. 1  **New Year's Day**

Jan. 6  **Epiphany** or **Day of the Kings**

Jan. 15  **Martin Luther King's Birthday**

Jan. 20  **Inauguration Day** (only the year following a presidential election)

Jan. 21  **Beginning of Chinese New Year**

Feb. 2  **Groundhog Day**

Feb. 12  **Lincoln's Birthday**

Feb. 14  **St. Valentine's Day**

Feb. 22  **Washington's Birthday** (celebrated in most states the Monday before the 22nd)

First Tuesday in March  **Town Meeting Day**

Mar. 17  **St. Patrick's Day**

Mar. 22  **Vernal Equinox**

Apr. 1  **April Fool's Day**

Apr. 14  **Pan American Day**

Third Friday in April   **Arbor Day**

Apr. 23   **Secretaries' Day**

Apr. 26   **Confederate Memorial Day**

May 1   **May Day**

May 5   **Cinco de Mayo**

Second Sunday in May   **Mother's Day**

May 30   **Memorial Day** (celebrated in most states the Monday before the 30th)

June 14   **Flag Day**

Second or third Sunday in June   **Father's Day**

June 23   **Midsummer's Day** or the **Summer Solstice**

July 4   **Independence Day**

July 14   **Bastille Day**

First Monday in September   **Labor Day**

Oct. 5   **Beginning of Oktoberfest**

Oct. 12   **Columbus Day**

Oct. 31   **Halloween**

Nov. 1   **All Saints' Day**

Second Tuesday in November   **Election Day**

Nov. 11   **Veteran's Day** (formerly Armistice Day)

Fourth Thursday in November   **Thanksgiving Day**

Dec. 21   **Winter Solstice**

Dec. 25   **Christmas Day**

Dec. 31   **New Year's Eve**

## Movable Christian Holidays

|                    | 1981    | 1982    | 1983    | 1984    | 1985    | 1986    | 1987    | 1988    |
|--------------------|---------|---------|---------|---------|---------|---------|---------|---------|
| Ash Wednesday      | Mar. 4  | Feb. 24 | Feb. 16 | Mar. 7  | Feb. 20 | Feb. 12 | Mar. 4  | Feb. 17 |
| Easter             | Apr. 19 | Apr. 11 | Apr. 3  | Apr. 22 | Apr. 7  | Mar. 30 | Apr. 19 | Apr. 3  |
| Pentecost          | Jun. 7  | May 30  | May 22  | Jun. 10 | May 26  | May 18  | Jun. 7  | May 22  |
| 1st Sunday in Advent | Nov. 29 | Nov. 28 | Nov. 27 | Dec. 2  | Dec. 1  | Nov. 30 | Nov. 29 | Nov. 27 |

## Movable Jewish Holidays

|  | 1981 | 1982 | 1983 | 1984 | 1985 | 1986 | 1987 | 1988 |
|---|---|---|---|---|---|---|---|---|
| *Purim* | Mar. 20 | Mar. 9 | Feb. 27 | Mar. 18 | Mar. 7 | Mar. 25 | Mar. 15 | Mar. 3 |
| *First day of Passover* | Apr. 19 | Apr. 8 | Mar. 29 | Apr. 17 | Apr. 6 | Apr. 24 | Apr. 14 | Apr. 2 |
| *First day of Shavuot* | Jun. 8 | May 28 | May 18 | Jun. 6 | May 26 | Jun. 13 | Jun. 3 | May 22 |
| *First day of Rosh Hashona* | Sep. 29 | Sep. 18 | Sep. 8 | Sep. 27 | Sep. 16 | Oct. 4 | Sep. 24 | Sep. 12 |
| *Yom Kippur* | Oct. 8 | Sep. 27 | Sep. 17 | Oct. 6 | Sep. 25 | Oct. 13 | Oct. 3 | Sep. 21 |
| *First day of Hanukkah* | Dec. 21 | Dec. 11 | Dec. 1 | Dec. 19 | Dec. 8 | Dec. 27 | Dec. 16 | Dec. 4 |

## Festival Notes

SPRING FESTIVALS: The *Easter festival* has both a religious and pagan heritage. On the first Sunday following the full moon that appears on or after the vernal equinox, Christ's resurrection and ascension into heaven are commemorated. The name Easter, however, comes from the Scandinavian word "Ostra" and the Teutonic "Ostern," both goddesses of myth who signify the coming of Spring.

*May Day* is a day to welcome Spring. Festivals held either on May 1 or during the first two weeks of May are marked by dances around the Maypole, sports events and games.

*Cinco de Mayo* is a festival day celebrated throughout much of California and the Southwest United States. It is a day for honoring the friendly relations between the United States and Mexico through lavish parades, music and feasting. The Fifth of May commemorates the victory of the Mexican army over a French invasion force in Pueblo on May 5, 1862.

SUMMER FESTIVALS: *Midsummer's Night,* celebrated traditionally in both Mexico and Sweden, is a festival of the summer solstice. Since pagan times it has been a night of rejoicing and feasting.

HARVEST FESTIVALS: The *Oktoberfest,* a festival of German origins, usually begins in late September or early October. It celebrates the annual harvest with festivities calling for enthusiastic consumption of beer and sausage.

The custom of harvest-time festivity goes back over 2,000 years, when the last day of the pagan calendar fell on October 31, *Halloween.* Although not observed in the United States until the last half of the nineteenth century, today Halloween is celebrated by costume parties and children trick-or-treating door to door.

*Thanksgiving* is more of a feast day than any other on the calendar. It is a family day marked by turkey dinners and parades throughout the country. The most famous is the Macy's Parade, begun in 1924.

WINTER FESTIVALS: *Christmas,* the birthday of Christ, is celebrated in many ways throughout the country. In New England, villagers carol and ring hand bells. In the South the night is filled with fireworks. In Yosemite National Park, bands of men dressed as Druids gather to enter the Ahwahnee Hotel, completed in 1927, carrying an enormous yule log covered in mistletoe. In the Southwest children break earthen jugs decorated to look like animals and filled with gifts. One interesting note: Xmas is not an abbreviation for Christmas. The use of "X" began when the early Christians were forced to become a secret society.

On *New Year's Day* there are two world-famous festivals. The first, the Tournament of Roses, is held in Pasadena, California. It is marked by a parade of fantastic floats covered with live flowers—prelude to the Rose Bowl Game. The Mummer's Parade, held in Philadelphia, is a ten-hour spectacle. "King Momus" leads a parade of colorfully costumed men (no women allowed), entertainers, musicians, and dancers, who vie for prizes for the best floats and costumes.

*Chinese New Year* begins the first day of the first moon (any time between January 21 and February 19) and lasts for fourteen days. Each day has a special theme, e.g. on the first day the family gathers together for a meatless meal, on the fifth day the house is completely cleaned, on the last day Chinatown is aglow with the light of thousands of lanterns—hence the name "Feast of Lanterns."

Carnival season begins on January 6th, *Twelfth Night*. Galas in New Orleans are held throughout this season in prelude to Mardi Gras, literally "Fat Tuesday," this celebration takes place on Shrove Tuesday, the day before the beginning of Lent. Torchlight parades, fantastic floats, lavish balls mark this period.

*St. Valentine's Day* was named after a young Roman, who was martyred for refusing to give up Christianity. He left a note for his jailer's daughter signed "From your Valentine," and this started a February 14 tradition.

JEWISH FESTIVALS: *Purim* is a Jewish "semi-festival," a time for rejoicing and thanksgiving commemorating the joyousness of the Jews when Queen Esther delivered her people from the vengeance of a Persian ruler named Haman. Purim means "lots," and the word refers to the casting of lots that Haman ordered to determine which Jews would be killed. Wooden rattles (greggers) are turned whenever Haman's name is mentioned during the reading of the Book of Esther in the synagogue.

*Pesach,* or *Passover,* celebrated more than 3,000 years of freedom. It is also known as the "Festival of Liberation." On the first and second nights of Passover, Jews come together to feast and pray at a gathering called a seder, during which the story of Passover (the Haggadah) is read. Lasting eight days, Passover is a time when matzos are eaten to remind the Jews that their ancestors once had to flee in haste before their bread could rise.

*Hanukkah,* the "Feast of Lights," is celebrated for eight days with the lighting of successive candles of the menorah. It commemorates the triumph for religious freedom more than 2,000 years ago, when the Maccabees recaptured Jerusalem. When they went to rededicate the Holy Temple, the oil they found only seemed sufficient for one day, but it burned miraculously for eight days.

## Special Freezer Tips

Freeze canapés in advance and save the work and bother of last-minute preparation. Cut day-old bread into desired shapes, butter before freezing; thaw slightly before adding spreads. Tray-freezing is ideal for canapés. Prepare dips and spreads and freeze; do not freeze salad dressings, crisp vegetables and hard-cooked eggs. These can be added when canapés are spread, if desired. If you use crackers, freeze the spread only. Thaw and spread on crackers just before serving.

Freeze bread crumbs, buttered or plain. Store in freezer bag or container.

Grate orange or lemon peel, a teaspoonful to a small piece of foil. Fold into packet and freeze. Store packets in labeled bag.

Freeze chopped nuts or meats in bags or rigid containers. Package citron or other candied fruits in foil or freezer bags and freeze.

Make up a pound of garlic butter, freeze in individual portions on cookie sheet and store in polyethylene bag.

Make up herb bouquets (small cheesecloth pouches filled with herbs), pack in bags or wrap in foil and freeze. Use while frozen. Used to flavor soups, stews, gravies, etc.

Use a plastic ice-cube tray to freeze soups, eggs, sauces, liquids, etc. When frozen, remove from tray and store in polyethylene freezer bags. Use as needed.

To keep foods such as individual steaks, hors d'oeuvre, chicken pieces, mushrooms, meatballs, etc., from sticking together when frozen, spread pieces in a single layer on a cookie sheet. Place in freezer unwrapped. Once frozen, remove food from cookie sheet and store in polyethylene freezer bags. Label and date. Return bags to freezer at once.

Fill ice trays with apple cider or fruit juices and freeze. Used instead of ice, the fruit juice cubes won't dilute your drink.

Don't discard foil wrappers when sticks of butter or margarine are used up. Freeze, and use for greasing baking dishes, cookie sheets, etc.

*From "How to Preserve Foods the Modern Way." Reprinted by permission of the Whirlpool Corporation.*

*This information is very useful for the hostess who likes to prepare double quantities of a dish and to keep half of it frozen for use at a future party. Casseroles and breads lend themselves particularly well to freezing, as do many desserts.*

## Food Storage Information

| FOOD | STORAGE TIME |
| --- | --- |
| *Fruits* | |
| berries | 12 months |
| cherries | 12 months |
| peaches | 12 months |
| pineapple | 12 months |
| citrus fruit and juices | 4 to 6 months |
| fruit juice concentrate | 12 months |
| commercially frozen | 12 months |
| | |
| *Vegetables* | |
| home frozen | 8 to 12 months |
| commercially frozen | 8 months |

(*Remember:* raw cabbage, celery, carrots, potatoes and tomatoes do not freeze well. Salad greens lose their crispness.)

| | |
| --- | --- |
| *Meat* | |
| bacon | 4 weeks or less |
| corned beef | 2 weeks |
| cured ham | 1 to 2 months |

(*Cured, smoked meats do not freeze well. The salt will speed rancidity.*)

| Food | Storage Time |
|------|--------------|
| frankfurters | 1 month |
| ground beef, lamb, veal | 2 to 3 months |
| *roasts* | |
| beef | 6 to 12 months |
| lamb | 6 to 9 months |
| veal | 6 to 9 months |
| pork | 4 to 8 months |
| sausage, fresh | 1 to 2 months |
| *steaks and chops* | |
| beef | 8 to 12 months |
| lamb | 3 to 4 months |
| veal cutlets | 3 to 4 months |
| pork | 3 to 4 months |

| *Fish* | |
|------|--------------|
| cod, flounder, haddock | 6 months |
| sole | 6 months |
| blue fish, salmon | 2 to 3 months |
| mackerel, perch | 2 to 3 months |
| breaded fish (*purchased*) | 3 months |
| clams, oysters, cooked fish, crab, scallops | 3 to 4 months |
| Alaskan king crab | 10 months |
| shrimp, uncooked | 12 months |

| *Poultry* | |
|------|--------------|
| chicken, whole | 12 months |
| turkey, whole | 12 months |
| duck | 6 months |
| giblets | 2 to 3 months |
| cooked poultry w/gravy | 6 months |
| slices (*no gravy*) | 1 month |

| *Main Dishes* | |
|------|--------------|
| stews, meat, poultry and fish casseroles | 2 to 3 months |
| TV dinners | 3 to 6 months |

| FOOD | STORAGE TIME |
|------|--------------|
| *Dairy Products* | |
| butter | 6 to 9 months |
| margarine | 12 months |
| *cheese* | |
| Camembert, cottage (*dry curd only*), farmer's, Roquefort, blue | 3 months |
| creamed cottage cheese | *Do not freeze* |
| Cheddar, Edam, Gouda | 6 to 8 weeks |
| (*Texture of cheese will change during freezing.*) | |
| ice cream, ice milk, sherbet | 4 weeks |
| | |
| *Eggs* | |
| whole (*yolk and white* mixed together) | 9 to 12 months |
| whites | 9 to 12 months |
| yolks | 9 to 12 months |
| (*Be sure to add sugar or salt to yolks or whole mixed eggs.*) | |
| | |
| *Baked Goods* | |
| yeast bread and rolls | 3 months |
| baked Brown 'n Serve rolls | 3 months |
| unbaked breads | 1 month |
| quick breads | 2 to 3 months |
| cakes, unfrosted | 2 to 4 months |
| cakes, frosted | 8 to 12 months |
| fruit cakes | 12 months |
| *cookies* | |
| dough | 3 months |
| baked | 8 to 12 months |
| *pies* | |
| baked | 1 to 2 months |
| pastry dough only | 4 to 6 months |

# Herb and Spice Table

| Herbs/Spices | Meat/Fish/Poultry/Eggs | Vegetables/Fruits | Breads/Cereals | Milk Products |
|---|---|---|---|---|
| *Allspice* | Fried chicken, glazed ham, egg custard, broiled haddock, shrimp | Beets, glazed carrots, broiled peaches, creamed cauliflower, pear pie, tomato juice, turnips, orange juice | Doughnuts, rolls, chocolate cake, rice pudding, cupcakes, bread pudding | Cream-cheese spread, banana milkshake, vanilla pudding |
| *Bay Leaf* | Lamb steaks, braised pork chops, chicken soup, clam chowder, baked haddock, shrimp cocktail | Beef stews, pea soup, tomato sauce, stewed carrots, pickled beets | Stuffings, herbed rice, corn bread | Cream soups, cheese soufflés, white wine sauce |
| *Caraway* | Ham salad, spare ribs, beef liver, kidney stew | Potato salad, cabbage, stewed onions, sauerkraut, boiled pears | Noodles, bread sticks, cheese rolls, refrigerator biscuits | Cheese spread, cheese soup, butter spread |
| *Celery* | Grilled sausages, cheese omelet, meat loaf, beef roast, broiled fish | Coleslaw, kohlrabi, French fries, tossed salads, mashed potato | Muffins, noodles, macaroni salad | Mayonnaise dressing, sour-cream sauce, white sauce |

| Herbs/Spices | Meat/Fish/Poultry/Eggs | Vegetables/Fruits | Breads/Cereals | Milk Products |
|---|---|---|---|---|
| *Cinnamon* | Chili, port steaks, fruited chicken, poached fish, spiced shrimp | Sweet potatoes, carrots, baked bananas, squash, apple sauce | Sweet rolls, cereals, coffee cake, cookies, brown bread, gingerbread | Vanilla milkshake, tapioca, whipped toppings, baked custard |
| *Dill* | Shrimp, short ribs, creamed eggs, lamb kabob, salmon salad, seafood stews | Sauerkraut, scalloped potatoes, shredded carrots, cucumber salad, parsnips | Macaroni salad, herbed biscuits, rice, casseroles | Brown gravy, sour-cream dip, potato soup, chowders, tartar sauce |
| *Garlic* | Baked oysters, meat sauce, beef hash, veal cutlets, swiss steaks, beef roast, chicken à la king | Caesar salad, fried spinach, marinated mushrooms, pickled vegetables | Pizza, cocktail crackers, popcorn | Butter spread, cheese fondue, cream-cheese spreads |
| *Mustard* | Broiled ham, deviled eggs, chicken mousse, hamburgers, duck | Guacamole, corn chowder, coleslaw, potato salad, broiled peaches, baked beans | Macaroni salad, buttered noodles, waffles, corn bread | Pork gravy, cheese sauce, Welsh rarebit, boiled dressing |
| *Nutmeg* | Meat pies, Swedish meatballs, ham steaks, sweet and sour pork | Green beans, creamed spinach, cauliflower, pineapple, cranberry sauce, fruit punch | Noodles, nut rolls, pie crust, angel food cake, fruit cake, French toast, rice pudding | Eggnog, baked custard, whipped cream, cream-cheese balls |

| | | | |
|---|---|---|---|
| *Onion* | Hamburgers, beef liver, meat loaf, chili, beef steaks | Vegetable soup, peas, marinated cucumbers, creamed vegetables, carrots, tossed salad | Hominy grits, buns, bread crumbs, dumplings | Cream gravy, cheese fondue, butter spread, sour-cream dip |
| *Oregano* | Pork chops, shrimp marinara, tomatoes, chicken, breaded veal, meat balls | Stewed tomatoes, eggplant, creamed potatoes, zucchini, baked onions, green beans, tossed salad | Corn bread, pizza, spaghetti, croutons | Cheese balls, cream sauce, quiche Lorraine |
| *Paprika* | Egg salad, fried chicken, broiled fish, goulash, spare ribs | Baked potato, creamed cauliflower, kohlrabi, tossed salad, onions | Canapés, rice, buttered noodles, pastry sticks, rolls | Cottage cheese, cheese soup, cream soups, Hollandaise sauce |
| *Parsley* | Crab salad, chicken salad, pot roast, broiled flounder, stews | Corn relish, pear relish, potato pancakes, eggplant, carrots, tomatoes | Biscuits, poultry stuffing, herbed rice | Cheese sauce, sour-cream dressing, mayonnaise dressing |
| *Pepper* | Beef steaks, soups, stews, scrambled eggs, chicken livers | Mashed potatoes, creamed carrots, succotash, marinated vegetables | Egg bread, spice cake, rice salad | Brown gravy, onion gravy, chicken gravy, Muenster cheese |
| *Sage* | Seafood salads, baked ham, roast pork, spare ribs | Tossed salad, cabbage slaw, yams, stewed tomatoes | Poultry stuffing, dumplings, bean soup | Cream of mushroom soup, sour-cream dip, white sauce |

## Table Wines

| WINE | DESCRIPTION | TASTE |
|---|---|---|
| *Red Table Wines* | | |
| **Barbera** | Mellow, full body | Dry |
| **Bardolino** | Delicate taste and bouquet | Dry |
| **Beaujolais** | Fresh, fruity, very popular | Dry |
| **Bordeaux** | Soft in taste, excellent flavor | Dry |
| **Burgundy** | Full body, full flavor | Dry |
| **Cabernet Sauvignon** | Excellent Bordeaux type | Dry |
| **Chateauneuf du Pape** | Sturdy, full body | Dry |
| **Chianti** | Round, full flavor | Dry |
| **Claret** | Bordeaux type, soft flavor | Dry |
| **Cold Duck** | Champagne mixed with sparkling burgundy | Sweet |
| **Lambrusco** | Fruity, mellow—slight "fizz" | Medium dry |
| **Margaux** | Full body, soft Bordeaux wine | Dry |
| **Médoc** | Delicate, medium-body Bordeaux | Dry |
| **Pinot Noir** | Warming Burgundy, pleasant wine | Dry |
| **Pommard** | Popular Burgundy, soft, full body | Dry |
| **Sangria** | Spanish fruit punch | Semi-sweet |
| **St. Emilion** | Bordeaux, full body, soft | Medium dry |
| **St. Julien** | Bordeaux, flavorful claret | Dry |
| **Spanish Rioja** | Often a unique, delightful flavor | Dry |
| **Valpolicella** | Velvet-like quality, delicate | Dry |
| **Zinfandel** | Fruity, delicate California wine | Medium dry |
| | | |
| *Rosé Wines* | | |
| **Mateus** | "Bubbly," soft wine | Medium dry |
| **Rosé d'Anjou** | Light body and flavor | Dry |
| **Tavel Rosé** | Pleasant, clean taste | Dry |
| | | |
| *White Table Wines* | | |
| **Asti Spumanti** | Italian Champagne | Sweet |

| WINE | DESCRIPTION | TASTE |
|---|---|---|
| **Chablis** | Medium body, crispy | Dry |
| **Chenin Blanc** | Soft and fruity | Medium dry |
| **Gewürztraminer** | Spicy flavor, Alsatian wine | Dry |
| **Graves** | Soft, light, pleasant flavor | Dry |
| **Haut Sauternes** | Full body | Sweet |
| **Johannisberg Riesling** | Fresh, flowery, soft | Medium dry |
| **Liebfraumilch** | Rhine wine, touch of sweetness | Medium dry |
| **Moselle** | Light, delicate flavor | Dry |
| **Muscadet** | Light, delicate and crisp | Very dry |
| **Pinot Chardonnay** | Finest full flavor, white Burgundy | Dry |
| **Pouilly-Fuissé** | Crisply dry, fruity bouquet | Dry |
| **Rhine** | Light body | Dry |
| **Sauterne** | Medium body, fruity and mellow | Medium sweet |
| **Soave** | Refreshing | Medium dry |
| **Verdicchio** | Very light body | Dry |
| **Vouvray** | Delicate, fresh | Medium dry |
| **White Bordeaux** | Smooth, refreshing | Medium dry |
| **Zeller schwarze Katz** | Light Moselle, refreshing | Medium dry |

## Wine Cookery Table

The amounts suggested are minimal, so add more little by little until it suits your taste.

Other dry wines may be substituted for Burgundy and Chablis. Although there are white Burgundies, this list calls for *red* Burgundy.

| FOODS | AMOUNT OF WINE | PREFERRED WINE |
|---|---|---|
| *Soups* | | |
| **cream** | 1 tsp. per cup | Sherry |
| **clear** | 1 tsp. per cup | Sherry |
| *Sauces* | | |
| **brown** | 1 tbs. per cup | Burgundy |

| Foods | Amount of Wine | Preferred Wine |
|---|---|---|
| cream or white | 1 tbs. per cup | Chablis or dry vermouth |
| tomato | 1 tbs. per cup | Burgundy |
| cheese | 1 tbs. per cup | Chablis |
| dessert | 1 tbs. per cup | Port, muscatel |

*Meats*

| | | |
|---|---|---|
| pot roast or stew beef | ¼ cup per lb. of meat | Burgundy |
| pot roast or stew lamb, veal | ¼ cup per lb. of meat | Dry white wine |
| baked ham | ½ cup per basting | Port, muscatel |
| liver, braised | ¼ cup per lb. | Burgundy, Madeira |
| kidneys | ¼ cup per lb. | Madeira, vermouth |

*Fish*

| | | |
|---|---|---|
| baked | ½ cup per lb. | Chablis |
| court bouillon for poaching | ½ cup per 1 qt. liquid | Chablis |

*Poultry*

| | | |
|---|---|---|
| coq au vin | 2 tbs. per cup liquid | Burgundy |
| chicken in cream sauce | 1 tbs. per cup sauce | Chablis |
| roast duck | ¼ cup per lb. | Burgundy |

*Game*

| | | |
|---|---|---|
| venison | ¼ cup per lb. | Burgundy |
| pheasant | 1 tbs. per cup sauce | Burgundy or Chablis |

*Fruits*

| | | |
|---|---|---|
| compotes | 1 tbs. per serving | Port, Madeira, sherry, sauterne |

# Wine and Cheese Table

| CHEESE | ACCOMPANYING WINES |
| --- | --- |
| **Appenzeller** | Burgundy |
| **Bel Paesi** | Beaujolais, Moselle, Rhine |
| **Bleu** | Chianti, Burgundy, Bordeaux |
| **Bonbel** | Chablis, Bordeaux |
| **Boursin, Boursault** | Moselle, Graves, Rhine |
| **Brie** | Chianti, Burgundy, sherry |
| **Camembert** | Burgundy, Chateauneuf |
| **Cheddar** | Bordeaux, Burgundy |
| **Crème Dania** | Moselle, Graves, sauterne |
| **Edam** | Bordeaux, Burgundy, medium-dry sherry |
| **Fontina** | Beaujolais, Moselle |
| **Gouda** | Beaujolais, Graves, Chablis |
| **Gourmandise** | Moselle, Graves, sauterne |
| **Feta** | Chianti, Burgundy, Bordeaux |
| **Gruyère** | Burgundy |
| **Jarlsberg** | Burgundy |
| **Liederkranz** | Burgundy |
| **Muenster** | Bordeaux, Chablis |
| **Port du Salut** | Burgundy, Chablis, Rhine |
| **Provolone** | Burgundy |
| **Swiss** | Burgundy, Bordeaux |
| **Tilsit** | Chablis, Pouilly-Fuissé |

# Ethnic Toasts

| | |
| --- | --- |
| **American** | Here's Luck! |
| **British** | Cheers! |
| **Chinese** | Wen Lie! |
| **French** | A votre santé! |
| **German** | Prosit! |
| **Greek** | Yasas! |
| **Hebrew** | L'Chayim! |
| **Hungarian** | Ege'sze'ge're! |
| **Irish** | Slainte! |
| **Italian** | Alla Salute! |

| Japanese | Kanpai! |
|----------|---------|
| Polish | Na Zdrowie! |
| Russian | Za vashe zdorovye! |
| Spanish | Salud! |
| Swedish | Skäl! |

## Place Card Designations at Formal Dinners

| PERSONAGE | DESIGNATION |
|-----------|-------------|
| **The President of the United States** | The President |
| **The President's wife** | Mrs. Lincoln |
| **Cabinet members** | The Secretary of the Treasury The Attorney General, etc. |
| **Senator** | Senator Howard |
| **Congressman** | Mr. Franklin |
| **Governor** | The Governor of (Idaho) |
| **Mayor** | The Mayor of (Chicago) |
| **Judge** | The Honorable James Crow |
| **Protestant bishop** | Bishop Farmington |
| **Protestant clergyman** | Mr. Jones, or, if he holds a degree, Doctor Jones |
| **Rabbi** | Rabbi Klein, or, if he holds a degree, Doctor Klein |
| **Monsignor** | The Right Reverend Ryan |
| **Priest** | Father O'Neal |
| **University professor** | Doctor Knowles, or Professor Knowles |
| **Physician, dentist, veterinarian** | Doctor Cassel |
| **Military personnel** | By their titles: General Brown, Ensign Black, Private White, etc. |

## Removing Common Stains

| STAIN | REMOVAL PROCEDURE |
|-------|-------------------|
| **Alcoholic Drinks** | Immediately sponge with cold water, then sponge with alcohol or, on acetates, with 1 part alcohol to 2 parts water. |

| STAIN | REMOVAL PROCEDURE |
|---|---|
| **Beer** | Sponge with soap and water or wash in machine. |
| **Berries and Fruit** | Immediately sponge with cool water. If the fabric is sturdy and washable, stretch it over a pot, secure with a rubber band, and pour on boiling water. With silk, wool and colored fabrics, apply hydrogen peroxide with a dropper every 5–7 minutes, testing after each application for color. |
| **Blood** | Wash in cold water. Then, if necessary, wash in warm water with detergent or apply hydrogen peroxide. |
| **Butter** | Wash or sponge with cleaning fluid. |
| **Coffee** | If colorfast and washable, soak in 1 part vinegar to 4 parts water. For non-washable fabrics, use cleaning fluid like carbon tetrachloride. |
| **Grease and Oil** | For washable fabrics, use warm water and soap containing naphtha or kerosene. For non-washable fabrics, use cleaning fluid or an absorbent like corn meal: sprinkle on the stain, let it sit, then wipe it off. Repeat if necessary. |
| **Scorching** | Hydrogen peroxide. |
| **Tomato (juice, catsup, sauce)** | Sponge with cold water; then apply glycerine and sponge with soap and water; rinse. |
| **Wine** | For washable sturdy fabrics, stretch fabric over pot and secure with rubber band. Pour on boiling water. Or you can cover with salt and clean with boiling water. For non-washable fabrics, sponge with alcohol or, for acetates, 1 part alcohol to 2 parts water. |

# Source Manual and Bibliography

This section provides a list of books, pamphlets, folders, etc., many available by mail order. The booklets cover a wide variety of subjects connected with entertaining, and they should be valuable assets and worthwhile additions to your reference shelf. Some are free, others require a self-addressed envelope or a small fee. Prices and availability are, of course, subject to change, but most of those noted as free will undoubtedly remain so, and other price changes can be ascertained by writing to the publishing company.

## Audio Equipment

*Annex Outlet Ltd.*
43 Warren Street, New York, NY 10007
*Catalogues of tape cassettes. Free.*

*Stereo Corporation of America*
1629 Flatbush Avenue, Brooklyn, NY 11210
*Catalogue of audio components and tapes. Free.*

*Stereo Discounts*
6730 Santa Barbara Ct., Baltimore, MD 21227
*Catalogue of records, tapes, audio and video equipment. Free.*

## Calendar

*300-Year Calendar, 1750–2059*
Arthur A. Merrill
P.O. Box 228, Chappaqua, NY 10514
*Self-addressed stamped envelope.*

## Calligraphy

*Scrolls Hand Lettered*
215 Park Avenue South
Department H-R, New York, NY 10003
*Booklet on Calligraphy.*

## Catering for Large Crowds

Wallace, James Young. *The American Quantity Cookbook*. Boston: Cahners
Books International, 1976.
*Regional American recipes in institutional or party quantities.*

West, Bessie Brooks, Grace Severance Shugart, Maxine Fay Wilson. *Food
For Fifty*, New York: John Wiley & Sons, 1961, 1979.
*The sixth edition of a leading source book for institutional cookery. Information on buying and preparing food for fifty; menus for parties and receptions, among other things; recipes, of course. Purchasing information is invaluable.*

# Coffees and Teas

*McNulty's Tea and Coffee*
109 Christopher Street, New York, NY 10014
*Price lists of teas, coffees and spices sold by mail. Free.*

*More Fun with Coffee*
National Coffee Association
120 Wall Street, New York, NY 10005
*Free.*

# Cleaning and Laundering

*Aids To Interior Decorating Fabric Care*
Aids International
2009 N. 14th Street, Arlington, VA 22201

*Energine Spot Remover Guide*
D-Con Company, Inc.
225 Summit Avenue, Montvale, NJ 07645

*The Facts of Laundry*
The Maytag Company, Home Economics Dept.
Newton, IA 50208

*Magic Laundry Booklet*
Armour & Company, Consumer Services Department
Greyhound Tower, 20th Floor, Phoenix, AZ 85077

*Removing Spots and Stains*
The Maytag Company, Form 194G
Home Economics Department, Newton, IA 50208

*Wood Floor Care Guide. 25¢.*
Oaks Flooring Institute, Department GSL-F
804 Sterick Building, Memphis, TN 38103

# Cookbooks

*Appetizers*

Beard, James. *Hors d'Oeuvres & Canapés.* New York: William Morrow & Co., Inc., 1967. Paperback.

Reed, Ann and Marilyn Pfaltz. *Your Secret Servant: Fix and Freeze Hors d'Oeuvres for Easy Entertaining.* New York: Charles Scribner's Sons, 1970. Paperback.

*The Great Cook's Guide to Appetizers.* New York: Random House, Inc., 1977.
*The country's best cooks share their favorite hors d'oeuvres.*

*Sunset Hors d'Oeuvres: Appetizers, Spreads and Dips.* Menlo Park, CA: Lane Publishing Co., 1976. Paperback.
*The whole range plus party menus, including nine tasty and ethnic themes.*

*Cooking with Appliances*

*The ABC of Chafing Dish Cookery,* Mount Vernon: The Peter Pauper Press, 1956. Paperback.
*Short and easy recipes.*

*The Amana Radarange Microwave Oven Cookbook.* Amana, IA: Amana Refrigeration, Inc., 1975.
*Tried and tasted quick-cooking meals. Covers complete meals and methods for the microwave oven.*

Anderson, Jean. *Jean Anderson's Processor Cooking.* New York: William Morrow & Co., Inc., 1979.
*Invaluable reference section on what processors can and can't do and how to process dozens of foods. Recipes are written with processor techniques incorporated into the instructions. Recipes chosen are those for which using the processor really saves labor or actually improves them.*

*Cooking with a Food Processor,* General Electric, 1978.
*A complete guide to how to prepare each type of food with the processor, plus 200 recipes.*

Hoffman, Mable. *Crockery Cooking.* Tucson: H. P. Books, 1975. Paperback.
*Complete menus and methods of crockery cooking. Takes into account the differences in models in describing the methods.*

Hoffman, William. *Gourmet Blender Cookbook.* New York: Galahad Books, 1974.

## Desserts

Burbridge, Cile Bellefleur. *Cake Decorating for Any Occasion.* Radnor, PA: Chelton Book Co., 1978.
*Step directions for twelve theme cake decorations for holidays and children.*

Heatter, Maida. *Maida Heatter's Book of Great Desserts.* New York: Alfred A. Knopf, Inc., and Warner Books, 1977. Paperback.
*The definitive dessert book.*

Lenotres. *Desserts & Pastries.* Woodbury: Barrons Educational Series, Inc., 1977.
*Every elegant dessert imaginable by the finest pastry chef since Carême.*

## Pamphlets

*Cake Decorating*
Nestle Co., Inc.
100 Bloomingdale Road, White Plains, NY 10605

## General

Axler, Bruce. *Adding Eye Appeal to Foods.* Indianapolis: Bobbs-Merrill Co., Inc., 1974. Paperback.

Beard, James A. *The Best of Beard.* Racine, WI: Western Publishing Co., Inc., 1974. Paperback.

*James Beard's Theory and Practice of Good Cooking.* New York: Alfred A. Knopf, Inc., 1977.
*Beard's cooking school between two covers. Invaluable basic techniques clearly presented, plus 300 excellent recipes.*

Claiborne, Craig. *The New York Times Cook Book.* New York: Harper & Row, Publishers, Inc., 1961.

*Nearly 1500 selected recipes that appeared in* The New York Times *between 1950 and 1960. Familiar classics, family recipes and European specialities. Good buffet and appetizer ideas.*

Claiborne, Craig. *The New York Times International Cook Book.* New York: Harper & Row, Publishers, Inc., 1971.
*Recipes from 45 countries for every day and special occasions. A cross-reference index, photos and drawings.*

Field, Michael. *Michael Field's Cooking School.* New York: Holt, Rinehart and Winston, Inc., 1965.
*Among the clearest of all how-to cookbooks and a classic by a famous chef and cooking school teacher.*

*The Gourmet Cookbook, vols. I and II.* New York: Gourmet Books, 1957, 1976.
*By the editors of that famous magazine. Lots of recipes suitable for entertaining.*

Rombauer, Irma S. and Marion Rombauer Becker. *Joy of Cooking.* New York: Signet Special, The New American Library, Inc., 1973. Paperback.
*Over 4,300 recipes from the most basic to the most exotic. When you can't find a recipe anywhere else, you'll find it in* Joy of Cooking.

Ungerer, Miriam. *The Too Hot To Cookbook.* New York: Funk & Wagnalls Publishing Co., Inc., 1966. Paperback.
*A small summer cookbook that's good all year. Excellent recipes, many geared to entertaining, and tidbits of interesting information.*

## Cookbooks for Dieters

Gibbons, Barbara. *The International Slim Gourmet Cookbook.* New York: Harper & Row, Publishers, Inc., 1978.
*How to prepare the best of world cuisine without hundreds of hidden calories.*

Nidetch, Jean. *Weight Watchers New Program Cookbook.* New York: New American Library, 1971, 1978.
*Cooking according to their program.*

Pappas, Lou Siebert. *Gourmet Cooking—The Slim Way.* Reading, MA: Addison-Wesley Publishing Co., Inc., 1977.
*200 international recipes for meals of 500 calories or less.*

## *American* (Regional)

Beard, James. *James Beard's American Cookery*. Boston, MA: Little Brown & Co., 1972.
*His favorites, plus epicurean reminiscences.*

Becker, Marion and Irma Rombauer. *Joy of Cooking*. Indianapolis: Bobbs-Merrill Co., Inc., 1931; New York: New American Library, Inc., 1975. Paperback.
*The standard soup-to-nuts guide to practically everything that could make its way into an American kitchen.*

Collin, Rima and Richard Collin. *The New Orleans Cookbook*. New York: Alfred A. Knopf, Inc., 1978.
*Great creole and cajun recipes with very clear instructions. The best New Orleans cookbook.*

Darden, Norman Jean and Carole Darden. *Spoonbread and Strawberry Wine*. New York: Doubleday & Co., Inc., and Anchor Press, 1978. Paperback.
*Recipes and reminiscences of black American family.*

Gruver, Suzanne Cary. *The Cape Cod Cookbook*. New York: Dover Publications, Inc., 1977. Paperback.
*Seafood chowders, cranberry pie, etc. Traditional recipes updated.*

Johnson, Ronald. *The Aficionado's Southwestern Cooking*. Albuquerque, NM: University of New Mexico Press, 1968.
*Special emphasis on Mexican-American dishes for entertaining.*

Lewis, Edna. *The Taste of Country Cooking*. New York: Alfred A. Knopf, Inc., 1976.
*One of the best of the personal cookbooks, it evokes post-slavery black family life in Virginia while explaining the delicious food that was an important part of that life.*

## *Chinese*

Claiborne, Craig and Virginia Lee. *The Chinese Cookbook*. Philadelphia: J. B. Lippincott Co., 1972.
*A good and authentic general survey.*

Kuo, Irene. *The Key to Chinese Cooking*. New York: Alfred A. Knopf, Inc., 1977.
*Careful guidance on technique and clear instructions, which are particularly important with an unfamiliar cuisine.*

Lin, Florence. *Chinese Regional Cookbook*. New York: Hawthorn Books, Inc.
*Excellent recipes and easy-to-follow format.*

Waldo, Myra. *The Complete Book of Oriental Cooking*. New York: Bantam Books, Inc., 1960. Paperback.
*Contains over 350 recipes covering thousands of miles of the Far East.*

## French

Child, Julia, Louisette Berthole, and Simone Beck. *Mastering the Art of French Cooking, Volume I*. New York: Alfred A. Knopf, Inc., 1961.
*The classic explication of French cooking to American cooks. Basic recipes and variations. Volume I is a must in your library.*

David, Elizabeth. *French Provincial Cooking*. New York: Penguin Books, 1960. Paperback.
*A classic by one of the great food writers.*

*Escoffier*. New York: Crown, 1969.
*The bible of French cuisine—for chefs and experts only.*

Mapie, The Countess de Toulouse-Lautrec. *La Cuisine de France*. New York: Orion Press, 1964.
*A practical modern adaptation of the French cuisine to the needs of today's housewife.*

Root, Waverly. *The Food of France*. New York: Alfred A. Knopf, Inc., 1958, 1966, and Vintage Press, 1977. Paperback.
*Gastronomic travelog which discusses, region by region, all the dishes that have made France famous for food. A classic on both food and France.*

## Italian

Giobbi, Edward. *Italian Family Cooking*. New York: Vintage Press, 1971, 1978. Paperback.
*A personal touch that makes the recipes seem extra tasty.*

Hazan, Marcella. *Classic Italian Cookbook.* New York: Alfred A. Knopf, Inc., 1978.
*A rare combination: the recipes are authentic, presented very clearly, absolutely delicious, and not terribly difficult.*

## Japanese

Ortiz, Elizabeth Lambert and Mitsuko Endo. *The Complete Book of Japanese Cooking.* New York: M. Evans and Co., Inc., 1976.

## Jewish and Kosher

Grossinger, Jennie. *The Art of Jewish Cooking.* New York: Bantam Books, Inc., 1972. Paperback.

London, Anne, Bishov London, and Bertha Kahn. *The Complete American-Jewish Cookbook.* New York: Thomas Y. Crowell Company, Inc., 1971.
*3500 tested kosher recipes. Most complete Jewish cookbook in English.*

## Mexican

Kennedy, Diana. *The Cuisines of Mexico.* New York: Harper & Row, Publishers, Inc., 1972.

Ortiz, Elizabeth Lambert. *The Complete Book of Mexican Cooking.* New York: M. Evans & Co., Inc., 1965.
*A classic volume.*

## Middle Eastern

Roden, Claudia. *A Book of Middle Eastern Food.* New York: Alfred A. Knopf, Inc., 1972, and Vintage Press, 1974. Paperback.
*Excellent recipes, exotic sounding but not difficult to prepare.*

## Special Meals

Billik, Crownie and Kathy Kaufman. *The Brunch Cookbook.* New York: Bantam Books, 1972. Paperback.

Weiland, Barbara. *The Picnic Cookbook*. New York: Butterick Publishing, 1979.
*Menus for all seasons—Labor Day Clambake, Japanese Celebration of Spring, Winter Ski Picnic, others. Gourmet backpack, Italian beach-blanket picnic, etc.*

## Specific Foods

Beard, James. *Beard on Bread*. New York: Alfred A. Knopf, Inc., 1973.
*The dean of American cookery on his favorite subject—bread.*

*James Beard's Casserole Cookbook*. New York: Fawcett Inc., 1955, 1968. Paperback.
*250 ideas for the oven.*

*James Beard's Fowl & Game Bird Cookery*. New York: Harvest, Inc., 1979. Paperback.

*James Beard's New Fish Cookery*. Boston: Little Brown & Company, 1954, 1976.
*One of the best fish books and one of Beard's best.*

Bradshaw, George. *Soufflés, Quiches, Mousses & the Random Egg*. New York: Harper & Row, Publishers, Inc., 1971.

Claiborne, Craig. *Cooking with Herbs & Spices*. New York: Harper & Row, Publishers, Inc., 1970, and Bantam Books, 1977. Paperback.

DeGouy, Louis P. *The Soup Book*. New York: Dover Publications, Inc., 1974. Paperback.
*Over 800 recipes from a master chef.*

Elkon, Juliette. *The Chocolate Cookbook*. New York: Barnes & Noble Books, 1975. Paperback.

Flagg, William G. *Mushroom Lover's Cookbook*. Cookbook, Inc., 1978.

Grigson, Jane. *Jane Grigson's Vegetable Book*. New York: Atheneum Publishers, 1979.
*An engaging writer tackles 75 varieties of vegetables.*

Harrington, Geri. *The Salad Book*. New York: Atheneum Publishers, 1977.
*Combination gardening and cookery book that tells you everything you ought to know about producing a salad.*

Hoffman, Mable. *Crepe Cookery*. Tucson: H. P. Books, 1976. Paperback.
*A versatile favorite for entertaining—crepes as appetizers, main dishes and desserts.*

Langseth-Christensen, Lillian. *Cold Foods for Summer & Winter*. New York: Doubleday, Inc., 1974.

Lobel, Leon and Stanley Lobel. *All About Meat*. New York: Harcourt Brace Jovanovich, Inc., 1975.
*The most famous butchers in America tell you how to select the best meat and how to cook it to perfection. Also how to store, freeze and carve.*

Pearl, Anita May, Constance Cuttle, and Barbara B. Deskins. *Completely Cheese: The Cheeselovers' Companion*. Middle Village: Jonathan David Publishers, 1978.
*Surveys the varieties, recipes, how to make it.*

## Vegetarian

*The Farm Vegetarian Cookbook*. Summertown, TN: The Book Publishing Co., 1975.
*An "absolute vegetarian cookbook with no meat, milk, eggs, cheese, fish or fowl." For hard-core vegetarians who really like beans.*

Lappé, Frances Moore. *Diet for a Small Planet*. New York: Ballantine Books, Inc., 1971. Paperback.
*Million-copy seller about high-protein, meatless cooking. Sets up meal plans for assuring the proper amount of protein in the diet.*

Thomas, Anna. *The Vegetarian Epicure* and *The Vegetarian Epicure Book II*. New York: Alfred A. Knopf, Inc., 1978; New York: Vintage Press, 1972, 1979. Paperback.
*Perhaps the most vegetarian cookbooks; charming drawings.*

## Costumes

*Dress for the Ages, a Guide to Historical Costumes.*
Brooks Van Horn Costumes
117 West 17th Street, New York, NY 10011
$1.00

House of Costumes
166 Jericho Turnpike, Mineola, NY 11501
*Costume catalogue. Free.*

# Decorations

*Books*

Cook, Harold C. *Decorating for the Holidays*. Milwaukee: Ideal Publishing Corp., 1976.

Pautz, Phyllis. *Decorating with Plant Crafts & Natural Material*. New York: Doubleday & Company, 1971.

Randlett, Samuel. *The Art of Origami*. New York: E. P. Dutton & Co., Inc., 1961.

Waugh, Dorothy. *Festive Decorations*. New York: Macmillan, Inc., 1962.

Weinberg, Julia. *Decorative Centerpieces to Eat and Enjoy*. New York: Butterick Publishing, 1978.
*How to transform everyday vegetables into bouquets that are beautiful and real conversation pieces.*

*Pamphlets*

*Catalogue of Art Supplies. Free.*
Polyart Products Company
1199 East 12th Street, Oakland, CA 94606

*Catalogue of Wooden Handcrafted Christmas Ornaments and Hawaiian Motifs. Free.*
Emgee Corporation
3210 Koapaka Street, Honolulu, HI 98619

*Catalogue of Danish Easter Ornaments. $1.00.*
Klod Hans
34 Hans Jensensstraede, DK-5000 Odense, Denmark

*Crafty Critters Folder. Free.*
Recycled Party Favors
Box RB, Texize
P.O. Box 368, Greenville, SC 29602

*"Dough-It-Yourself" Christmas Decorations. Free.*
Morton Salt, Consumer Affairs Department
110 N. Wacker Drive, Chicago, IL 60606

*Easter-egg Decorating and Party Idea Pamphlet. Free.*
PAAS, Department RB
Plough Avenue, P.O. Box 377, Memphis, TN 38151

*Christmas Decorations Made with Plant Materials.*
Science and Educational Administration
U.S. Department of Agriculture
The National Arboretum
Washington, DC 20250

Toy Balloon Co.
204 East 38th Street, New York, NY 10016
*Animal-shaped personalized balloon catalogue and price lists. Free.*

## Flags

*Our Flag* (Booklet #052-071-00476-9). *$1.50.*
Government Printing Office
Superintendent of Documents
Washington, DC 20402
*Flag history and etiquette guidebook. Free.*

## Flowers

*Books*

Ascher, Amglie A. *The Complete Flower Arranger.* New York: Simon & Schuster, Inc., 1977. Paperback.

Buffet-Challic, Lawrence. *Flower Decoration in European Homes.* New York: William Morrow & Co., Inc., 1969.

Hirsch, Sylvia. *Art of Table Setting & Flower Arrangement.* rev. ed. New York: Thomas Y. Crowell Co., 1967. Illustrated.

Gordon, Leslie. *Green Magic.* New York: Viking Press, 1977.

Morrison, Winifrede. *Flower Arrangements for Special Occasions.* New York: Hippocrene Books, Inc., 1976.

*Pamphlets*

*Catalogue for Flower Arrangers. 10¢.*
Dorothy Biddle Service
DBS Building
Hawthorne, NY 10532

*Selection Guide & Tips on Caring for Cut Flowers. Free.*
Florist's Transworld Delivery Association
Advertising and Public Relations Division, P.O. Box 2227
29200 Northwestern Highway, Southfield, MI 48037

# Food Suppliers

*Food Preparation*

*Cake Cutting Guide*
The American Institute of Baking
400 East Ontario Street, Chicago, IL 60611

*Freezing Tips*
Standard Brands, Inc.
Box 2695
Grand Central Station, New York, NY 10017

*How to Prepare Maine Lobster and/or*
*How to Eat a Maine Lobster*
The Maine Publicity Bureau
State House, Augusta, ME 04333

*Pamphlets*

*American and Pennsylvania Dutch Specialties. Catalogue $1.00.*
Colonial Gardens Kitchens
270 West Merrick Road, Valley Stream, NY 11582

Briggs Way Company
Ugashik, Alaska 99683
Fresh Alaska seafoods packed in glass.
*Price lists and information. Free.*

*Cheese and maple syrup products. Free.*
Sugarbush Farms
Woodstock, VT 05091

*Cheese of the Month Club. Free.*
Cheese of All Nations
153 Chambers Street, New York, NY 10003

*Chinese Food Ingredients. Free.*
Kam Shing Company
2246 Wentworth Avenue, Chicago, IL 60616

*Creole Delicacies. Free.*
Creole Delicacies Company
533 St. Ann Street, New Orleans, LA 70116

Paprikas Weiss Importer
1546 Second Avenue, New York, NY 10028
*Food and utensils imported from Hungary and Czechoslovakia. $1.00.*

*French Gourmet Food Catalogue. Free.*
Les Echalottes
Ramsey, NJ 07446

*Fruit of the Month Catalogue. Free.*
Harry & David
Bear Creek Orchards
Medford, OR 97501

*German Specialties. Free.*
Bremen House
218 East 86th Street, New York, NY 10028

*Imported Food and Specialty Appetizers. Free.*
Zabars
Broadway at 80th St., New York, NY 10024

*Ingredients for Mexican Cooking.*
La Semillera Horticultural Enterprises
P.O. Box 34082, Dallas, TX 75234

*Italian Food Specialties. Free.*
Manganaro Foods
488 Ninth Avenue, New York, NY 10018

*Natural Foods. Free.*
Walnut Acres, Inc., Penns Creek, PA 17862

*Wild Game, Poultry Specialties, Elk, Elephant.*
Maryland Gourmet Mart
414 Amsterdam Avenue, New York, NY 10024

## Card Games

Gibson, Walter B. *Hoyle's Modern Encyclopedia of Card Games.* New York: Doubleday & Company, Inc., 1974.

Morehead, Albert H. *Official Rules of Card Games.* New York: Fawcett Books, 1978. Paperback.

## Children's Games

Johnson, June. *Eight Hundred Thirty-Eight Ways to Amuse a Child.* New York: Macmillan, Inc., 1962. Paperback.

Webb, Alison and Leary Shulagh. *Fun for Kids.* Los Angeles: Reed Books, 1975. Paperback.

## Games and Amusements

*Books*

Abraham, Robert M. *Easy-to-Do Entertainments and Diversions with Cards, Strings, Coins, Paper, and Matches.* New York: Dover Publications, Inc., 1961. Paperback.
*Winter nights entertainments.*

Anderson, Ken and Morry Carlson. *Games for All Occasions.* Grand Rapids: The Zondervan Corp., 1951, 1967. Paperback.

Burnes, Lorell Coffman. *The Indoor Games Book.* Salem, NH: Merrimack Book Service, 1973.

McWhirter, Norris and Norvin Pallas. *Guinness Game Book.* New York: Sterling Publishing Inc., 1971.

Mulle, Margaret E. and Marian S. Holmes. *The Party Game Book*. New York: Harper & Row, Publishers, Inc., 1951.

## Pamphlets

*American Contract Bridge League and Easy Guide to Duplicate Bridge*
220 Democrat Road, Memphis, TN 38116

The Athletic Institute
200 Castlewood Drive, North Palm Beach, FL 33408
*Source of official rules for all sports. 50¢.*

## Invitations

Goudy, Frederick W. *The Alphabet and Elements of Lettering*. New York: Dover Publications, Inc., 1952.
*A concise introductory book of styles and how-to. Beautifully illustrated chapters on the beginnings of the alphabet.*

*Pocket Pal*. New York: International Paper Company, 1934, 1980.
*An authoritative introduction to printing and typesetting. Covers all of the graphic arts processes, each new addition reflecting technological advances. Everything you need to know about printing in one invaluable and inexpensive little book.*

## Measures

*Household Weights & Measures*. SP 430
U.S. Department of Commerce
National Bureau of Statistics
Office of Technical Publishing
Washington, DC 20234

## Movies

Audio Brandon
334 MacQuesten Parkway, Mt. Vernon, NY 10550
*American and International film-rental catalogue. Free.*

Blackhawk Films Digest
1235 West 5th Street, P.O. Box 3990
Davenport, IA 52808
*Hollywood films from 1896 to 1980. Catalogue. Free.*

# Music

Chesterfield Music Shop
12 Warren Street, New York, NY 10007
*Record catalogue. Free.*

House of Oldies
267 Bleecker Street, New York, NY 10014
*World Headquarters for out of print 45's. Catalogue $1.50.*

*Singing Telegrams.*
Music Box
212–620–7970. 800–221–9820.
Special services: roses, champagne, tap dancing.

# Napkin Folding

Belgian Linen Association
280 Madison Avenue, New York, NY 10016
*Napkin folding pamphlet. 25¢*

Kemp & Beatley
1040 Avenue of the Americas, New York, NY 10018
*Napkin folding brochure. 35¢.*

Vera, Inc.
5 East 37th Street, New York, NY 10018
*Brochure of classic napkin folds. Free.*

# Novelties

D. Robbins and Co., Inc.
70 Washington Street, Brooklyn, NY 11201
*Catalogue of magic tricks, books, jokers' novelties, puzzles, party fun items.*
*$1.00.*

The Fun House
P.O. Box 1225, Newark, NJ 07101
*Magic tricks, novelties and souvenirs. Catalogue. Free.*

The Game Room
P.O. Box 4290, Washington, DC 20012
*Humorous gifts for adults. Catalogue 50¢.*

Johnson Smith Company
35075 Automation Drive, Mount Clemens, MI 48043
*Catalogue of tricks and novelties. Free.*

## Occult

New York Astrology Center
127 Madison Avenue, New York, NY 10016
*Astrology catalogue—books, tables, wall charts. Free.*

Templestar Company
Times Plaza Station
Box 224, Brooklyn, NY 11217
*Collection of psychic arts. Free.*

U.S. Games System, Inc.
38 East 32nd Street, New York, NY 10016
*Catalogue of tarot cards, games, posters; occult books; bridge decks; magic cards; children's cards. $1.00.*

## Parties

*Children's Parties*

Bioff, Dorothy A. *Birthday Parties for Children.* Grand Rapids, MI: Baker Book House, 1978. Paperback.

Carlson, Bernice. *Let's Plan a Party.* Grand Rapids, MI: Baker Book House, 1978. Paperback.

Fiarotta, Phyllis and Noel. *Confetti: The Kids' Make It Yourself, Do-It-Yourself Party Book.* New York: Workman Publishing Co., Inc., 1978. Paperback.
Grades K-4. Illustrated.

Hedges, Sid. *Popular Party Games*. New York: Grosset & Dunlap, Inc., 1975. Paperback.
Grades 1 and up.

## Party Planning

*Books*

Burros, Marian Fox and Lois Levine. *The Elegant but Easy Cookbook*. New York: Collier, 1967.
*Stresses advance preparation so that hostesses can relax with guests. Hints for successful entertaining.*

Chase, Ilka. *The Care and Feeding of Friends*. New York: Doubleday & Co., Inc., 1973.
*Ilka Chase presents a great deal of information in this "not really a cookbook." The recipes and menus are mixed with entertainment ideas and spiced with anecdotes and travel tips.*

Follett, Barbara Lee. *Checklist for Entertaining*. New York, Doubleday & Co., Inc., 1976.
*A quick survey of the major areas of entertaining with some interesting checklists for equipment and liquor.*

Jones, Jeanne. *Party Planner and Entertaining Diary*. San Francisco: 101 Productions, 1979.
*Spiral-bound party diary with spaces to record seating chart, menu, expenses, decorations, plus four typical party menus.*

MacDonald, Barbara. *Parties for All Seasons*. Chicago: Culinary Arts Institute, 1976.
*From the main event to the casual grouping, this book will provide recipes and service ideas in a month-by-month party guide format.*

Ross, Diane and Elyse Schaffer. *The Birthday Party Book*. Maplewood, NJ: Hammond, Inc., 1979.
*From 1 to 100 details on themes, games, costumes, decorations, cakes and food.*

Saunders, Rubie. *The Calling All Girls Party Book*. New York: Young Readers Press, 1966. Paperback.
*This is geared to the young hostess, and provides recipes for food, fun and games for the young teens.*

*Guides & Kits*

Abbey Rents
3216 El Segundo Blvd., Hawthorne, CA 90250
*Party planning guides for all occasions. Free.*

American Rental Association
2920 23rd Avenue, Moline, IL 61265
*Your party rental guide.*

*Let's Have a Party. Booklet.*
Canada Dry Corporation
100 Park Avenue, New York, NY 10017

Gravymaster, Inc.
599 Connecticut Avenue, Norwalk, CT 06854
*Party planning guide and wall chart for teens and pre-teens.*

*Balloon Sculpture.*
La Wain's House of Magic
522 South Fifth Street, Monmouth, IL 61462
*A complete guide to balloon sculpture for amateur and professional children's party entertainers.*

*Kentucky Derby Party Kit*
2239 Millvale Road, Louisville, KY 40205
*Complete party kit with napkins, swizzle sticks, posters and more. $12.00.*

The Pillsbury Co.
Box 916, Minneapolis, MN 55460
*Party ideas.*

*Your Entertaining.*
Scott Paper Company
Home Service Center
Philadelphia, PA 19113

*Time for Hospitality*
Womens Division, LBI
155 East 44th Street, New York, NY 10017
*How to plan a party without even trying.*

*Party Themes*

Almaden Vineyards
Alcoa Building
1 Maritime Place, San Francisco, CA 94111
*Beach parties, soup and wine buffets, patio picnics and May wine festivals.*

*The First Steps*
Board of Jewish Education
426 West 58th Street, New York, NY 10019
*Ideas and recipes for parties, celebrations, Jewish festivals. $5.75.*

*Luau Guidebook*
305 Seventh Avenue, New York, NY 10001
*Luau history, recipes and practices. Free.*

*Mardi Gras Guide*
P.O. Box 8058, New Orleans, LA 70182
*$2.95.*

Paradise Products, Inc.
P.O. Box 568, El Cerrito, CA 94530
*Catalogue picturing favors, decorations and costumes for 120 kinds of parties —Oktoberfest, Calypso Nights, the Roaring 20's. $2.00.*

*Parties in Motion and Beer Party USA*
The U.S. Brewers Association
535 Fifth Avenue, New York, NY 10017

## Posters

Chinese Information Service
159 Lexington Avenue, New York, NY 10016
*Chinese posters. Free.*

Food and Wines from France
1350 Avenue of the Americas, New York, NY 10019
*Food and wine posters.*

Irish Tourist Board
Box 273, Dublin 8, Ireland
*Irish posters. $6.00.*

Israel Ministry of Tourism
350 Fifth Avenue, 19th floor, New York, NY 10118
*Map of the Holy Land.*

Kenya Tourist Office
60 East 56th Street, New York, NY 10022
*Kenya posters. Free.*

Organization of American States
General Secretariat
Department of Publications
Washington, DC 20006
*Flags and coats of arms of the American nations.*

Scandinavian National Tourist Office
75 Rockefeller Plaza, New York, NY 10019
*Scandinavian posters. Free.*

Union Pacific Railroad Company
1416 Dodge Street, Omaha, NE 68179
*Giant map of the U.S.*

## Protocol

McCafree, Mary Jane and Pauline Innis. *Protocol: The Complete Handbook
of Diplomacy.* Englewood Cliffs, NJ: Prentice-Hall, 1977.

## Recipes

Alaska King Crab Promotion Committee
190 Queen Anne Blvd.
Suite 110
Seattle, WA 98109
*King Crab recipes.*

*Amazing Magical Jello Desserts. $1.00.*
JELL-O
Box 5074, Kankakee, IL 60908

*Anything You Like Can Be Pie. 25¢.*
Ready Crust
P.O. Box 868
Department CCP
Mundelein, IL 60060

The Art & Secret of Chinese Cookery
La Choy Recipe Booklet
Archbold, OH 43502


Bee Honey Wise
California Honey Advisory Board
P.O. Box 32, Whittier, CA 90608
Bee honey recipes.


Children's Recipes
Carnation Co., Department E-BB
P.O. Box 330, Pico Rivera, CA 90666
48-page book. 50¢.


Cooking for Small Groups #001-000-03210-1. 35¢.
Superintendent of Documents
U.S. Government Printing Office
Washington, DC 20402


Create a Difference. 50¢.
Real Lemon
P.O. Box 775, Young America, MN 55399


El Paso Co.
Mountain Pass Canning Co.
El Paso County, TX 88021
Mexican recipes. Free.


Jolly Time Popcorn
American Pop Corn Company
Box 178, Sioux City, IA 51102
15 Jolly Time recipes for pop corn lovers. Free.


Kitchen Tricks, HW487
Oster, Advertising Service
5055 N. Lydell Avenue, Milwaukee, WI 53217


La Fondu
Switzerland Cheese Association Inc.
444 Madison Avenue, Room 2203
New York, NY 10022
Recipes for entertaining with fondue.

Lenders Bagel Bakery, Att: Peter Donohue
Post Road, West Haven, CT 06516
*Bagel recipes.*

*New Idea Cookbooks. Free.*
Borden, Inc.
P.O. Box 451, Jersey City, NJ 17303

*Outdoor Cooking*
Trappey's Sons, Inc. B.F.
Department EPS, Box 638, New Iberia, LA 70560

*Pilafs, Pilaus & Perlas*
Uncle Ben's Foods
P.O. Box 11756, Chicago, IL 60611
*Rice dishes.*

*The Quickbook*
Underwood Co.
1 Red Devil Lane, Westwood, MA 02090
*30 recipes for making hot and cold sandwiches.*

*They'll Love It. 50¢.*
Eagle Brand
P.O. Box 775, Young America, MN 55399

*Allergy Recipes*

The American Dietetic Association
620 North Michigan Avenue, Chicago, IL 60611

*Baking For People with Food Allergies. S/N 001–000–03362. 35¢.*
Superintendent of Documents
U.S. Government Printing Office
Washington, DC 20402

*Cholesterol-Free Menus*
P.O. Box 1K, Elm City, NC 27898

*Cooking with Imagination for Special Diets*
Grocery Store Products Company
West Chester, PA 19380

Council on Family Health
Department MW
633 Third Avenue, New York, NY 10017
*Free emergency chart.*

*Diets Unlimited for Limited Diets*
Allergy Information Association
3 Powburn Place, Weston 627
Ontario, Canada

*Good Recipes to Brighten the Allergy Rut*
Department GRA-1001
Box 307, Coventry, CT 06238
*Leaves out wheat, milk and eggs.*

*125 Great Recipes for Allergy Diets. 75¢.*
Good Housekeeping
969 Eighth Avenue, New York, NY 10019

# Table Settings

*Books*

Forsyth, Anne. *Table Settings for All Occasions.* Levittown: Transatlantic Arts, Inc., 1976.

*The New Tiffany Table Settings.* New York: Doubleday, 1981. *$35.00.*

*Pamphlets*

*Maximize the Minimums. 50¢.*
Baccarat
55 East 57th Street, New York, NY 10022

*To Have and to Hold: Romance of Table Settings*
Fostoria Glass Co.
1200 1st Street, Maidsville, WV 26041

Gorham Company
Total Tabletop
P.O. Box 2823, Providence, RI 02907
*Gorham sterling, china and crystal described in Hostess Tips. Free.*

Steuben Glass
717 Fifth Avenue, New York, NY 10022
*Pictures of table settings. Free.*

# Wines and Spirits

*Pamphlets*

*A Personal Guide to the Wines of the Wine Spectrum. Free.*
The Wine Spectrum
P.O. Box 1734
Atlanta, GA 30301

Southern Comfort Corporation
1220 North Price Road
St. Louis, MO 63132
*Entertaining with Comfort.*

*Books*

*The Art of Mixing Drinks.* New York: Bantam Books, Inc., 1967. Paperback.
*Truly a classic in this category. Lists over 1,000 drinks in a style that has brought the book to nearly two dozen printings.*

Bergeron, Victor J. *Trader Vic's Bartenders' Guide.* New York: Doubleday & Company, 1972.
*All the standards plus Trader Vic's original exotic concoctions.*

Craddick, Harry. *The Savoy Cocktail Book.* New York: Arno Press, Inc., 1976.
*Updated and expanded version of the 1930 guide by the famous bartender of the Savoy Hotel in London. Beautiful Art Deco illustrations.*

Lichines, Alexis. *New Encyclopedia of Wines and Spirits.* New York: Alfred A. Knopf, Inc., 1978.
*The 1967 classic updated with greatly expanded section in American wines.*

Lichines, Alexis. *Guide to the Wines and Vineyards of France.* New York: Alfred A. Knopf, Inc., 1979.
*Supersedes his 1963 classic* Wines of France. *Updated and authoritative account of each of France's wines by America's foremost wine connoisseur.*

Misch, Robert J. *Quick Guide to Wine.* New York: Doubleday & Company, Inc., 1968.

Powell, Fred. *The Bartender's Standard Manual.* New York: Harper & Row, Publishers, Inc., 1979.
*Compilation of over 700 recipes for drinks and punches.*

Thomas, Mario. *Playboy's Bar Guide.* Chicago: Playboy Press, 1971.
*Introduction with tips on setup and serving. Hundreds of recipes to quench the thirst.*

Waugh, Alec. *Wines and Spirits.* New York: Time-Life Books, 1967.

Weiner, Michael. *The Taster's Guide to Beer: Brews & Breweries of the World.* New York: Macmillan, Inc., 1977.

# Index

## About the Authors

Elizabeth L. Post, granddaughter-in-law of Emily Post, is director of the famed Emily Post Institute and the author of *The New Emily Post's Etiquette, The Emily Post Book of Etiquette for Young People, Emily Post Wedding Etiquette,* and *Please Say Please: A Common Sense Guide to Bringing Up Your Child.* She writes a nationally syndicated column "Doing the Right Thing," and a regular feature for *Good Housekeeping,* where she is a contributing editor. She lectures frequently and is often a guest on radio and television shows throughout the country. She and her husband, William G. Post, make their home in Vermont.

Anthony Staffieri's expertise in event and party coordination developed while he was employed by Abbey Rents, one of the world's largest party and catering equipment rental agencies. During his tenure as a party consultant he became the chief party planner for the east coast, coordinating a variety of events from airport openings to political fund raisers to small at-home soirees. Mr. Staffieri is now president of his own public relations firm, Savvy Management, Inc., in New York City.